DESIGN-CENTERED ENTREPRENEURSHIP

Supported by extensive research and field-testing, *Design-Centered Entrepreneurship* presents a concise, problem-solving approach to developing a unique business concept. Step-by-step guidelines provide insight into exploring market problem spaces, uncovering overlooked opportunities, reframing customer problems, and creating business solutions.

Basadur and Goldsby present students with a creative and practical approach to problem finding and design in the entrepreneurial field. Plenty of useful diagrams help to organize key concepts, making them easily accessible to readers.

Drawing on methodologies from the design field, the book will help students of entrepreneurship fill in the missing piece that transforms opportunity recognition into a viable business concept.

Additional support for students and instructors, including a virtual Creative Problem-Solving Profile, can be found at www.basadurprofile.com.

Min Basadur is Professor Emeritus of Organizational Behavior and Innovation at McMaster University, Canada, and founder of Basadur Applied Creativity.

Michael Goldsby is the Stoops Distinguished Professor of Entrepreneurship, Chief Entrepreneurship Officer and Executive Director of the John H. Schnatter Institute for Entrepreneurship and Free Enterprise at Ball State University, USA.

An old adage reads, "give a man a fish, feed him for a day; teach him how to fish, feed him for a lifetime." With these words in mind, Goldsby and Basadur go beyond traditional entrepreneurship texts, not only providing information to the reader, but drawing from design theory to teach the aspiring entrepreneur how to recognize a legitimate opportunity and develop it into a viable business concept.

Christopher P. Neck, *Arizona State University, USA*

Basadur and Goldsby provide all of us with the tools to be "creative." In an increasingly complex world, it is more important than ever to truly understand the problem before coming up with knee-jerk solutions. If you want to confidently solve complex problems in emotionally charged environments, read *Design-Centred Entrepreneurship*.

Paul Heinrich, *President and CEO,*
North Bay Regional Health Centre, Canada

I believe that this book charts a path to entrepreneurial success. Its value lies in starting *before* the big idea that many aspiring entrepreneurs feel they need to begin. By quickly dismissing the necessity of beginning with a fully realized "game changing" idea in the first chapter, it sets the reader at ease and plants the notion that entrepreneurship is actually possible *for them*. From there it lays out a reasonable, doable, systematic path forward towards entrepreneurial success that is applicable across various fields, industries, and personal situations. I highly recommend this book to anyone wishing to begin or accelerate their entrepreneurial career.

Thomas E. Nelson, *University of Cincinnati, USA*

Only firms that recognize innovation begins with a problem and utilize this approach to empower their teams to develop thoughtful, creative, and timely solutions are truly positioned for long-term success in the new manufacturing sector. I first learned of Min's approach to problem solving some 25 years ago and having worked with it over this time. It is a critical tool enabling our survival and success and I would encourage anyone committed to building a world class organization to familiarize themselves with Goldsby and Basadur's methodologies and empower their teams through its use.

Jim Campbell, *President, Adventec Manufacturing Inc., Canada*

Goldsby and Basadur offer hope that entrepreneurs can cleanly navigate the mire created from having too much information with too little time to make good decisions. Their innovation process is not only easy to use, but it allows me to be consistent and effective in my approach to driving organizations forward.

Shawn A. Noble, *Lenovo, USA*

The collaborative design processes and problem-finding skills this book teaches are fundamental to creating new value. Even if you skillfully apply Lean Startup methods, learning the framework in *Design-Centered Entrepreneurship* will amplify your entrepreneurial effectiveness.

Kate Hammer, *Co-founder, KILN, USA*

DESIGN-CENTERED ENTREPRENEURSHIP

Min Basadur and Michael Goldsby

Routledge
Taylor & Francis Group

NEW YORK AND LONDON

First published 2016
by Routledge
711 Third Avenue, New York, NY 10017

and by Routledge
2 Park Square, Milton Park, Abingdon, Oxon, OX14 4RN

Routledge is an imprint of the Taylor & Francis Group, an informa business

© 2016 Taylor & Francis

The right of Min Basadur and Michael Goldsby to be identified as authors of this work has been asserted by them in accordance with sections 77 and 78 of the Copyright, Designs and Patents Act 1988.

Library of Congress Cataloging in Publication Data
Names: Goldsby, Michael G., author. | Basadur, Min, author.
Title: Design-centered entrepreneurship / Michael Goldsby & Min Basadur.
Description: 1 Edition. | New York: Routledge, 2016.
Identifiers: LCCN 2016000889 | ISBN 9781138920521 (hbk) |
ISBN 9781138920552 (pbk) | ISBN 9781315686912 (ebk)
Subjects: LCSH: New business enterprises. | Strategic planning. |
Problem solving. | Entrepreneurship.
Classification: LCC HD62.5 .G644 2016 | DDC 658.1/1—dc23
LC record available at http://lccn.loc.gov/2016000889

ISBN: 978-1-138-92052-1 (hbk)
ISBN: 978-1-138-92055-2 (pbk)
ISBN: 978-1-315-68691-2 (ebk)

Typeset in Bembo
by codeMantra

Eleanor, Bob, Steve, and Tim
Molly, Dougie and Tim Jr.
Phyllis, Marg and Bruce.
                              Min

To Elizabeth, my greatest teacher
                           Michael

CONTENTS

List of Figures   ix
Acknowledgments   xi

   Introduction   1

1 Step 1: Problem Finding   24

2 Step 2: Fact Finding   51

3 Step 3: Problem Definition   78

4 Step 4: Idea Finding   105

5 Step 5: Evaluate and Select   132

6 Steps 6, 7, and 8: Solution Implementation   163

7 Conclusion   191

Index   235

FIGURES

I.1 The Innovation Wheel: A Complete Process of Creative
     Problem Solving   6
I.2 The Four Quadrants of the Innovation Process   9
I.3 Basadur Creative Problem-Solving Profile   10
I.4 Basadur Creative Problem-Solving Profile: Your Unique
     Blend of the Four Quadrants   11
I.5 Real-World Example 1   14
I.6 Real-World Example 2   15
I.7 Real-World Example 3   16
I.8 Real-World Example 4   16
I.9 Real-World Example 5   17
I.10 Which Might Be Your Most Preferred Style?   18
I.11 The Three Critical Process Skills   19
I.12 The Result of Content Without Process   20
I.13 The Result of Content Plus Process   21
I.14 The Result of Content Plus Process Plus Process Skills   21
I.15 The Quality Results Equation   21
1.1 Adaptability   27
1.2 The *Real* Customer   35
1.3 Customer Fieldnotes   41
1.4 Telescoping   46
2.1 Key Fact-Finding Behaviors   52
2.2 Questions to Clarify a Fuzzy Situation   58
2.3 The Results of Heavy Orientation Toward Quadrant 3
     and Quadrant 4 Thinking Styles   66
2.4 Balancing Orientations Toward All Four Thinking Styles   67
2.5 Digging Out the Hidden Facts   68
2.6 Finding Facts by Experiencing   70

2.7   Pyramiding   73
3.1   The "Why-What's Stopping" Analysis   83
3.2   An Example of Using the "Why-What's Stopping" Analysis
      to Broaden and Narrow a Challenge   84
3.3   Coast   85
3.4   8-Step Process   86
3.5   Broadening the Scope   89
3.6   Practice Challenge Map   90
3.7   Aerospace Senior Management   93
3.8   The "Why-What's Stopping" Analysis   96
3.9   The "Why-What's Stopping" Analysis—Strategic Perspective   97
3.10 Four Boilers from Eight   98
3.11 Customer Challenge Map   102
3.12 Using the Challenge Map   103
4.1   Four Techniques for Generating Ideas   106
4.2   Guidelines for Converging on Best Ideas   109
4.3   Breaking Through Patent Barriers   110
5.1   What Criteria Might Be Used to Evaluate?   134
5.2   Selecting the Most Important Criteria   135
5.3   Converging by Consensus   135
5.4   Integrating and Building   136
5.5   Evaluation of Car Options Using the Criteria Grid Method   138
5.6   Telescoping   140
5.7   Too Many Ideas?   140
5.8   Which Option?   141
5.9   Paired Comparison Analysis   143
5.10 Customer Feedback Form for Product/Service Concept   151
5.11 Expert Feedback Form for Product/Service Concept   155
5.12 Refined Product/Service Concept Form   157
6.1   Psychological Roadblocks that Impede Action   165
6.2   Action Plan   167
6.3   Prompter Questions for Anticipating Difficulties
      in Implementing a Solution   167
6.4   Action Plan Divergence   168
6.5   Example: Lubricants Distribution Division   171
6.6   Proof of Concept and Legitimacy   173
6.7   Legitimacy and Risk   174
6.8   Certainty and Valuation   174
6.9   Reducing Others' Discomfort with New Ideas   175
6.10 Selling Your Idea   176
6.11 Ways to Spur Yourself to Action   181
7.1   Two Parts of a Continuous Process   195
7.2   The Four Stages of the Simplexity Innovation Process   198
7.3   Selected Criteria   209
7.4   Problem Definition Map   220

ACKNOWLEDGMENTS

I would like to acknowledge many individuals whose collective efforts have helped make this book by Mike and me come together. I am sure I have accidently left out several deserving people and I apologize to them in advance for the omissions.

To begin, I would like to acknowledge my colleagues Larry Crase, Tim and Bob Basadur, Garry Gelade and George Graen who have participated with me over the years to create the experiences, thoughts, words, stories, research studies and pictures that were chosen for the book and Brenda Andrew who spent countless hours inserting rewrite after rewrite.

Next, I have been fortunate to work with several world-class leaders who have taken bold risks to build entrepreneurship and innovation capability in their organizations. The following stand out in their fields. In industry, Jim O'Neal, Bruce Paton, Jim Jarratt, Richard Perez, Shannon Wagers, David Trigg, Phillip Sawin, Doug Barber, Bob Lane, Shawn Noble, Jerry Lee, Penny Armstrong, Ian Brookes, and Jim Thyen; In healthcare, Paul Heinrich, Sue Lebeau, Bill Evans, Mark Berry, and Jean Ann Larson; In government, Dave Augustyn, Darren Ottaway, Peter Papp, Cari Pupo, Patrick Kane, and Sue Ellspermann; In corporate insurance, Les Herr and Jatinder Parhar; In banking, Torjus Jensen and Emma Movitz; In high-tech, Charles Warren, Dane Howard, Michael Lenahan, Kent Sullivan, and Michael Corning; In consulting engineers and scientists, Mike Soligo, Jon Galsworthy, and Ian Tudhope; in community economic development, Janet Scott and Mark Breen; In executive and entrepreneurship education, Paul Bates, Donna Muirhead, Dave Mammoliti, Ed Leach, Mary Kilfoil, Sergei Korolev, Peter Jones, Mohan Nadarajahand, Glen Drummond, and Pam Pringle; in energy utilities, Don Dalicandro and Gerry Smallegange. I have learned great deal from everyone.

I have also had the opportunity to learn directly from real life entrepreneurs already highly successful in their own fields: Doug Leggat, Jim Campbell, Randall

Craig, Sam Malatesta, Philip Conklin, Sergio Alanis Rueda, and Chris Bart. They have been generous in sharing of their experiences.

. Finally, I have been privileged to enjoy the luxury of being surrounded by a cast of supporting thought leaders who continue to open up new ways of perceiving and communicating with the world and who provide expert feedback on new ideas and choices: Kate Hammer, Paul Almas, Peter Nixon, Evette Cordy, Jacquie Lloyd-Smith, Silje Kamille Friis, Olga Modesto, Bill Flack, Wayne Fisher, Gene Recker, Mike Karpinski, Tonya Peck, Lorraine Weygman, Gwen Speranzini, Marie Bacot, Milena Head, Mark Runco, Peter Austin, Mitzi Short, Sylvie Gelinas, Debra Pickfield, Mindy Morrow, Brad Grant, Jennifer Spear, Debbie Elliott, Kim Arnott, and Phyllis Conklin.

To all, my heartfelt thanks!

Min

The content of this book developed over a 15 year period of bringing creative problem solving into entrepreneurship education. First, I want to thank my coauthor, Dr. Min Basadur, for sharing his extensive knowledge on creativity and innovation with me. Second, I want to thank Dr. Donald F. Kuratko for his mentorship in my professional career as an entrepreneurship educator. Any success I have achieved in my field is a result of the time and support they have given me in developing my craft. I will always be indebted to them.

I also want to thank the incredible support given to me by the outstanding people I work with at Ball State University. President Terry King has always encouraged me to be innovative in the classroom and pursue my research interests. My Institute teammates Rob Mathews and Margo Allen have been great partners to work with on the many initiatives we try to bring to our University and the state of Indiana. I also want to recognize Bob Morris, Rick Hall, Jen Bott, Julie Halbig, Cheri O'Neill, Kathryn Kennison, Kelly Favory, Ronda Smith, Matt Marvel, Ted Baker, Jen Blackmer, and Suzanne Plesha for their good work in supporting entrepreneurial learning at Ball State.

There have been many good people who have given me great advice and direction over the years. Jon Shepard, Brian Burton, Rich Wokutch, John Chrisman, and Chris Neck were instrumental in the attainment of my doctorate. These gentlemen pushed me to think more deeply about business and society and made my career opportunities possible.

I have also had incredible support and encouragement from the business world. Specifically, John Schnatter ("Papa John") and Charles Koch have provided generous support for my educational initiatives at Ball State by funding the John H. Schnatter Institute for Entrepreneurship and Free Enterprise. It is an honor to lead the Institute, and I am also appreciative of the support of Adam Kissel of the Charles Koch Foundation and Paul Ferguson for their help in establishing this special institution. Several friends from world class companies have had a tremendous impact on my thinking about innovation and business. In particular, Kevin Lansberry, Dan Cockerell, and Scot Reynolds at the Walt Disney Company have been very generous with their time and support in teaching me about how a legendary company stays impactful and relevant. Richard Perez and Shannon Wagers at Procter & Gamble have taught me about the creative process of inventing new products for large markets. And Chuck Schmal of Woodard Emhardt Moriarty McNett & Henry has provided me with a better understanding of the intellectual property issues that occur in any creative pursuit. I also appreciate Brian Geiselhart, Kyle Kuntz, and Jacob Schpok, my former students and now business executives, for keeping me apprised of the latest goings on in the corporate world.

Several education colleagues have been helpful in shaping my thinking over the years, such as: Alex Bruton and Stephen Kenny of Mount Royal University in Calgary, Alberta; Ed Leach, Mary Kilfoil, and Aaron Newman at Dalhousie University in Halifax, Nova Scotia; Jim Bishop of New Mexico State University; Jeff Hornsby of the University of Missouri-Kansas City; Kevin McCurren of Grand Valley State University; and Tom Nelson of the University of South Alabama. I always enjoy the company of these scholars and teachers.

I also appreciate the support of the literary expertise and guidance of Sharon Golan, Erin Arata, and Francesca Monaco in making this book possible. They run a first class operation, and it was a pleasure to work with them during the writing process.

Finally, I would like to thank my friends and family who have always supported me in my life. I am blessed to have great friends like Karl Mesarosh, Seth Burris, Rich Chumley, Martin and Meribe Nyberg, Stephen Gregory, Bob Helfst, Carol Dean, and Luke Smelsor. And my amazing family has always made life fun and exciting, so special thanks to my wife Beth and Will, Andy, and Sarah; parents Joe and Sujane Goldsby; brother Tom Goldsby and Kathie, Emma, and Aiden; Uncle Hugh McNeely; Ivis and Mary McNeely; and in-laws Bill and Jan Swinney. Thank you for your encouragement of me to pursue my dreams and crazy ideas.

Michael

INTRODUCTION

No matter where you look around the world today, entrepreneurs[*] face a common challenge: the need to stand out from their competitors and win over customers. For example, in Europe, recessions force startups to compete for limited funds in tight capital markets. In China and Southeast Asia, companies seek to gain market share in previously undeveloped regions on their continent. In Japan, companies redefine themselves in order to remain relevant as their neighboring competitors aggressively grow. South American companies feel pressured to roll out new products to live up to the expectations that come up with being the surprise success story of the twenty-first century. African entrepreneurs bring professional solutions to overlooked markets but in the process must create customers from scratch. The situation is no different in North America. Entrepreneurs try to stand out from bigger and more well-known corporations, managers try to build their reputation by better serving their customers, and executives ponder over which new lines of business to support for growing the bottom line.

Further complicating the situation is that graduating college students are faced with challenges their ancestors didn't have. The days of getting a degree in a specific area, meeting with a human resources representative, and working for one company for a lifetime are no more. Many economic and sociological developments brought this societal shift. The re-engineering and downsizing movement of the 1990s created leaner companies that add and subtract jobs as needed. Every relationship and transaction is analyzed based on its efficiency and returns. But that

---

[*] In this book, *entrepreneur* will refer to someone starting or running a business or someone working inside a company who behaves like an entrepreneur. The second type of person is known as a *corporate entrepreneur*. The process of developing new products and services works much the same way for both groups. However, how an idea is brought into the world may vary depending on whether it is someone's own company or whether they are working for someone else. A plethora of books exists for the mechanics of starting a business. This book focuses on the process of finding and developing the opportunities that new business revenue is built on.

was just the beginning of the massive changes taking place in business. The next decade brought the digital revolution. The creative economy of the twenty-first century has added speed and complexity to the game of business as well. Competitors are now springing up in all corners of the world. International supply chains and digital technologies make it possible for anyone with an Internet connection to start their own business. While this situation can be stressful, it can also be liberating. People have the opportunity to chart their own course in the world like never before. Whether starting their own company or working inside one, people have to *think* like entrepreneurs.

This sentiment is easier said than done because the industrial model of business worked quite well for so many people for a long time. Churning out incrementally improved products for existing customers over a lifetime ensured steady growth and dependable returns on investment. However, mechanical, utilitarian models are simply not effective today. We live in a world of customized experiences, choice, and high expectations. Customers expect more from companies today, which requires entrepreneurs to uncover people's *real* problems and design elegant solutions to those problems. This approach requires integrating knowledge across many disciplines, collaborating with diverse groups of people, and managing projects to completion. Economic security is no longer dependent on merely working hard but on creating new value for their customers, and the best way to create new value is to connect in relevant and impactful ways with these customers.

All of these groups recognize that creativity and innovation are essential for success today. Simply put, selling the same products in the same way over a long period of time is a recipe for disaster. Yet, many very smart people in these situations do not know what steps to take to come up with that next big idea. They usually can't rely on what they learned during their university years because most training in business schools is oriented toward managing instead of creating. After all, it's no coincidence that graduate business degrees are called "Masters of Business Administration" instead of "Masters of Innovation." The pedagogy is focused on controlling what you currently have and do to get desired results rather than learning how to develop and implement new ideas in a state of uncertainty.

The business press is also lacking books that provide systematic approaches to developing innovative ideas. As a result, professors and coaches often rely on common creativity tools such as brainstorming and mind mapping to generate winning ideas. Unfortunately, they often experience only frustration with the lack of actionable ideas derived from the exercises. Other books on innovation share motivating stories of maverick entrepreneurs creating the next business revolution but then do not explain how to generalize those approaches to other industries. While the books are effective in getting people fired up to find that next big idea, detailed steps are often lacking in how to actually bring it to life.

Fortunately a few scholars in entrepreneurship have provided more prescriptive ways to pursue opportunity. What these scholars have found is that opportunities do not typically appear in final form but instead emerge through individual insights and develop through learning.[1] Some ideas are abandoned while others are shaped and progressed until they show promise in feasibility, desirability, and viability. To date, the two leading prescriptive models are systematic search and effectuation. Systematic search describes how individuals with specific domain knowledge, unknown to others, can constrain their search for viable opportunities to consideration sets.[2] Conversely, effectuation is another method that emphasizes how expert entrepreneurs leverage their resources to create opportunities, whereby they focus on resources under their control rather than on specific preplanned goals.[3] However, both of these theories are specific to individuals who possess specialized domain expertise or prior startup expertise with resources under their control. Unfortunately there is a dearth of prescriptive models available to guide nascent entrepreneurs who lack expertise due to youth or inexperience or for entrepreneurs or managers who are struggling to find the next idea that gives them a competitive advantage in their industry. This book addresses this gap and puts forward a prescriptive approach of opportunity development based on the principles and methodologies from research on applied creativity, innovation, and design. We've practiced these methodologies in industry and the classroom for many years.

Innovation: A Creative Process for Solving Customer Problems

Innovation is the driver of business growth, but there is little guidance on how to make it happen. Yet, we know it happens in successful companies because we read about the exploits of business mavericks every day. How can they do it while others struggle so much? Perhaps they have access to research labs and scientists that the average company doesn't. But we know this isn't true. Fledgling biotech companies close their doors every year because they couldn't develop a new product the market wanted. Maybe they have more money to throw at ideas. If this was the case, the same companies would always remain at the top, but that doesn't happen either. So if it isn't about resources, then maybe it's simply about brain power. Might breakthroughs happen because some companies are led by geniuses who have the uncanny ability to see opportunities others can't? Maybe their brains are simply wired differently, and the best solution is to lure those geniuses to your company. Fortunately, our research and experience with innovation over the years proves this isn't true either. After working with many students and businesses, we have found that anyone with the right attitudes and skills applying an effective process can create innovative products.[4] An even better finding is that these attitudes, skills, and processes can be learned and applied in any setting, and the best insight is that you don't have to be blessed with money to make money. You just have to be patient in learning how to apply a time-tested methodology for creating products and services customers will love. This book offers you an approach to do that. We adapt the Simplexity Creative Problem-Solving Process that Basadur Applied Creativity has honed over 40 years to entrepreneurship. This process has helped entrepreneurial companies around the world create products and services millions of people around the world use every day. It has also been the foundation of our entrepreneurship and management courses at our respective universities. Whether in the classroom or the boardroom, the process works.

Imagine a creative approach that helps your business thrive in your chosen market by solving problems no one has figured out yet. Think about it: a company dedicated to finding and solving the problems in the world around it. It's quite a vision, and it's one you can build by developing the skills and applying the process in this book. Our entrepreneurial approach is right for where the world is today. It prepares you for an economy and world where empathy, creativity, smart risk taking, and savvy execution are needed to thrive and flourish. It's an approach that helps you take charge of your future and connect deeply to the world around you, just as an entrepreneur should do every day.

We base our methodology on the premise that entrepreneurial activity is first and foremost about creative problem solving. No matter how great your technology or idea, if it does not solve an important problem for enough people, you have little chance for success. However, with very limited means but the right insights, you can build a successful business. This perspective is wonderfully evidenced in a book by Clifton L. Taulbert and Gary Schoeniger. *Who Owns the Ice House? Eight Lessons from an Unlikely Entrepreneur* tells the story of Taulbert's Uncle Cleve. Uncle Cleve was an unlikely entrepreneur during the Jim Crow days in the Mississippi Delta. While his neighbors were working in the cotton fields, Uncle Cleve ran a successful icehouse business. How was he fortunate enough to live a more prosperous life than his contemporaries? He knew that opportunities existed within problems. As Taulbert recollects,

> At the time, I didn't view Uncle Cleve's ownership of the Ice House as a solution to a problem. I simply saw it as a good business for him and a great job for me. Looking back, I now know that at some point along the way, before his business materialized, an opportunity existed within a problem. Everybody needed ice. The heat in the delta was overwhelming and the humidity was everywhere. Without ice for cold water to keep food from spoiling, life would have been unbearable.[4]

Like Taulbert's Uncle Cleve, we will teach you how to solve the problems of your target customers and then offer ways to solve your company's own problems in getting to market. You may find it odd to talk about innovation and problem solving in the same breath. For most people, problem solving is a distasteful task they have to do when something goes wrong. By contrast, most people think of innovation as an exciting pursuit that results in something new. Yet innovation is actually a problem-solving process. Innovation begins when you recognize a challenge your customers are facing. It happens further when you design a breakthrough solution for meeting the challenge, and it ends when you provide your solution. From that premise, a successful business can be built.

Think of the many problems that challenge your potential customers. Why hasn't someone capitalized on these opportunities? Some of these problems might be obvious, but a good solution has not been discovered yet. On the other hand, some are more difficult to perceive, so no one even considers ways to better serve the customer. If an entrepreneur could tackle and uncover more problems and find better solutions, innovation would result in new or better products and services. However, most people work with a limited view of problem solving, due mostly to using a restricted set of tools to handle problems. You've probably picked up various tools along the way—things like listing pros and cons to decide between alternatives, brainstorming solutions to a problem, and analyzing statistical data. Such techniques are all useful in helping to solve problems, but they are only pieces of a process. Gathering and analyzing statistical data, for example, is an excellent way to find facts to help define problems, but it leaves you short of developing a solution. Brainstorming is a wonderful technique for developing solution ideas once you've defined a problem, but it leaves you short of action and often yields off-target ideas. Listing pros and cons of various solutions is only useful if you have already created alternatives, and it still leaves you short of ways to implement them. Instead, we will teach you a *complete* process of creative problem solving that encompasses finding problems, developing creative solutions, and implementing your solutions. We divide the process into eight separate steps that make up sections of a wheel, as in Figure I.1.

We use a wheel to emphasize the circular nature of problems. Think of how often a product hits the market only to have a company modify it later. Even when a product seems perfect, it may have unforeseen problems that have to be addressed later. Ongoing problem solving like this is the source of tenacity and grit that separates the successful entrepreneur from the run-of-the-mill dreamer. As any experienced entrepreneur can attest, the road to a successful launch is chock-full of obstacles and challenges that have to be addressed for a product to be accepted in a market. Consider products that we practically take for granted in our daily lives. Their usefulness seems obvious now, but the path to acceptance was likely strewn with new needs. The microwave oven, for example, was a wonderful solution to the problem of speeding up food preparation, but consider the problems it created in turn. It required new kinds of cookware and compatible food products, it took up space in kitchens already filled with appliances, and it posed new safety hazards. For making microwave ovens or anything else, problem solving is a never-ending creative process.

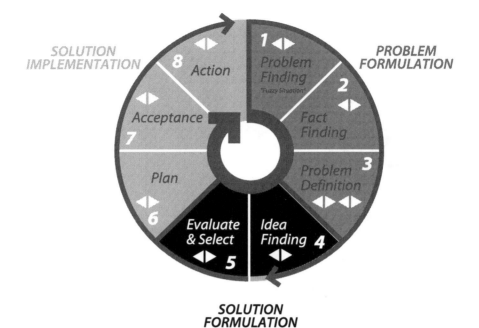

FIGURE I.1 The Innovation Wheel: A Complete Process of Creative Problem Solving

Eight Steps to Solving Problems

This book will dedicate a chapter to each step of the creative problem-solving process. Before learning the eight steps of the process in detail in the following chapters, let's take a quick look at what each of them means.

Step 1

Problem finding means sensing, anticipating, and seeking out customer problems and needs, social changes, technology trends, and opportunities for improvement in the chance to offer a new product or service. With a confident attitude, a creative entrepreneur seeks out complex problems other companies are shying away from. He or she is comfortable with "fuzzy" situations.

Step 2

Fact finding involves gathering information about a fuzzy situation without prematurely judging its relevance. Too many entrepreneurs and managers develop new products without fully considering the various aspects of a problem they are attempting to solve. A skilled fact finder avoids unwarranted assumptions, examines a solution from a wide variety of viewpoints, listens to and accepts others' versions of the facts, extends effort to dig out hidden information, and shows no reluctance to ask simple questions. Establishing what is *not* known is as vital as determining what is known or thought to be known. Only later does he or she worry about choosing the most relevant facts.

Step 3

Problem definition means composing clear, insightful challenges from a few key facts. These challenges reveal directions for solutions. An individual skilled in defining problems can create unusual ways to view them. He or she can broaden the problem's scope by asking why it needs to be solved (the intent) and narrow its scope by asking what stands in the way of solving it (the stumbling blocks). This individual creates optional ways of formulating the problem until a superior angle has been developed.

Step 4

Idea finding means creating a variety of ways to solve a defined problem. A skilled idea finder is never content with a single good idea but continues to hunt for more. The idea finder is able to build on and complete fragments of other ideas. Seemingly radical, even "impossible" ideas can be turned into more unusual but workable solutions. A few of the more promising ideas are selected for evaluation and further development into possible solutions.

Step 5

Evaluating and selecting involves converting selected ideas into practical solutions. An individual skilled in evaluation and selection considers plenty of criteria in order to take an unbiased look at the ideas. They avoid leaping to conclusions based on a single criterion or on unrelated hidden motives. Interesting but flawed solutions are creatively improved, then reevaluated.

Step 6

Action planning means creating specific action steps that will lead to successful implementation of a solution. An individual skilled in action planning can see the end result in a specific, concrete way that motivates people to act on the plan. Within an entrepreneurial context, Step 6 begins the process of getting the solution to market.

Step 7

Gaining acceptance means understanding that even the best ideas and plans can be scuttled by resistance to change. Someone skilled in gaining acceptance creates ways to show people how a particular solution benefits them and how possible problems with the solution can be minimized. Guidance will also be given as to how to gain legitimacy and credibility among various stakeholders. Effective stakeholder management can better ensure acceptance in the market when it's time to launch the company.

Step 8

Taking action means "doing" the steps in the action plan and continually revising and adapting the plan as things change in order to ensure the solution is successfully implemented. An individual skilled in taking action avoids getting mired in unimportant details and minor roadblocks on the way to implementing the solution. They do not fear imperfect solutions, knowing that even ingenious solutions can be revised and continuously improved (think of the microwave). An action-oriented entrepreneur or manager knows that they can improve the solution as they adapt to customer feedback and learn better ways of making it work over time.

Because innovation is like a wheel, it actually has a ninth step: the first step of the next rotation. Each solution that you bring to your customers changes things. It results in a new array of problems, customer expectations, opportunities for improvement, and competitive reactions. We can't expect a breakthrough idea to work perfectly the first time out of the box. Thus, we're back to Step 1. But it is this ongoing iterative process that ensures the entrepreneur does not fall too in love with their idea. Rather, they learn what is not working with the product or service and work through the wheel as often as is needed to solve each problem that arises.

Getting the Process Skills You Need

Now that we've discussed the creative problem-solving process, let's look at how you can make it work well for you. After all, it's one thing to know about the innovation process, but it's another to master the thinking skills needed to carry it out. The innovation process consists of four distinct parts or quadrants (Figure I.2): the generation of new problems and opportunities; the conceptualization of new, potentially useful ideas; the optimization of solutions; and the implementation of the new solutions. Each quadrant requires different kinds of thinking and problem-solving skills. If an entrepreneur hopes to create a big hit, he or she must employ the skills of all four quadrants to make it happen. Think about it. A great idea that's not well developed and executed gets an entrepreneur nowhere. A common idea that's well executed has a limited window for growth. However, few people are equally skilled or comfortable in all four quadrants. This insight provides good reason for entrepreneurs to think about building a management team that has not only a diversity of knowledge and experience but of creative problem-solving styles as well. Therefore, we encourage entrepreneurs to strongly consider having partners who are comfortable and skilled in varying degrees of idea generation, conceptualization, optimizing, and implementation. A well-balanced team in thinking styles builds a more creative company with potential for not only a breakthrough idea but also solid execution.

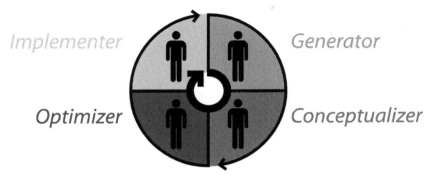

Implementer *Generator*

Optimizer *Conceptualizer*

FIGURE I.2 The Four Quadrants of the Innovation Process

Building these teams is possible with a profile to help recognize your own and others' problem-solving styles. In order to better understand these quadrants and to determine your own blend of problem-solving preferences, either (1) fill out the problem-solving inventory in Figure I.3 then follow the instructions or (2) click on the link to take it on line at no charge for a one time only usage. https://www.basadurprofile.com/jointeam.aspx?KEY=BMEKRFPS. We've given this inventory to over 40,000 people over the years at companies such as Ebay, Microsoft, and Frito Lay. The assessment of problem-solving preferences present in product development teams and startup companies has provided guidance to these entrepreneurs in recognizing where they could use assistance. You can do the same as you consider how to build your own company, new product development team, or classroom project teams.

Now, after you have filled out the inventory in Figure I.3, follow the instructions to score and interpret your creative problem-solving profile provided in Figure I.4. Please be doubly sure that after you have filled out the eighteen rows of Figure I.3, *you must stroke out rows 1, 2, 5, 10, 14, and 17 BEFORE totalling the four vertical columns.* These rows are not to be counted in the addition. Then plot the four column totals on the corresponding four axes of the grid in Figure I.4.

Now, connect the four points you have plotted on the grid with curved lines to create your profile (Figure I.4). If you have identical column scores—an extremely unlikely result—your profile will be a perfect circle. However, your profile is probably skewed toward particular quadrants. The largest of the four quadrants indicates your strongest orientation. The others represent your secondary thinking and problem-solving styles. For example, if the area of the circle in quadrant 1 is larger than in the other three, you are oriented toward generating; if quadrant 2, then conceptualizing; if quadrant 3, then optimizing; and if quadrant 4, then implementing. Here's a description of each quadrant to help you further interpret and define your blend.

This inventory is designed to describe your method of problem solving. Give a high rank to those words which best characterize the way you problem-solve and a low rank to the words which are least characteristic of your problem-solving style.

You may find it hard to choose the words that best describe your problem-solving style because there are no right or wrong answers. Different characteristics described in the inventory are equally good. The aim of the inventory is to describe how you solve problems, not to evaluate your problem-solving ability.

Instructions

Eighteen rows of four words are listed horizontally. Fill this questionnaire out **horizontally**, not vertically. That is, going **across** each row, assign a **4"** to the word which **best** characterizes your problem-solving style, a **3"** to the word which **next best** characterizes your problem-solving style, a **2"** to the **next most** characteristic word, and a **1"** to the word which is **least characteristic** of you as a problem solver. Be sure to **assign a different number to each** of the four words in each **horizontal** row. **Do not make ties in any row. Every row must have a 4, 3, 2 and 1.**

	Column 1	Column 2	Column 3	Column 4
1	Alert	Poised	Ready	Eager
2	Patient	Diligent	Forceful	Prepared
3	Doing	Childlike	Observing	Realistic
4	Experiencing	Diversifying	Waiting	Consolidating
5	Reserved	Serious	Fun-loving	Playful
6	Trial & Error	Alternatives	Pondering	Evaluating
7	Action	Divergence	Abstract	Convergence
8	Direct	Possibilities	Conceptual	Practicalities
9	Involved	Changing perspectives	Theoretical	Focusing
10	Quiet	Trustworthy	Responsible	Imaginative
11	Implementing	Visualizing	Describing	Zeroing-in
12	Hands-on	Future-oriented	Reading	Detail-oriented
13	Physical	Creating Options	Mental	Deciding
14	Impersonal	Proud	Hopeful	Fearful
15	Practicing	Transforming	Thinking	Choosing
16	Handling	Speculating	Contemplating	Judging
17	Sympathetic	Pragmatic	Emotional	Procrastinating
18	Contact	Novelizing	Reflection	Making sure

FIGURE I.3 Basadur Creative Problem-Solving Profile

Generating

Generating involves getting the innovation process rolling. Generative thinking involves gathering information through direct experience, questioning, imagining possibilities, sensing new problems and opportunities, and viewing situations from different perspectives. Legendary entrepreneurs are famous for dreaming up ideas others have never considered. Entrepreneurs strong in generating skills prefer to

SCORING:

LEGEND: Column 1 scores indicate the orientation to getting knowledge for
           solving problems by Experiencing (direct personal involvement).
           Column 2 scores indicate the orientation toward using
           knowledge for solving problems by Ideation (the generation of
           ideas without judgment).
           Column 3 scores indicate the orientation toward getting
           knowledge for solving problems by Thinking (detached
           abstract theorizing).
           Column 4 scores indicate the orientation toward using
           knowledge for solving problems by Evaluation (the application of
           judgment to ideas).

Post your total scores for each column on the appropriate axis below.

           In each column, add up all the items except items 1, 2, 5, 10, 14,
           and 17 to get your column scores.

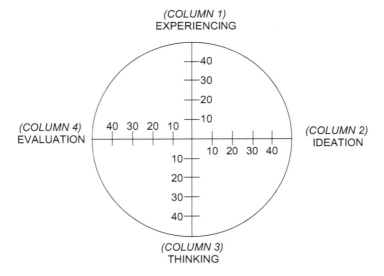

To develop your personal creative problem-solving profile, simply connect the 4
points in sequence with 4 curved lines to make a 'warped' circle accordingly. (If
you have identical column scores, you will have a perfect circle. This is unlikely.)
The quadrant in which your profile is most dominant indicates your strongest
orientation. The other quadrants represent secondary styles accordingly. Your
profile is your own unique blend of the four quadrants.

FIGURE I.4 Basadur Creative Problem–Solving Profile: Your Unique Blend of the
           Four Quadrants

come up with options, or diverge, rather than evaluate and select, or converge. They see relevance in almost everything and think of good and bad sides to almost any fact, idea, or problem but are willing to let others take care of the details. They enjoy ambiguity and are hard to pin down. They delight in juggling many new projects simultaneously. Every solution they explore suggests several new problems to be solved. Thinking in this quadrant includes problem finding and fact finding.

Conceptualizing

Conceptualizing keeps the innovation process going. Like generating, it involves divergence. But rather than gaining understanding by direct experience, it favors gaining understanding by abstract thinking. It results in putting new ideas together, discovering insights that help define problems, and creating theoretical models to explain things. Entrepreneurs strong in conceptualizing skills enjoy taking information scattered all over the map from the generator phase and making sense of it. Conceptualizers need to "understand": to them, a theory about what the business can be must be logically sound and precise. They prefer to proceed only with a clear grasp of a situation and when the problem or main idea is well defined. They dislike having to prioritize, implement, or agonize over poorly understood alternatives. They like to play with ideas and are not overly concerned with moving to action. Thinking in this quadrant includes problem defining and idea finding. As a result, they're very good at creating the overall concept of what a startup can sell.

Optimizing

Optimizing moves the innovation process further. Like conceptualizing, it favors gaining understanding by abstract thinking. But rather than diverge, an individual with this thinking style prefers to converge. This results in converting abstract ideas and alternatives into practical solutions and plans. These individuals rely on thought experiments, mentally testing ideas in their heads rather than testing them in the outside world. Entrepreneurs who favor the optimizing style prefer to create optimal solutions to a few well-defined problems. They are masterful at planning systems and operations that will support the concept created by a conceptualizer. They prefer to focus on specific problems and sort through large amounts of information to pinpoint "what's wrong" in a given situation. They are usually confident in their ability to make a sound, logical evaluation and to select the best solution to a problem. Entrepreneurs strong in optimizing will address the realities needed to get an idea to market. They often lack patience with ambiguity and dislike "dreaming" about additional ideas, points of view, or relations among problems. They believe they "know" what the problem is. Thinking in this quadrant includes idea evaluation and selection and action planning. As a result, entrepreneurs good at optimizing recognize that even the best products will have specific challenges in getting to market. They are realists when it comes to starting a business and can help a team plan ahead to potential roadblocks to success.

Implementing

Implementing completes the innovation process. Like optimizing, it favors converging. However, unlike optimizing, it favors learning by direct experience rather than by abstract thinking. This results in getting things done. Implementers rely on trying things out rather than mentally testing them. They see the world as their laboratory. Implementers do not live inside their heads like conceptualizers and optimizers do. Entrepreneurs strong in implementing prefer situations in which they must somehow make things work. They do not need complete understanding in order to proceed, and they adapt quickly to immediately changing circumstances. Implementers enjoy "thinking on their feet." When a theory does not appear to fit the facts, they will readily discard it. Others perceive them as enthusiastic about their product or service but also as impatient or even pushy as they try to get their businesses off the ground. They will try as many different approaches as necessary and follow up or "bird-dog" as needed to ensure that the product or service is on the market. Thinking in this quadrant includes gaining acceptance and implementing.

Understanding the Blend of Your Team's Creative Problem-solving Styles

All individuals and organizations have peculiar blends of these four distinct orientations. In which quadrant is your team dominant? What blend does it exhibit? How appropriate is this blend? Have you seen your team's blend change over time from one situation to another? In order to succeed in creative problem solving, a startup team requires strengths in all four quadrants. Team members must learn to use their differing styles in complementary ways. For example, generating ideas for new products and services must start somewhere, with individuals scanning the environment, picking up data and cues from customers, and suggesting possible opportunities for change and improvement. Thus, the generator raises new information and possibilities—usually not fully developed but in the form of starting points for new products. Then the conceptualizer pulls together the facts and idea fragments from the generator phase into well-defined problems and challenges. They use this understanding to develop the big picture and offer ideas worth further evaluation. Good conceptualizers give sound structure to fledgling ideas and opportunities. The optimizer then hones a well-defined idea into a more practical solution and provides a detailed plan for efficiently proceeding to market. Finally, implementers carry forward the practical solutions and plans to the marketplace. This includes selling customers on the benefits of the new product or service, managing supply chain relationships, and overcoming operational issues in making the company a reality. They take action and adapt the company's solutions to customer feedback and discovered market realities as they go.

Skills in all four quadrants are equally valuable. Startup teams must appreciate the importance of all four quadrants and find ways to fit together their members' styles. Teams should capitalize on each individual's strengths, as well as tapping resources in all four quadrants to help the individual, team, or company cycle through the complete innovation process.

Thus, each of the four quadrants in the creative problem-solving profile is characterized by two activities:

- Generating: problem finding and fact finding
- Conceptualizing: problem definition and idea finding
- Optimizing: idea evaluation and action planning
- Implementing: gaining acceptance and implementation

These eight activities make up the complete innovation process. Let's look at some real examples of how each quadrant can have an impact on a company.

Real-world Example 1: *Wanting New Products but Lacking Generators*

Figure I.5 is the distribution of creative styles of a typical group of managers within a large aerospace company serving aircraft, airline, and aerospace industries. The company says it wants to expand faster into new products and new markets. With this spread of managers, how likely is this team to surface customer problems and find fresh commercial opportunities?

Faced with this, senior leadership introduced Creative Problem-Solving Process training and also began to recognize and reward people who achieve skills and demonstrate success in Generator activities. Also, central headquarters offered to fund new projects of high potential, which alleviated the subdivisions from spending from their own budgets.

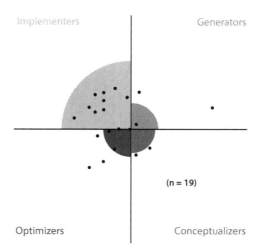

FIGURE I.5 Real-World Example 1

Real-world Example 2: *Great Ideas but No Action*

A manager inside an old fashioned company that desperately needs a break-through idea forms a team. He chooses well, insofar as the team generates a raft of problems worth solving and creative ideas to meet those needs. But now the manager has a new dilemma: nothing changes, and no new ideas ever get implemented. Looking at his team, we can see why (Figure I.6).

When change starts and then stalls, the reason may be an incomplete team. Ambitious leaders need to anticipate this and build the best possible teams to move innovative thinking all the way into effective implementation.

Real-world Example 3: *No Interest in Optimizing*

A very profitable manufacturing plant has a top management team that tolerates many quality defects, much rework and waste, duplication of effort, firefighting, makeshift steps, and resource under-utilization in an environment with little accountability. In this setting, people work in silos and sit idle if work is unbalanced. When assessed using the CPSP (Figure I.7), only one of the fourteen top managers prefers optimization, and most of the managers are implementers capable of flexing but lacking efficiency. The plant could be even more profitable if management would do what it takes to optimize their work processes and thus lower their costs.

Real-world Example 4: *Heavy on Implementing and Optimizing*

Problem recognition: At a pan-national symposium of Lean Six Sigma leaders, the CPSP is offered to 79 delegates ahead of a workshop (Figure I.8). The majority of Continuous Improvement (CI) professionals have creative styles that support

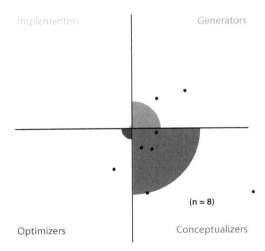

FIGURE I.6 Real-World Example 2

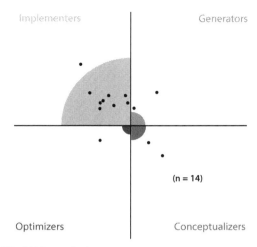

FIGURE I.7 Real-World Example 3

solution development and implementation. They are good at driving efficiency and making incremental improvements. With fewer generators and conceptualizers, however, this tribe is less likely to create disruptive innovation or discontinuous change.

Real-world Example 5: *Finding a Balance to Put It All Together*

By contrast, a regional hospital seeking innovation as well as continuous incremental improvements appointed a Transformation Leaders team to work across the hospital surfacing problems and exploiting ideas (Figure I.9).

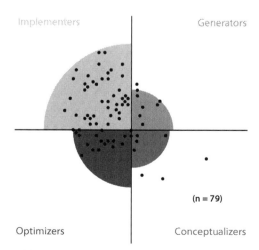

FIGURE I.8 Real-World Example 4

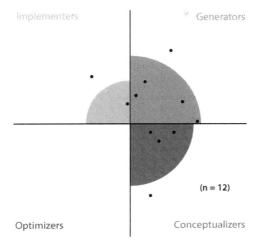

Implementers   Generators

(n = 12)

Optimizers   Conceptualizers

FIGURE I.9 Real-World Example 5

The profile of this change-making team differs markedly from the CI leaders example. Yet, providing you had reliable insights about the creative problem-solving styles of everyone, you could compose a complete dynamic team.

In order to lead people through this process in a synchronized fashion, entrepreneurs must learn to become process leaders rather than subject matter experts.[5] Simply defined, content is what we do, and process is how we do it. To leverage the thinking skills of a team, leaders need to engage them in the process of learning to think innovatively, rather than telling them what to do. This is called leading by being "the guide on the side" instead of the "sage on the stage". When leaders focus on continuously finding and solving important problems, they concentrate on process. Leaders who focus all of their attention on content typically solve the wrong problems. Understanding the crucial difference between content and process allows entrepreneurs to involve others in the creative process in a way that will maximize the use of their content expertise and uncommon sense.

Building Capability by Understanding Preferences

As discussed earlier, innovation is a continuous, circular, creative problem-solving process that begins with the deliberate seeking out (generating) of new problems and opportunities. The second stage of the process is conceptualizing, or formulating, defining, and constructing a newly generated problem. In the third stage, problem solving, evaluation and selection of solution ideas takes place, while the fourth stage results in solution implementation. The process then begins anew, as every implemented solution (action) results in the opportunity to discover (generate) new problems and opportunities.

While effective innovation requires strong performance in each of the four stages of the creativity process, our research has found that individuals, teams, and organizations may prefer some stages of the creative process more than others. We call these preferences "styles" and suggest that effective entrepreneurs must learn to synchronize the different creativity styles. In teams, for example, the members must learn to combine their individual preferences and skills in complementary ways. Our previous research found that teams composed of members with a diverse range of preferences performed better than teams made up of members with similar preferences but had less enjoyment working together due to their different styles.[6]

While most people enjoy some stages more than other stages, it is typical to see preferences that combine or blend styles. It is also common for people to prefer one style in particular but also have secondary preferences for one or two adjacent styles. An individual's unique, creative problem-solving style blend shows only their preferred activities within the creative process. These activities are illustrated in Figure I.10.

No single quadrant or style is to be considered any more "creative" than the others. Skills are needed to execute all stages. All four stages of the process require creativity of different kinds and contribute uniquely to the overall innovative process and innovative results. Successful entrepreneurs will recognize and communicate the key message that everyone has a different but equally valuable creative contribution to make to the innovation process. By allowing teammates to capitalize on their preferred orientation, entrepreneurs can turn the journey to market into a satisfying experience, as well as pinpoint individual development opportunities along the way.

Which might be your most preferred style in the **Process ?**

Implementer
- action, results
- understanding not necessary
- adapt to changing circumstances
- enthusiastic but impatient
- bring others on board, but…
- dislike apathy

Optimizer
- analytical thinking
- practical solutions to well-defined problems
- find the critical few factors
- evaluate options rather than diverge
- see little value in "dreaming"
- dislike ambiguity

Generator
- new problems, challenges
- different perspectives
- create options (diverge) rather than evaluate
- enjoy ambiguity
- keep all options open

Conceptualizer
- abstract thinking
- create new insights
- problem definition; big picture
- clear understanding necessary
- high sensitivity to and appreciation of ideas
- not concerned with moving to action

FIGURE I.10 Which Might Be Your Most Preferred Style?

- **DEFERRAL OF JUDGMENT**
- **ACTIVE DIVERGENCE**
- **ACTIVE CONVERGENCE**

FIGURE I.11 The Three Critical Process Skills

By tapping resources in all four styles, entrepreneurs can also help a team cycle skillfully through the full innovation process. Skillful synchronization of the preferred creative styles and activities (Figure I.10) of interdepartmental and interdisciplinary team members is particularly important.

In order to make this innovation process work, entrepreneurs and teams must learn and apply several specific process skills within each of the four quadrants and within each of the eight steps. These specific process skills are deferral of judgment, active divergence, and active convergence (Figure I.11).

Your skill in deferring judgment shows up in several ways, as follows:

- an open-mindedness to new opportunities;
- deferral of action on a problem in order to seek out facts;
- willingness to look for alternative ways to define a problem;
- willingness to try unusual approaches to solve a problem; and
- open-mindedness to new solutions.

Active divergence shows up when you demonstrate the following:

- continually seek new opportunities for change and improvement;
- view ambiguous situations as desirable;
- seek potential relationships beyond the known facts;
- show awareness of gaps in your own experience and tolerate situations in which things are less than clear-cut;
- realize that the early stages of innovation require the patience to discover the right questions before seeking the right answers;
- extend yourself to seek out additional possible solutions to problems and additional factors for evaluating solutions beyond the obvious.

Active convergence shows up when you:

- take reasonable risks to proceed on an option instead of waiting for the "perfect" answer;
- show willingness to help your team reach consensus by viewing differences of opinion as helpful rather than as a hindrance;
- follow through on implementation plans; and
- do whatever it takes to ensure successful implementation.

The Big Secret: Separating Process from Content

Now that we've discussed the innovation process and the skills needed to make it work well, it would appear we're ready to get started working on new product ideas, but there's still one more important point we need to cover. We call this "the big secret" of innovation, and you must master it before you can come up with truly breakthrough ideas. When you concentrate on continuously finding and solving important problems, you concentrate on process. Most of us, however, ignore process and focus only on content. Simply defined, content is *what* you work with, and process is *how* you work on it. When you focus all of your attention on content, you create no better than mediocre products. In order to distinguish yourself from your competition, you must understand the crucial difference between content and process.

How do you distinguish between process and content? Let's take an example from an automobile assembly plant. A good company will put a lot of thought into the elements of an efficient and effective assembly line. The assembly line itself is how *(the process)* all the parts *(the content)* are put together to make the automobile *(the product)*. If the parts are flawed, or if the workers lack the technical knowledge to run the machines, the product will be poor quality. If the line itself *(the process)* is flawed, the product will again be lower quality (Figure I.12).

Perhaps both the parts and the technology, and the assembly line, are high quality. But if the assembly line workers and their managers lack teamwork skills in running the line *(process skills),* the result will be the same: a poor-quality automobile (Figure I.13). What you need for a high-quality result is a combination of good content, a good process, and good process skills (Figure I.14). We can express the idea as the quality product equation (Figure I.15).

Similarly, if the plant managers focus only on content and lack skills in managing process, poor quality will result. It is not enough, for example, for managers to concentrate only on the number of cars produced and the associated costs. If they neglect to maintain and upgrade the auto assembly process and neglect to develop their skills in cooperating with their fellow managers, employees, customers, and

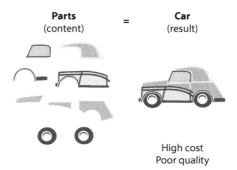

Parts   =   **Car**
(content)   (result)

High cost
Poor quality

FIGURE I.12 The Result of Content Without Process

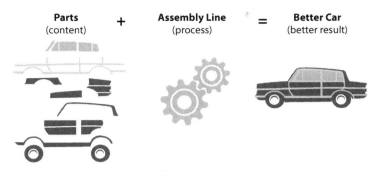

FIGURE I.13 The Result of Content Plus Process

suppliers *(their process skills),* what will result are poor-quality cars, poor sales, and low profits. When the managers pay equal attention to maintaining quality parts, machinery and technical skills, creating and maintaining efficient assembly lines, and ensuring that people are motivated and collaborative, then they are managing both content and process.

For world-class managers, in this assembly line or anywhere else, today's quality products are never good enough. These managers strive to improve both content and process throughout the organization in order to continuously improve the quality of its offerings. They make the effort to interact with customers to unearth new or hidden problems and to invent new products and procedures to solve them.

Now let's consider the assembly line metaphor within an entrepreneurial context. Many entrepreneurs are savvy enough to bring content experts onto the founding team for collaboration and idea generation. But how many entrepreneurs use a process or develop process skills among the team to systematically move an idea from raw possibility to actionable breakthrough? The answer is not

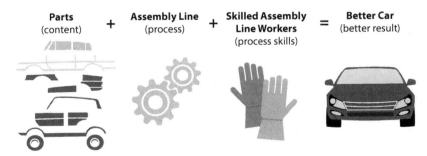

FIGURE I.14 The Result of Content Plus Process Plus Process Skills

Quality Results = Content + Process + Process Skills

FIGURE I.15 The Quality Results Equation

very many, as intuition and experience become most entrepreneur's guideposts. As a result, the opportunity stage of a startup becomes inefficient and stressful. This is where an innovation process employed by content experts with creative problem-solving skills can bring winning products and services to market in an efficient and satisfying way.

Thus, the "big secret" of this book is the ability to separate process from content—not just in a four-hour product development session but twenty-four hours a day, in all your dealings with customers and investors, and in all of the marketing, operations, and financial problems you're trying to solve. An effective process is often invisible to an onlooker. Think of the major leaguer who makes baseball look easy, or the actor who makes the audience forget that he's only acting. Their years of practice have given them high process skills. Few people, however, will truly understand the process-content dichotomy just by reading about it. Most people are too eager to jump into content without considering process. As with most things, what you need to do is practice, practice, and practice. Become self-aware that process leads to better outcomes. Be deliberate. Slow down and methodically work through the process. Over your startup journey, you'll likely find yourself passing those companies that moved too quickly executing poorly conceived plans that don't truly address what their market wants.

This book is about managing the entrepreneurial process of developing new sources of revenue for a startup or already existing business—thinking about *how* you are creating new products and services and about ways to continually improve the how. We hope you understand the concept of process and develop the process skills that drive it. While the implementation of an idea may vary between a startup and an existing business, the process of finding and developing ideas will be very similar regardless of the organization. In the following chapters, we will examine in more depth each step of the innovation process involved in the early stages of entrepreneurial activity. We dedicate Chapters 1 through 5 to explaining how to design new products and services through identifying and solving important customer problems. Chapters 6 and 7 share steps for preparing the idea for market acceptance, as well as providing skills for creating an organizational culture that centers on collaboration and efficient problem solving. Many other books exist for building enterprises, but this book will concentrate on the design of the original concept that the business is built around. Therefore, we do not cover business planning, financing, legal issues, and a myriad of other "nuts and bolts" startup issues.

Throughout the book we also incorporate design principles and practices (such as ethnographic research, prototyping, and iteration) to complement our creative process. However, we utilize a more explicit method than how most design is practiced. Design is typically executed in an approach that might be called "directed serendipity." That is, there are stages in design approaches that utilize tools, but the processes are fairly unstructured. Our creative process provides a systemized method with more structure and guidance than the average design approach. Each chapter will also provide examples illustrating how the steps are performed. We are confident that if you learn and apply this book's creative process that you will design and deliver more breakthrough ideas your customers will love. Good luck!

Notes

1 Dimov, D. (2007). "From Opportunity Insight to Opportunity Intention: The Importance of Person-Situation Learning Match." *Entrepreneurship Theory and Practice,* 31(4): 561–83.
2 Fiet, J. O. (2007). "A Prescriptive Analysis of Search and Discovery." *Journal of Management Studies,* 44(4): 592–611.
   Fiet, J. O., and Migliore, P. J. (2001). "The Testing of a Model of Entrepreneurial Discovery by Aspiring Entrepreneurs." *Frontiers of Entrepreneurship Research.* Bygrave, W. D. Autio, E., Brush, C. G., Davidsson, P., Greene, P. G., Reynolds, P. D., and Sapienza, H. J. (eds.). Wellesley, MA: Babson College, pp. 1–12.
   Fiet, J. O., and Patel, P. C. (2008). "Entrepreneurial Discovery as Constrained, Systematic Search." *Small Business Economics,* 30(3): 215–29.
3 Sarasvathy, S. (2008). *Effectuation: Elements of Entrepreneurial Expertise.* Northampton, MA: Edward Elgar Publishing.
4 Schoeniger, G. and Taulbert, C. (2010). *Who Owns the Ice House: Eight Life Lessons from an Unlikely Entrepreneur,* Cleveland, OH: ELI, p. 27.
5 Basadur, M. S. (2004). "Leading Others to Think Innovatively Together: Creative Leadership." *Leadership Quarterly,* 15: 103–21.
6 Basadur, M. S., and Head, M. (2001). "Team Performance and Satisfaction: A Link to Cognitive Style within a Process Framework." *Journal of Creative Behavior,* 35: 1–22.

1
STEP 1: PROBLEM FINDING

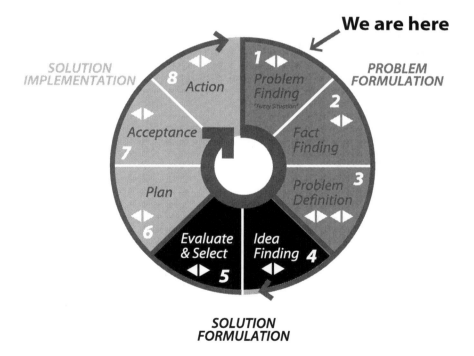

Entrepreneurs that design innovative products and services are first and foremost good problem solvers. They anticipate customer problems and market opportunities and develop timely solutions. They continually seek out ways to improve their customers' lives, and they search for changing circumstances that they can turn to their advantage. Rather than wait to see what their competitors do, they shake up their industry. Simply put, problems are the clay that entrepreneurs shape into new products and services.

Successful entrepreneurs are comfortable with the word *problem*. Most people are not. Think of the negative words we normally associate with a problem: crisis, disaster, barrier, bottleneck, trouble, deviation, fear. Our negative perceptions cause us to avoid problems rather than seek them out. A negative view of a problem also causes us to do a poor job in solving it because we might grasp for a hasty answer to make it go away. However, being comfortable with ambiguity and uncertainty and deliberately addressing problems lead to better designed products and services. This positive mindset helps entrepreneurs expand their horizons of opportunity. Let's think of some positive words associated with problems: challenge, goal, objective, opportunity, desire, wish. With imagination, skill, and open-mindedness, we can often turn apparent impossibilities into opportunities for new and exciting products. We must keep an open mind toward "fuzzy situations" as the first inklings of barely sensed problems and opportunities. Remaining neutral about problems leaves room for us to define them in creative, challenging, and productive ways. Customer problems represent new situations that entrepreneurs can turn to their advantage.

Positives and negatives can be found in any problem. However, if we think of problems as fuzzy situations filled with opportunities, we will be more likely to anticipate and seek them out. This cannot help but improve our customers' lives and our bottom line. We would also do well to remember this Chinese proverb: "If one does not begin with a right attitude, there is little hope for a right ending."

In our field research,[1] Toshiba Corporation provided the following insights to their innovation success: "When we hire new scientists and engineers, we keep them out of R&D for two years. Instead, we place them into the sales department to begin their careers. We want them to learn that their job is to learn the problems of the customer. We want them to know we are not going to hand them problems to solve. We want them to know that innovation begins with finding problems to solve." In innovative companies, the word *problem* is synonymous with need, challenge, want, desire, opportunity, puzzle, change, trend, observation, and many other triggering terms.

STORY: No One Gives Us Problems to Solve Anymore!

I visited a former student in New York City and spoke to senior partners at the advertising and communications firm where he was now interning. They told me that their clients were increasingly uncertain about how to continue to grow their businesses. "In the old days, General Motors would come to us and say, 'Here is what we want, go do it. Run some focus groups and send us the results'. But nowadays, they often ask us to tell them what they should be doing. Our people are having trouble coping. They used to be able solve problems well. But nowadays, no one gives them a problem. More often our customers are looking for help in discovering the right problems to solve." The firm was discovering that solution formulation was no longer the name of the game. Instead problem formulation—made up of problem finding and problem definition—was the new key skill they had to master to differentiate themselves in their workplace.

Programmed vs. Non-programmed Problems

There are two very different kinds of problems people encounter in business, industry, and their personal lives. The first kind is of a more "programmed" nature. In these situations, solutions are found by applying what was learned from rigorous on-the-job training or professional schooling. They require analytical skills and knowledge of rules and procedures pre-designed to handle similar situations. The second kind is more "non-programmed." Non-programmed problems often have never been encountered before and have no preset rules and procedures to guide their handling. They are sometimes caused by changing circumstances. Such problems are typically less structured, unpredictable, and ambiguous as to "what is wanted." Solutions require additional skills, such as problem sensing and defining, open-ended fact finding, and creating and selecting from brand new diverse options. They require the use of imagination, nonlinear thinking, and some risk taking. The main challenge is to discover and define "what is wanted" because nobody really knows. Often, sensing and defining the problem is more difficult than solving it. Skills in both of these kinds of problems are vital for effective performance. However, our traditional formal training and education primarily address the former, more "programmed" kind of problems. We tend to learn formulas and turn to handbooks for advice on problem types, rules, and procedures. More training in complex, non-programmed problem solving is needed in today's world. The following is an excerpt from an address by an officer of a major corporation to a prestigious high school faculty. He articulates the gap in our formal education, which the Simplexity creative problem-solving process attempts to fill.

STORY: Prestigious High School Faculty

In a keynote address, a corporate executive urged a prestigious high school faculty to prepare their students for the uncertainty they will face in their future working lives.

> In business—and in industry, government, and institutions—in the world outside this campus, nobody defines your assignment. And you almost never get a grade. There are rewards for a job well done—raises, perquisites, eventual prestige and position; but those come with less frequency, perhaps, than they do in school. This can provoke frustration, particularly in younger people unfamiliar with the anxiety of navigating uncharted territory without specific and certain directions and in the face of continual, accelerating change. Please help your students learn how to find out what to do by themselves. Help them learn how to operate independently.

Organizations whose main virtues during previous times were predictability and reliability are finding it difficult to adapt to this increasingly dynamic environment. In previous decades, the role of the manager was to improve efficiency and maximize the next quarter's results. Those goals required routine-based, analytical thinking and decision-making. These skills were widely taught in most business and engineering schools and universities and were rewarded and reinforced in most organizations. But while still valuable, an organization's efficiency is now recognized as only one-half of the formula for success in today's shifting economy. The other half of the success formula demands that organizations develop proactive adaptability skills.[2,3]

Efficiency means perfecting routines in order to attain the highest quantity and quality for the lowest possible cost. On the other hand, adaptability means continually and intentionally changing routines and finding new things to do and innovative ways to do current work. Adaptability means scanning the environment[4] to anticipate new problems, trends, customer needs, and opportunities, and then deliberately changing methods in order to attain new levels of quantity, quality, and cost and new innovative methods, products, and services. To develop adaptability and build competitive edge, entrepreneurs must expand their thinking to include non-routine-based, imaginative creative thinking and problem-solving skills.

As shown in Figure 1.1, the key to adaptability is problem finding.

Problem finding does not come easily to many people.[5] People tend to wait for others to find problems for them to solve rather than take the initiative to seek out or anticipate problems, changes, trends, and opportunities for improvement or innovation. Leavitt[6] suggested this tendency is, in large part, due to the fact that managers find their desks loaded with problems every day, making it easy for them to be reactive rather than proactive. In fact, people often avoid important problems that cut across organizational functions and department lines. The phrase "that's not our problem" becomes a second-nature response for them. They also tend to avoid addressing complex or "wicked" problems[7]—that is, messy problems that do not lend themselves to analytical problem-solving techniques. Even on less daunting but not obviously solvable problems, people often assume prematurely that

Adaptability

- · **Anticipating** new problems, trends, opportunities
  (and creating new products and services in advance)
- · Pro-actively **seeking** new methods and technologies
- · **Deliberately** changing and disrupting routine
- · **Finding** new and better work
- · **Prompt** acceptance of new ideas
- · Acceptance **across** the whole organization

FIGURE 1.1 Adaptability

"it can't be done" simply because of their unwillingness to challenge conventions or step beyond the boundaries of their current work.

Can problem-finding performance be developed? Recall the Toshiba story placing newly hired R&D engineers and scientists into the sales department to begin their careers so that they gain awareness that innovation begins with discovering customers' problems. Later, solutions to those problems become new products. Other top companies in Japan also teach new employees in first-day orientation training sessions that problems are "golden eggs." They are provided encouragement and simple structures to identify problems as opportunities for improving processes and products. Employees are then encouraged to solve them and implement the solutions themselves. In North America, the 3M Corporation sets goals that provoke problem finding for its managers. For example, one goal calls for 25 percent of the company's products to be new every 5 years. As well, 3M employees are required to spend 15 percent of their working time exploring new opportunities of personal interest to them.[8]

The bottom line is that innovation is a process, not an event or an outcome. It is a process of finding and defining internal and external customer needs, developing solutions to address those needs, and successfully implementing those solutions. The needs—or problems to be solved—can be found across a broad spectrum of areas, including, but not limited to, technology, products, markets, packaging, design, manufacturing processes, new business models, and new ways to go to market.

Using an effective innovation process will help you tackle customer problems other companies avoid … or can't even find! In the next section, we look at some legendary entrepreneurs who were great at finding worthwhile customer problems to solve.

Legendary Problem Finders

Steve Jobs

Steve Jobs is one of the most innovative entrepreneurs in history. He transformed seven industries over an illustrious career. Personal computing, animated movies, music, phones, tablet computing, retail stores, and digital publishing were all impacted by the creations of the Apple and Pixar teams he led. Many experts debate what the source of his ingenuity was. Was it his drive to "make a dent in the universe?" Maybe. His motivation of building empires that improved the world around him did inspire him, but this drive doesn't explain how he made his breakthroughs. So was it his love of design? Indeed, great attention to aesthetics, functionality, and simplicity led to many of his successful products, and design was the guiding philosophy of how Jobs worked with his management and R&D teams. But design does not address the fundamental way he found great opportunities for Apple and Pixar. To understand how Jobs designed great products for his companies, you have to go a layer deeper: you have to understand how Jobs found problems to direct his teams' efforts.

In *Steve Jobs,* Walter Isaacson starts the book by sharing how the entrepreneur approached him for the idea of writing his biography. Isaacson had invited Jobs to a summer conference at the Aspen Institute in Colorado. Jobs agreed to come, but he didn't want to speak at the conference. He wanted to go there to take a walk and talk about something very personal with the author. Isaacson thought that was a bit strange, but he discovered that taking a walk with Jobs was serious business. Walks were when he would think through with others what his next big projects would be or how to work through the issues with current projects he was completing. At other times in his career, he took walks with Bill Gates to discuss an Apple partnership with Microsoft, or he walked around his neighborhood before dinner with technology experts from industries he was thinking about entering. In this case, it was to have his authorized biography written before he died. What was Jobs doing on these walks? He was thinking deeply about what challenges he wanted to pursue. He was problem finding.

Let's learn how Jobs found interesting problems to solve by looking at the iPhone, one of his most iconic products. The iPhone was such a revolutionary product that when it first launched a lot of the business press and industry experts thought it would be a complete failure. Many complained that the iPhone had a solid screen on its entire face. They thought that smartphone users liked the tactile sensation and surety of button pushing and that customers would reject the new invention. But that's exactly the problem Jobs was trying to address with the iPhone. He reimagined the smartphone industry by asking the question, "How might we create a phone that is more interactive and has more space for visuals?" He solved a new problem in the phone industry that others had overlooked. And as a result, customers loved it. As Isaacson reports, "By the end of 2010, Apple had sold 90 million iPhones, and it reaped more than half of the total profits generated in the global cell phone market."[9]

Once Jobs got his head around a challenge he wanted to pursue, he would direct all his energy to understanding everything he could about it. With regard to the iPhone, solving the full screen problem would require learning a lot about new materials, supply chains, software, and hardware. At this point, he tasked his team and himself with finding out all they could about the issues related to the problem he was trying to solve. We call this "fact finding," and we will discuss that important step in the next chapter. But as history shows, thinking hard about what challenges you want to pursue can pay off by sending you down a path others have overlooked. Jobs was always searching for that problem his competitors weren't willing to address.

Edwin Land

One of Steve Jobs's personal heroes was Edwin Land, the inventor of the Polaroid camera. Jobs was fascinated by Land's ability to create a product others during his time could not even imagine possible. He even met Land in person and quizzed him on his process. Jobs applied those lessons in building Apple into an innovation powerhouse. Some years ago, a Life Magazine cover story told the tale of the invention of the Polaroid camera. Having snapped the last exposure on his film, Land suggested to his three-year-old daughter that they take the film for processing so they could see the pictures in about a week's time. Her response was, "Why do I have to wait a week to see my picture?" Like a flash bulb going off in his mind, her simple question sparked a challenge that had never occurred to him: "How might I make a camera that yields instantaneous pictures?" Within about an hour, he had formulated several solutions, and within about four years, he had commercialized a product that changed lives.[10] Looking back, the then-chairman of Polaroid said the most important part of the process was not finding the solution itself—the camera—but finding the problem: how to get instantaneous pictures. The moral of the story, in Land's words: "If you can define a problem, it can be solved."

Thomas Edison

Think of Thomas Edison's invention of the phonograph in 1878. Until then, the world had revolved perfectly well without this device. But Edison was always looking for ways to create inventions that changed the world around him. One important market he immersed himself in was communication technology. Edison came naturally to pursue this industry, as he had been a telegrapher as a young man. As an adult, he feverishly looked for ways to advance the telegraph beyond commercial use to households. He also had interest in perfecting the telephone, which had already been invented by Alexander Graham Bell. Using his experience as a telegrapher, Edison thought that the telephone could be very useful as a new product for telegraph companies. He imagined telegraph officers working with the human voice rather than dots and dashes. It would be a much richer form of communication. However, the use of the new invention would lead to some difficulties for the operators. They would have to transcribe the conversation, or repeat the message to an assistant who would write it down. That sounded like a lot of work, so Edison started thinking about how he could make the telephone easier to use for telegraphers. So he took it upon himself to tackle the problem, "How might I record the human voice?"

After sensing the opportunity, it didn't take him long to come up with the solution. He rigged a test combining parts of a telephone with telegraph recording equipment and used wax paper to record the transmission. He said, "Mary had a little lamb," into the mouthpiece, and when he looked at the wax paper he saw irregular markings on it. Imagine his own surprise when his first solution actually worked.[11] When he put a needle on top of the paper and pulled the strip under it, his voice could be heard coming from the telephone equipment. He later refined this solution into a waxed disk and phonograph that could play back music or the human voice anytime the listener chose. It was a monumental achievement in entrepreneurship history; however, observers believe the real creativity in this invention was not the discovery of the solution but the discovery of the problem.

Henry Ford

Henry Ford is another member of the American entrepreneurship pantheon, and he had a connection to Thomas Edison as well. At the age of 28, he worked for the Edison Illuminating Company as an engineer. In his spare time, he worked on developing gasoline engines for automobile prototypes and was even later supported by Edison himself in doing so. However, being the entrepreneur he was, he left Edison's company to start the Detroit Automobile Company. Over the years he would start and close a few automobile companies as he experimented with ways to improve the performance, quality, and cost points of the new product. At the age of 40, he received the help of more supportive investors and formed the Ford Motor Company. Building on his experiences in the industry and with the support of his management team, he experimented and perfected innovations that revolutionized the automobile industry. His cars set speed records and competed in races against other manufacturers. On October 1, 1908, he introduced the country to the Model T, his crowning achievement in the automobile industry.

The Model T's steering, engine, and transmission became the standard for what a car was to be. It was a huge success, and its growth was further propelled by Ford's promotion of it in newspapers and advertisements. However, a challenge many successful entrepreneurs face when their companies take off is how to meet the increasing demand while maintaining the quality and performance their customers have come to expect. Ford had advantages in addressing this challenge though. He had vast experience as an engineer and entrepreneur. Thus, he could facilitate the needs of the business with the design challenges the technicians faced. He was obsessed with not only building the best car in the world but also doing it in a very cost efficient way. As sales increased, he had to ask himself, "How might I meet the increasing demand of my customers by making my cars much more quickly?" The answer became the moving assembly line. Until then, Ford had increased efficiencies through the use of advanced machinery like stamping machines and specialized labor, but the assembly of the cars was still very labor intensive. By moving a car chassis to a worker's station rather than the worker coming to the car, the Ford Motor Company was able to drastically reduce the time it took to build it. The improved efficiency led to more customers and greater profitability for the company. The moving assembly line became so successful that companies in other industries began to copy Ford's manufacturing philosophy too. The manufacturing revolution that started in his Highland Park plant became a model for other companies. Because of his impact on his contemporaries' practices, Henry Ford once proclaimed that *he* created the modern world. So it's not a stretch to say that the world we live in is largely a result of Henry Ford tackling the problem of making the mass production of his day even more massive.[12]

Walt Disney

Another legendary entrepreneur who tackled the problem of mass production was Walt Disney. Many people do not realize this because of his affiliation with entertainment. We think of movies and the arts as a place for craftsmen and tinkerers, and it is. But to have worldwide and cross-generational impact like Disney, it also requires building a system to deliver it to all those admiring fans. For this reason, Disney has similarities to Henry Ford, in that both entrepreneurs were able to make innovative leaps in technology in their chosen fields while also scaling their product to the masses. Walt made significant contributions to the art of filmmaking by introducing the storyboard and other innovations in the use of color, sound, and camerawork for animated and live-action films. However, while Disney was proud of these accomplishments, he thought his greatest creation was the studio he built to produce and deliver the movies and related products. And for this objective, Walt used the Ford factory model as his inspiration for how to more efficiently scale animated movie production. As Neal Gable chronicled in *Walt Disney*, "Walt had always been as concerned with the process of making cartoons as with the cartoons themselves, and in comparing his studio to a factory production line, he was acknowledging the new pressure on him to streamline that process. ... It was precisely because he didn't want to sacrifice his status as the best cartoon maker that he was driven to find a better way to make cartoons, effectively trying to mass-produce excellence."[13] The philosophy worked, and Disney was able to apply it to television and live-action movies as well.

With cartoons, animated movies, live-action films, television, soundtrack albums, and licensed merchandise and books emanating from the Disney company, Walt started ruminating on his next foray into American entertainment. He loved that his products provided an avenue for children and adults to be entertained and educated while also offering an escape from their everyday lives. But Disney was never satisfied, and he was always looking for his next big challenge to tackle. When you've conquered movies, music, and television, what else is there to do? That's when it occurred to Walt that instead of bringing his dreams and visions to the customers, what if the customers were to come to him? What if they became part of his show? Disney's insight drove him to offer a different type of place than had ever existed before in the world: the theme park. Amusement parks had been around a long time, and Walt was a fan of them as a child, but once he became a parent he saw their shortcomings. Amusement parks were dirty and loud with a lot of disjointed attractions. The problem Walt tackled by building a theme park might be framed as "How might I offer a place that provides an escape from daily life that both children and adults can enjoy?"

The solution became Disneyland. It was a major challenge to conquer, but once Disneyland was built the world had another form of entertainment to love thanks to Walt. As Gabler notes, "Disney reconceptualized the amusement park as a full imaginative experience, a *theme* park, rather than a series of diversions, and just as his animation revised graphic design, his park eventually revised urban design." Walt had so successfully solved the problem of building a three-dimensional form of entertainment that he had enough money to pursue his next big problem of interest: the American community. Just as he saw shortcomings in amusement parks, he thought cities could be designed better too. Disneyland's success afforded him the opportunity to build a new form of city, which was to be called E.P.C.O.T., which stands for the Experimental Prototype Community of Tomorrow. It was to be an actual community where people would live in a real life urban design experiment where leading corporations would design and test breakthrough technologies in the setting. Unfortunately, Disney died before constructing it, but the company did proceed with building the EPCOT theme park at Walt Disney World. The park stands as a testament of Walt Disney's endless pursuit of solving big problems.

As these stories demonstrate, many of history's most impactful entrepreneurs started their journeys by finding big problems to solve. They approached the world with a mindset that they could change it for the better. A major issue for an entrepreneur is finding a good starting point. Attitudes and motivation help in knowing where to start. After all, you can't solve a problem until you find it—and finding problems requires motivation and a collaborative spirit. Taking delight in discovering problems to solve, being "constructively discontented" with the status quo, and looking for "golden eggs" are important traits in creating breakthrough products. However, most people aren't intuitively successful in doing this like a Walt Disney or a Steve Jobs. Fortunately, entrepreneurs don't have to be born with this ability; they can attain it by learning a process and applying it to the world around them. In the rest of this chapter, we will provide step-by-step guidance on how you can find worthwhile problems for your startup to address. The first step is to discover whose problem you're going to solve.

Who's the *Real* Customer?

Before you start solving problems, you have to decide whose problems you actually need to solve. This sounds obvious, but it's actually a much deeper assignment than it appears. Most people think of the customer as the person who pays for a product or service, and technically that is true. However, just because someone pulls money out of their pocket, that doesn't mean that they are the one making the *real* decision. The *real* customer is someone who has the most influence on a buying decision. When we approach the buying decision from this perspective, we might uncover an entirely new set of problems that others are overlooking.

Let's look at an example we're all familiar with. Think about some of your trips wandering up a grocery aisle looking for your favorite breakfast cereal. Have you ever had trouble finding it because of all of the choices on the shelves? And this is just when you're shopping for yourself. Now imagine you're buying a cereal for a picky child. You want to buy something healthy for your daughter, but you also know that if she doesn't like it, you'll be throwing away a lot of cereal over the next week. Who is making the real decision in this situation? Many consumer goods companies would lead us to believe it's the child. After all, breakfast cereal advertising is a staple on children's television. Now think about how many commercials for a sugary breakfast cereal you have seen during an episode of an adult show like *The Walking Dead*. The answer is not very many. Clearly, a consumer goods company knows that influencing a child's interest in their product will affect which cereal the parents buy. So who's the *real* customer of sugary breakfast cereal? Oftentimes it's the child.

Let's examine another common buying decision: buying a car. The average person buys many cars during their lifetime, but the type of car purchased will vary depending on what stage of life they're in. Even if a person has a dream car lodged firmly in their heart, they may not get to buy it when others have more say on the purchase.

Imagine you have a buddy named Frank. Frank is a fan of German sports cars and always dreamed of owning a Porsche 911. When Frank was in high school, he worked part-time jobs so he could save up to buy his own car. He spent his free time cruising car lots and checking out which car he'd buy when he had enough money. Because his father appreciated his son's work ethic, he made Frank a deal. When Frank bought his car, his father would pay for the insurance. One day Frank decided it was time to buy his dream car. He thought he could get a good one with $10,000 and rushed down to the used car lot. When Frank pulled into the lot, he saw a black Porsche 911 with 110,000 miles on it, and it only costs $9,000. He called his dad to approve the purchase, but much to his dismay Frank was told not to buy the car. The insurance would be too much. Frank ended up buying a different car that he liked but didn't love. With the guidance of his dad, Frank bought a used Subaru Outback. It was sporty, had good gas mileage, and was very reliable. The Subaru lasted him a long time. A couple years into his marriage, it was time for Frank to trade in for a new car again. This time he had to think about his new family and bought a minivan. Frank experienced this situation a few more times until years in the future when he retired. As a reward to himself, he bought a brand new 911. It took Frank 40 years before he was the *real* customer of the vehicle he drove.

Now let's take a look at how one of our colleagues determined who her customer was. Sylvie is a successful process consultant who frequently travels on business, but she would prefer more consulting jobs in her home city. In order to make this transition worthwhile, she would need to find clients who would pay enough to offset the revenues she would give up by not traveling to see former customers. After giving it much thought, she determined that the best consulting contract in her home city would be with the city itself. Sylvie lives in a booming city led by a very charismatic mayor with a big vision. If she could explain how her services would help him make his vision possible, maybe she could secure a long-term contract to assist with new projects. Unfortunately, many other consultants in town would also like to sit down with the mayor and pitch their ideas. When Sylvie asked for our advice in how she could get a contract with the mayor, we asked her to think about who had influence on creating the mayor's schedule. Sylvie divulged a list of possible influential people, such as his P.R. people, his secretary, his wife, the human resources department, the local newspaper, and the mayor's chief advisor. When we asked her who was *really* the most influential person in determining who met with the mayor, she thought about it a while and then confidently said the mayor's chief advisor. She explained that the chief advisor filtered through what information the mayor considered, and if she could win him over, then the meeting with the mayor would be a cinch. Thus, Sylvie determined that the *real* customer of her consulting services with the city was the mayor's chief advisor.

Figure 1.2 provides a template for discovering who the real customer of your product is. It demonstrates that whenever we want to design a new product or service, we start by asking, "Who do we intuitively think is our customer?" Keep in mind that sometimes the obvious person that we think is the customer oftentimes is. However, we should not make that assumption until we've examined who has influence on the buying decision. Thus, we next ask, "Who has influence on this person's buying decision?" In answering this question, we want to write everyone that comes to mind. Diverge on as many people and organizations as you can think of (include the intuitive answer on the list as well). Now look at the list and ask yourself, "Out of all these people, who is the most influential person in determining what is purchased?" If you are having a hard time deciding, you can also ask yourself, "So, who do I have to really win over to get this business?"

Who do we intuitively think is our customer? _____

_____

Who has influence on this person's buying decision?_____

_____

Out of all these people, who is the most influential person in
determining what is purchased? _____

_____

So, who do I have to really win over to get this business? _____

_____

FIGURE 1.2 The *Real* Customer

When we have decided who on the list is the best answer to these questions, we have found our *real* customer. We also call this person the "owner" of the problem. This is who we fill focus on creating a solution for.

Now that we know who the real customer is, we will need to better understand them. Acquiring deep knowledge of the customer is the keystone of a well-designed solution. Only through such deep understanding can we pinpoint the best problems to solve for the customer. Well-established companies have constructed extensive profiles of their customers, but anyone can generate knowledge on a potential market if they are willing to do their fieldwork. All it requires is the willingness to find potential customers, talk with them, and record the findings.

Remember the legendary entrepreneurs we discussed earlier? Who were their real customers? With regard to Jobs and the iPhone, we might intuitively think the general public was. However, studying the history of the iPhone reveals that Jobs had to convince one important person to get it made. Wendell Weeks, the CEO of Corning, controlled the manufacturing of Gorilla Glass, the only material that could work on the all-encompassing face of the iPhone. Without Weeks's approval, there would be no iPhone. In this case, the *real* customer might be Weeks.

What about Edwin Land and Polaroid? Again, the obvious answer is the general public, which bought up the first 56 cameras sold at the Jordan Marsh department store in Boston on November 26, 1948. However, before that big day could happen, Land had to convince its future competitor Eastman Kodak to manufacture the film for him. At the time, Polaroid had an insignificant presence in the film industry, but the originality of the product enticed Kodak to take a chance on him. Can you imagine the moxie Land must have had to get an agreement from not only a competitor but one of the world's largest firms?

Now let's re-examine Thomas Edison's invention. When Edison developed the phonograph, his Menlo Park laboratory was in its startup stage. He wasn't known as the Wizard of Menlo Park yet, so he had to hustle to find capital for his R&D activities. Edison was trying to draw attention to his lab's innovation capabilities and was looking for ways to promote his inventions. At the time, he was working feverishly to develop a telephone that would rival his competitor Alexander Graham Bell. In need of business orders and investment funds, Edison turned his attention to making the American public aware of who he was and what his lab could do. Although he had not yet put much thought into how to commercialize the phonograph, he recognized the publicity possibilities he could receive by promoting it. In Edison's case the real customer was someone who could persuade the American public that Edison was a genius whose products should be anticipated and bought. For the phonograph idea, he identified the editors of *Scientific American* as his target for winning worldwide fame. His business partner Edward Johnson sent the magazine a letter with an engraved illustration that described the phonograph. It worked. The idea of a device that would allow the public to replay music and the voices of great orators, even if they were dead, captivated the American imagination. Edison became a celebrity and was better able to secure orders for his many inventions that followed later. Therefore, it might be observed that *Scientific American* was the *real* customer of the phonograph.

Henry Ford was another entrepreneur we recognized for addressing key problems. His most successful product, the Model T, was in production well before he addressed the assembly line challenge. In 1912, it took 12.5 hours to assemble his car with traditional methods. But in 1914, after the assembly line process was refined, the task took only 93 minutes to complete. Efficiency was not new to Ford. He was innovative in adopting the use of metal stampings, machine tools, repetitive work, and time studies in his factories. However, he was always looking for better ways to manufacture his product. In the case of the Model T assembly line problem, the real customers were his chief mechanics … and Henry Ford himself.

You see, Ford didn't come up with the assembly line idea himself. The actual innovator of the assembly line car approach was company executive Charles Sorenson. Sorenson thought it would be easier and faster to move a chassis along different stations rather than clustering all the parts around a chassis for assembly. He tested the idea on a Sunday in 1908 when production was shut-down. Sorenson had parts distributed across the factory and had a makeshift assembly line organized. He had a chassis tugged along on a skid as workers added parts at the various assembly locations. Ford and his chief mechanics observed the exercise but were hesitant about adopting it. In the end, Ford was the one person in the group who gave the go-ahead to Sorenson to continue experimenting with the concept.

The first actual product made via assembly line production was a flywheel magneto. Twenty-nine men turned a 20-minute job into 13 minutes using the assembly line approach. Over the next year, modifications enabled the production time to drop to 5 minutes. Ford was impressed by the results and was convinced that assembly line production was the key to success in the automobile industry. Once Henry Ford had sold *himself* on the idea of the assembly line process, his sheer will and leadership as an entrepreneur transformed the industry. He gave the green light to modernize the entire assembly process in 1914, and by 1925 the company was producing over 2 million cars per year.

Now let's look at Walt Disney. When Disney decided to tackle the problem of creating a family-friendly theme park, it was a concept most people couldn't get their head around. Amusement park operators thought the idea was destined for failure because of the expansive sets and gardens proposed in the design. They didn't think Walt had thought through the economics of running such a park. Even his own wife thought the idea was too much of a stretch to pull off. But another family member who had more influence on whether the park was built was his brother and business partner Roy. Roy was responsible for financing Walt's dreams, and he thought this one would require more money than they could afford to risk. Most of the other executives in the company agreed with Roy. So the real customer for Disneyland was actually the Walt Disney Company itself.

In order to convince his company that the idea was worthwhile, Walt started his own organization called WED Enterprises (which stands for Walter Elias Disney). Hiring some of the studio's best animators and model makers, he designed concepts of what Disneyland could be. Once his brother saw the ideas and how committed Walt was to fulfilling it, Roy convinced the rest of the company to pursue Disneyland. From there, Walt and Roy were able to take the drawings and models to the Bank of America and the ABC television network to arrange the financing they needed to build the park.

As these stories evidence, we need to think beyond the end user or the person with the purchasing decision when trying to gain support for our products and services. You have to think about who you *really* have to win over to make your business a success. Recognizing the real customer and what their problems are helps the entrepreneur in uncovering possibilities their competitors may be overlooking. However, this recognition is difficult unless you clearly understand the world that the customer inhabits. To really get inside their heads, you have to have knowledge on where they live and work, what they do, and what they think. Creative problem solvers can attain this knowledge by immersing themselves in those environments. In the following section, we explain how an entrepreneur can acquire this knowledge via a "deep dive" into the customers' world.

The Deep Dive

A winning business concept begins with recognizing the problems of a customer and concludes with creating a delightful solution. Unfortunately, all too often entrepreneurs reverse this process. They devote a lot of brain power and money into an invention that nobody really wants. The entrepreneur falls in love with their idea at the expense of the business. We call this the "Great Product, No Market" mistake. You might love your new idea, but is there a customer out there somewhere with a problem it will solve? Target customers may find the product interesting, but no wants to write a check for it. Until these people are converted into actual customers, there is no business.

Consider the following scenario.[14] A consumer products company was trying to expand from retail into the institutional market. Market research indicated that the size and number of hospitals and schools afforded great opportunities for revenue growth. The plan was to approach this new market with the same routine they had used many times in retail: make a superior product, promote it like crazy, and watch the customers pour in. So the company began a project to offer a better disinfecting and cleaning product than was currently used in institutions. Their testing showed that all current competitor products provided only marginal cleaning but passed the government laboratory germ-killing tests. Their field performance was marginal. The solution was to produce a product that was both a cleaner and a disinfectant and thus killed germs much better than the competitors did.

The technical difficulty was that normal cleaning ingredients were not compatible with standard disinfecting ingredients. The company had great technical prowess in cleaning, and their competitors did not. Combining cleaning and disinfecting ingredients was recognized as a formidable challenge. The company chose to take it on as a way of building a competitive edge using their technical core strength.

After two years of intensive effort, the R&D department completed the project and a breakthrough, patentable formula was finally achieved. Field testing proved that the new product killed germs significantly better than competitors' because it was able to get after germs unearthed by its better cleaning performance. The company was eager to unveil the new product to customers who surely would be excited by its breakthrough performance. Floors and walls would be cleaner and more germ free than ever possible. When the product went to test market, the company was unable to sell even a gallon of it. As it turned out, purchasing administrators in hospitals and schools were searching far less for improved cleaning and disinfecting than they were for lower cost. The new product was more than double the price of the product they were currently using. Their current products were satisfactory in performance (no one was complaining), and purchasing decisions were made on price and service. So the team had devoted two years on a great solution to a non-existing problem. Perhaps if the team had studied the customer more thoroughly before developing the product, they would have known to focus more on improving cost and service for hospitals and schools and less on improving cleaning and disinfecting. Great product, no market!

So how can entrepreneurs keep from making this gaffe? The design field offers an approach. Legendary design firm IDEO avoids the "Great Product, No Market" mistake by undergoing a "deep dive" and immersing themselves in the problem space of a market. They study and interact with the customer and their surroundings in any way possible. General manager Tom Kelley says they act like anthropologists, "getting out of the office, cornering the experts, and observing the natives in their habitat."[15] In a classic *Nightline* episode, Ted Koppel covers how they do this. He presents IDEO with a distinct challenge: "Take something old and familiar, like say the shopping cart, and completely redesign it in five days."[16] After visiting grocery stores, talking to managers, watching parents and children, talking to professional buyers who purchase shopping carts, and interviewing a cart repairman, three design challenges emerged from the research: make the cart more child friendly, redesign the shopping cart experience so that traversing the aisles is more efficient, and increase safety. The team then broke into different groups and diverged on possible ways to meet these challenges in a new shopping cart design.

The team did not develop a solution until it thoroughly understood the customers and their problems. This immersive problem-finding approach, also known as ethnography, has served IDEO well over the years. The company is famous for designing such iconic products as the first Apple mouse. Anthropologists, sociologists, and videographers are just a few examples of ethnographic specialists the company employs to help their design teams. Rich observation brings deep understanding of customer problems for IDEO, helping the firm to become a global powerhouse in the design field.

But what if you don't have access to research professionals or have no experience gathering qualitative data? Can you gather enough information on your customers to know what they truly care about? Fortunately, the answer is a big "Yes!" if you are willing to dedicate the time and energy to knowing your target customer the way IDEO does theirs. The first place you can start is by interacting with customers. As you interact with your customers, document everything you learn. This practice is called journaling, and it is especially important in the early stage of concept development. In a trusty notebook, capture everything you come across that pertains to your customer and their problems. You're trying to understand the landscape of your industry and the culture of your market. As you immerse yourself in their territory, you may at times be overwhelmed by the mass of information you gather. However, keeping information and thoughts in notebooks and folders can alleviate that problem. After all, your memory is fallible. If you don't maintain notebooks, you are likely to incorrectly recall the information or forget it all together. Also, notebooks allow you to periodically re-examine your observations, which helps you pull together new ideas and insights. Notebooks are a wonderful way of reminding us of important points on our projects. They lessen the strain that comes with gathering and managing massive amounts of information. We don't have to worry about forgetting anything because it's in our notebooks. Think of these notebooks as "Thought Catchers." This allows you to focus on what you are currently observing rather than trying to remember what you have already done. Journaling keeps you present on the task at hand. In the long run, this practice can move projects along much faster because you don't risk retreading familiar ground because of forgetfulness or sloppiness. Your market and industry research becomes more efficient.

You may find note taking intimidating at first, but it is a skill that can be developed. Once you start writing down observations, you'll likely develop your own symbols and shorthand for becoming more efficient in using your notebook. Each person has their own style that works for them. The ability to observe and capture your thoughts is crucial for creating useful profiles of the customer. Figure 1.3 provides a customer fieldnote form we often use to document interactions with customers. The customer fieldnote form provides a template for reflecting on what you've captured in your notebook. The forms also allow you to methodically sift through the customer interactions. After you have a thorough collection of customer fieldnote forms, search for patterns in the answers. Pay special attention to common statements, phrases, or words that start to regularly appear, and note anything that elicits an emotional response from the interviewee. Be open to what they tell you, and look for clues in your notebook that start to show who the customer really is. As you study your customer, you can also include articles and pictures that pertain to their problems in your notebook.

1. Customer's name (if interviewed)

_____

2. Customer's address (if interviewed)

_____

3. Place of interview or observation

_____

4. Date of interview or observation

_____

5. Why did you choose to interview or observe this customer(s)?

6. Describe this customer(s).

7. What did you learn from observing or interviewing this customer(s)?

8. What surprising information did you gather that was interesting or unexpected?

9. How did the information you gathered modify your concept of the customer?

10. What one word or phrase best describes the customer or what you saw?

FIGURE 1.3 Customer Fieldnotes

This journaling practice may be new to many readers, so you might be asking yourself what you should look for or ask in the interactions. The following questions serve as prompts for gathering insights about your customers' basic attitudes and behaviors:

- What common physical features do the customers have, if any?
- What common activities do they do?
- What do they typically wear?
- What are typical jobs they hold?
- Where do a lot of these customers typically live?
- What is the most interesting thing about these customers?
- What one word or phrase best describes these customers?

Interviews, observation, and consultation can be used in answering these questions. In this stage, be open to whatever you can find out. It is important to have an open mind. Use divergent thinking to list as many answers to the questions as you can, and then converge on the most interesting facts, gaps, and revelations. You can also study others who may have knowledge about the customer, such as coworkers, friends, family members, industry experts, suppliers, distributors, and academics.

When we understand who our customer is, our next step is to understand why they purchase particular products and services in the first place. Deep philosophical questions to answer are why does this industry even exist? What purpose does it serve customers? The simplest answer is that it probably makes customers' lives better. But how? Some transactions are simply to meet the physiological and safety needs of survival, such as food, water, sex, a constant body temperature, safety from dangerous elements, and medical attention. People need to eat, clothe, and shelter themselves. Markets for satisfying these needs will always exist, but differing tastes, life goals, and means will lead to different ways this is done. For example, one person may like Colby jack cheese while another prefers pepper jack. When survival and safety needs are met, most people turn their attention to buying things to meet their desires and wants. These transactions often account for a large share of people's consumption as they buy products they want but don't necessarily need. As social critic Arthur Asa Berger summarizes, "It boils down to this: Needs are finite but desires are infinite. We don't need all the stuff we buy; but we feel that having things will make our lives better, make us feel more alive." So in a capitalistic society where desires are never fully met, companies will always have the opportunity for product and service innovation. People play many roles in society, but in order to make it manageable, we will break it up into public and private. By studying the public and private lives of customers, you will have a better understanding of what problems to address.

Public Life

One way customers pursue their vision of the "good life" is by buying products and services that signal to others their values, rank, and preferred self-image. Everyone covets their uniqueness and wants to feel special. This goal is often achieved in our society through the purchase of the things we wear, the objects we use, and the things we do. Evolutionary psychologist Geoffrey Miller[17] asserts that the underlying drive of this consumer behavior is to demonstrate to others your worth. The clothes you wear, the car you drive, and the home you live in are visible indicators of your professional and financial status. From an evolutionary perspective, these are signs or proxies of good genes, good health, and high social intelligence, which others are drawn and attracted to. As Miller notes, "Almost every animal species has its own fitness indicators to attract mates, intimidate rivals, deter predators, and solicit help from parents and kin. Male guppies grow flag-like tails, male lions sport luxuriant manes, male nightingales learn songs, male bowerbirds build bowers, humans of both sexes acquire luxury goods." In a consumer society, this will likely be an ongoing shopper arms race that will offer unlimited innovative opportunities for companies, with marketing providing the vehicle for persuading customers that the new products and services meet these underlying desires. Corporations even evidence this behavior through branding and symbols of prestige. Banks are often housed in large, marble buildings to show stability and wealth, and Fortune 500 companies host professional golf events that bring celebrities and athletes together under a corporate presence.

While Miller addresses the competitive nature of people in pursuing mates, status, and possessions, he also notes the social side of human nature. As social creatures, we seek products and services that allow us to communicate and socialize with more frequency and ease. Music preferences, webpages, and clothing help us to advertise our interests so that we can interact with people like ourselves. Coffee shops and other social settings allow us to have places to meet and socialize. Smartphones and tablet computers make it easier for people to stay in touch on a more regular basis. LinkedIn is a social networking website that brings professionals together to share ideas and contacts. There will always be business opportunities for creating new ways to help people come together and share their dreams, concerns, and aspirations. The following questions serve as prompts for attaining insights into your customer's public goals:

- How does this customer usually communicate with others?
- What are the customer's favorite places to go?
- Why do they like these locations so much?
- What about the locations they frequent stand out to you?
- Is there anything unusual about these locations?
- Is there anything about these locations that could be applied in different settings?
- Is there anything interesting about the people that could be applied to a different group of people?
- Is there anything from a different setting or group of people that could be applied to this setting?
- How do the people interact with each other in this setting?

Use divergent thinking to list as many answers to the questions as you can, and then converge on the most intriguing facts, gaps, and revelations. Answers can come from fellow employees, outside experts, customers, suppliers, and your team. You might be surprised by what trends begin to appear. Uncovering an unmet, and perhaps consciously unknown, want is a big step in making a breakthrough innovation.

Personal Life

Beyond the social nature of consumption, shopping plays an immensely personal role in people's lives. As author Jim Pooler[18] asserts, "Shopping is important, and it is underestimated. It's one of the most common things we do, and it dominates our lives. ... Never before has so much emphasis been placed on shopping and never before has it assumed the central place in our lives that it now does. Shopping for emotional and psychological reasons has become the new mantra of modern society." In short, shopping has become a pathway toward the good life and feeling fulfilled … at least in the short term. People shop to attain health and alleviate illness, to achieve gusto and thrills and reduce sluggishness and misery, to feel secure and avoid physical threats, to feel loved and admired and not hated and shunned, to be considered an insider and not an outsider looking in, to feel confident and not insecure, to feel serene and relaxed and not tense and anxious, to feel beautiful and not ugly, to feel wealthy and not poor, to feel clean and not dirty, to feel knowledgeable and not ignorant, to feel in control of life and not at the mercy of events, to feel entertained and not bored, among other reasons.

Shopping also serves as a self-reward for enduring the trials and challenges of life. In a busy world where people take on the responsibilities of work and family, they often do not receive the recognition from others they may feel they deserve. Shopping provides an opportunity to indulge in buying something extra like an unneeded tool, gadget, or piece of clothing. Savvy marketers advertise this theme in many commercials broadcast in the middle of people's busy days. Although at the opposite ends of the entertainment spectrum, Las Vegas and Disney theme parks pamper their customer base in meeting this underlying motivation with escapism and self-renewal. Ironically, some people even reward themselves for doing a good job of shopping. Finding bargains gives psychological comfort for buying more goods and services. While some people struggle to find a new business idea, the aforementioned discussion on shopping motivations evidences that there should never be a shortage of opportunities if human nature is understood and exploited. The following questions serve as prompts to find out more about your customers' life goals:

• What do they seem to enjoy doing?
• What are their hobbies?
• What activities do they pay to do?
• What are they passionate about?
• How could customers improve themselves physically, intellectually, or spiritually?
• What seems to be missing in their lives?
• What changes, issues, problems, and opportunities for improvement do you visualize for them?

Again, use divergent and convergent thinking to uncover the most intriguing facts, gaps, and revelations. Talk to many constituencies who you think may have insight to help answer these questions.

Uncovering Problems

The previous section provided guidance for gaining a better understanding of your customers. If you've completed these exercises, you should have a deeper knowledge of who they are, what they think, and what they do. Now that you have a good understanding of the customer, you can uncover the problems that really matter to them. Always remember that problems are great sources for innovation. Since it's so important for developing an innovative mindset, let's contemplate the nature of problems a little more. A problem is a situation where there is a gap between where a person is now and where they want to be; however, on their own, they haven't found a way to cross that gap. The bigger that gap is or the more difficult it is to figure out how to cross it, the bigger the problem. If it's a big enough problem, then finding a solution to it will be very important to a person. They will be willing to pay a lot to have it solved. If enough people feel the same, great market opportunity exists for the company that can solve it. Common mistakes entrepreneurs often make with a lot of serious innovation attempts are (1) the chosen solution doesn't adequately cross the gap, (2) the gap is not a big enough concern to the customer to warrant interest, and (3) there are not enough people who have the problem to make it profitable for the company. Thus, successful entrepreneurship requires finding high impact problems to solve and offering solutions that are worthwhile to enough people to justify the existence of a business.

So how do you discover worthwhile customer problems to solve? You ask the customers. A very effective way to discover problems worth solving is to gather a group of customers and other people who may have knowledge of the market and industry together in a room. With this group, you can explain to them who the customer is you plan to serve. Remember, you're going to be referring to the *real* customer. Then ask, "What problems does this customer have?" On an easel pad, capture everything the group says. Once the group has exhausted its answers, have each member select the biggest problems they think the customer has. (Depending on the size of the group, the number of selections per person will vary, but it should be small, forcing people into a convergent mode. Often the 10% rule holds: that is about 1 selection per person for every 10 problems on the list.) Once everyone has made their selections, take each selection and ask who chose it. Allow each person who chose that problem to explain their selection to the group. This is called clarifying, not judging or defending, as it provides more thought to what the problem really means to the group. After all the chosen problems have been discussed, facilitate the group to choose the top 1 or 2 problems to consider further. This 3-step converging method is called "telescoping" and is shown in Figure 1.4.

Telescoping is a powerful technique for individuals and groups to learn to apply. Experience and scientific research[19,20] provide empirical evidence that, *if performed skillfully*, a creative problem-solving group can significantly improve the quality of the options being evaluated *while they are being evaluated*. As clarification occurs ("Oh, now I understand better what you meant by that choice!"), new or improved options often begin emerging. Thus, quality convergence often breeds quality (secondary) divergence.

After you've diverged and converged on selecting the customer's biggest problems, you'll want to make sure there's strong interest in finding a solution to the chosen problems. If there isn't a lot of energy in the room, you can ask this penetrating question to draw out a more honest response: "We've looked at a lot of possible problems the customer might have, and they are all good things to think

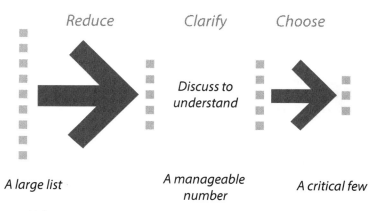

FIGURE 1.4 Telescoping

about, but what's the customer's *real* problem? What really needs to be addressed for them?" This question usually gets the group to get to the root problem the customer has.

If you have the time and want to do a deeper problem-finding session, you can ask more detailed questions instead of simply asking, "What problems does your customer have?" The following prompter questions are useful tools to immerse deeper into the problem space of the customer. The questions are broken into business to consumer (B2C) and business to business (B2B) classifications, depending on the type of business you're pursuing.

Problem Classification 1a (B2C)

Questions to uncover the present problems the customer may have if they are a consumer

- What are the customers' major gripes and difficulties?
- What opportunities are the customers missing in their lives?
- What small problems do your customers have that could grow into big ones?
- What barriers impede your customers from being more successful?
- How could you improve the quality of the products or services they currently buy?
- What are their most difficult people problems?
- What goals do they fail to attain year after year?
- What crises do these customers often face in their lives?
- What issues are these customers often afraid or embarrassed to bring up?
- What areas of their life are hard to plan for?
- What problems do people like themselves have that they'd like to avoid?
- What solutions could you modify that are currently serving the customers?

Problem Classification 1b (B2B)

Questions to uncover the present problems the customer may have if they are a business

- What are the organization's major gripes and difficulties?
- What opportunities is the organization missing for better performance?
- What small problems does the organization have that could grow into big ones?
- What barriers are preventing the organization from growing?
- How could you improve the quality of the products or services they currently sell?
- What are the organization's most difficult people problems?
- What goals does the organization fail to attain year after year?
- What is likely to be the next crisis in the organization's industry?
- What issues is this organization likely to ignore or bury?
- What makes planning difficult for this organization?
- What problems experienced by other organizations would they like to avoid?
- What competitors' ideas could the organization adapt?

Some entrepreneurs such as Steve Jobs believe that customers consciously don't always know what they want, so the management team makes a strategic decision to address particular problems they feel have opportunity for generating new business. They like to peer into the future and predict problems the customer might one day have. Many of these business people also prefer this approach because they believe they can surprise the customer with a never-before-seen solution to a problem they didn't even realize they had.[21] A deep understanding of the customer reveals the problems you'd like to prepare to address in the future. In a sense, you are creating the future for your customers.[22] When you know your customers so well that you know how they think and behave and what they value, you can often anticipate what they'll like.

But you don't have to be Steve Jobs to anticipate what tomorrow will look like. Let's look at questions that can prompt you to predict the future problems customers may have. These questions are also broken into B2C and B2B categories.

Problem Classification 2a (B2C)

Questions to uncover the future problems the customer may have if they are a consumer

- What changes, issues, problems, and opportunities do you visualize this customer having three years down the road?
- As the customer's life changes, what new problems and changes will arise?
- Who might feel threatened by the idea of you selling to the customer?

- What skills and knowledge will the customer need to meet challenges two years from now?
- What product or service would simplify the customer's life?
- What customer needs will increase in the next three years? Five years? Ten years?
- What will be your customers' biggest challenges over the next three years? Five years? Ten years?
- What products or services would your customers most like to see come to them in the next three years?
- What new pressures might you encounter from your customers?
- What might cause the customer to avoid you?

Problem Classification 2b (B2B)

Questions to uncover the future problems the customer may have if they are a business

- What changes, issues, problems, and opportunities do you visualize this organization having three years down the road?
- As the organization's industry changes, what new problems and changes will arise?
- Who might feel threatened by the idea of you selling to the organization?
- What training might the organization need to meet challenges two years from now?
- What product or service would simplify the organization's work?
- What organizational needs will increase in the next three years? Five years? Ten years?
- What will be the organization's biggest challenges over the next three years? Five years? Ten years?
- What would the organization most like to see happen in the next three years?
- What new pressures might the organization encounter from their customers? Their community? Politicians? The media?
- What might cause the organization to cancel an account with you?

This is a third category of questions for entrepreneurs who may be creating businesses in the coaching, counseling, or consulting industries. These questions address personal concerns that are limiting customers' quality of life or professional achievements.

Problem Classification 3 (B2C and B2B)

Questions to uncover more personal problems that apply to customers

- What existing risks and uncertainties do they face?
- What risks and uncertainties might they face in the future?

- What changes do they feel they need to make?
- With whom do they want to get along better?
- What would make them happy or proud?
- What makes them worry?
- What takes too much time?
- What has bothered them recently?
- What would they like to know more about?
- What goals have been lying fallow?

Asking "What problems does your customer have?" can unveil a plethora of answers. After you have found an important customer problem to address, you may want to start working on a solution. This is a common impulse for entrepreneurs, but it often leads to the development of an inferior product. Before we solve the problem, we first need to better understand it. Our next step requires that we gather facts that shed more light on the problem so that we approach it from the best angle possible. We must first understand before we act. The next chapter will cover fact finding, Step 2 of the creative entrepreneurial process.

Summary

Legendary businesses are built around solving an important customer problem others have overlooked. Entrepreneurs like Ford, Edison, and Disney made a career of pushing their companies to find problems their predecessors and contemporaries had overlooked. While these entrepreneurs seemed to be naturals at doing this, most people are not skilled in this important activity. Fortunately, you can develop your ability to sense problems and to seek out opportunities just as you can hone any other skill. The innovation process, and the mental skills that make it work, can be learned and become a daily habit that results in ongoing creative disruption and problem solving. The first important aspect of problem finding is developing an attitude of being an active problem seeker. Successful entrepreneurs are constantly scanning the world around them for problems to solve.

Problem finding is taking the initiative to discover new problems instead of tackling the same old problems everyone else does. Creative entrepreneurs take pride in setting themselves goals and challenges for finding problems others overlooked. This chapter provided guidance on how to find important customer problems that an entrepreneur could pursue. We first challenged the reader to think about whose problem they are actually solving. Thinking about who the real customer is opens up new areas of problems competitors may have overlooked. By finding the problems of the real customer, the company secures a good foundation for later developing products and services the market will embrace. Once the real customer is identified, a deep dive into their world is encouraged. The entrepreneur should study the real customer to uncover where they are, what they think, and what they do. Prompter questions for guiding observation and interaction with the real customer in their personal and public lives were provided. When the entrepreneur has identified key customer problems, they are now encouraged to learn more about those problems. The next chapter on fact finding addresses Step 2 in the creative entrepreneurial process.

Notes

1 Basadur, M. S. (1992). "Managing Creativity: A Japanese Model." *Academy of Management Executive,* 6(2): 29–42.
2 Mott, P. E. (1972). *The Characteristics of Effective Organizations.* New York, NY: Harper and Row.
3 Basadur, M. S., Gelade, G., and Basadur, T. M. (2014). "Creative Problem Solving Process Styles, Cognitive Work Demands and Organizational Adaptability." *Journal of Applied Behavioral Science,* 50(1): 80–115.
4 Simon, H. A. (1977). *The New Science of Management Decisions.* Englewood Cliffs, NJ: Prentice Hall.
5 Csikszentmihalyi, M. (1988). "Motivation and Creativity: Toward a Synthesis of Structural and Energistic Approaches to Cognition." *New Ideas in Psychology,* 6(2): 159–76.
6 Leavitt, H. J. (1978). *Managerial Psychology,* 4th ed. Chicago, IL: University of Chicago Press.
7 Rittel, H., and Webber, M. (1973). "Dilemmas in a General Theory of Planning." *Policy Sciences,* 4: 155–69.
8 Nayak, P. R., and Ketteringham, J. (1997). "3M's Post-it Notes: A Managed or Accidental Innovation?" In R. Katz (ed.), *The Human Side of Managing Technological Innovation.* New York, NY: Oxford University Press, pp. 367–77.
9 Isaacson, W. (2011). *Steve Jobs.* New York, NY: Simon & Schuster.
10 Land, E. (1972). From Sean Callahan's article "Dr. Land's Magic Camera." *Life Magazine,* 27 (October): 42.
11 Jonnes, J. (2004). *Empires of Light: Edison, Tesla, Westinghouse, and the Race to Electrify the World.* New York, NY: Random House Trade Paperbacks.
12 Brinkley, D. (2003). *Wheels for the World: Henry Ford, His Company, and a Century of Progress, 1903–2003.* New York, NY: Viking Press.
13 Gabler, N. (2006). Walt Disney: *The Triumph of the American Imagination.* New York, NY: Knopf Doubleday Publishing Group.
14 Basadur, M. S. (1995). *The Power of Innovation.* London, UK: Pitman Professional Publishing.
15 Kelley, T. (2001). *The Art of Innovation: Lessons in Creativity from IDEO, America's Leading Design Firm.* New York, NY: Crown Business.
16 Nightline. http://www.ideo.com/work/shopping-cart-concept.
17 Miller, G. (2009). *Spent: Sex, Evolution, and Consumer Behavior.* New York, NY: Penguin.
18 Pooler, J. (2003). *Why We Shop: Emotional Rewards and Retail Strategies.* Westport, CT: Greenwood Publishing Group.
19 Basadur, M. S., and Basadur, T. M. (2008) "Telescoping: Enabling Groups to Achieve Creative Decisions with High Consensus and Commitment." Presented at the Academy of Management Annual Conference, Anaheim, California.
20 Basadur, M. S., Basadur, T. M., and Beuk, F. (2014). Facilitating High Quality Idea Evaluation Using Telescoping. *Wirtschaftspsychologie (Business Creativity),* 16(2): 59–71.
21 Isaacson, W. (2011). *Steve Jobs.* New York, NY: Simon & Schuster.
22 Hamel, G., and Prahalad, C. K. (2013). *Competing for the Future.* Boston, MA: Harvard Business Press.

2
STEP 2: FACT FINDING

Introduction

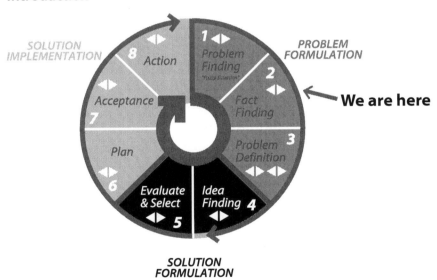

Once the entrepreneur understands who their real customer is and what problem they want to address, it is time to better understand their situation. Finding good problems to solve means more than anticipating and sensing opportunities in the marketplace. It means going a step further to see if there are details in the problem space that need further consideration. These details might not be as visible on the surface, but on further examination the entrepreneur uncovers something competitors may have missed. Beyond finding a problem that serves as an indicator of an opportunity, entrepreneurs must uncover and absorb as much information about the problem as they can. Therefore, Step 2 of the creative entrepreneurial process is fact finding.

Alert and with an open mind, the entrepreneur must gather unbiased, comprehensive data about their fuzzy situation instead of making the fatal mistake of investing too quickly in a solution. There is a big difference between a fuzzy situation and a well-defined problem. The bridge between the two is called fact finding.

Seven Strategies for Finding Facts

Deferring judgment on the final definition or formulation of the problem, the entrepreneur must exercise seven fundamental fact finding process strategies, as outlined in Figure 2.1.

Search Divergently for Possibly Relevant Facts

One of the biggest mistakes entrepreneurs make is bringing an idea into the marketplace without having a good understanding of the realities it will face upon implementation. If the entrepreneur can keep their excitement for an idea in check, they can prevent making costly mistakes later. Successful entrepreneurs mitigate risk, which is achieved by reducing the uncertainty and ambiguity surrounding their enterprise. Uncovering facts about the personal, organizational, and competitive dynamics entrepreneurs will face in bringing the product or service to market gives them understanding that improves their odds of success. As clarity is gained and uncertainty is reduced, entrepreneurs gain more credibility and legitimacy among their stakeholders, all of which helps them gain needed resources and support needed to make the business a success.

1. Search divergently for possibly relevant facts.
2. Use several viewpoints.
3. Beware assumptions.
4. Avoid a negative attitude toward problems.
5. Share information.
6. Say what you think.
7. Look for the truth, not just ways to boost your ego.

FIGURE 2.1 Key Fact-Finding Behaviors

A critical strategy for gathering good data is to defer judgment and logic. Do not prejudge information. Simply capture it for later consideration. Therefore, entrepreneurs must consider any information that might relate to their fuzzy situation. It is not enough to say, "I know the facts, let's get on with it." They must push beyond the obvious to get as many bits and pieces of knowledge as they can. Entrepreneurs must ask questions about the problem, whatever comes to mind.

Entrepreneurs must assume that whatever they think about the problem is automatically relevant. In later steps they can analyze the information. A metaphor for understanding the importance of deliberately separating these steps might be helpful in acquiring this skill. Think of the Saturn rocket that launched Apollo missions to the moon during the 1960s. Soon after the rocket left the ground, its first stage dropped off. The second stage took over to lift the rocket higher before falling off in turn. The third stage then propelled the landing craft on a course to its final destination. Becoming aware of a new opportunity or problem is like the first rocket stage. It's enough to get the entrepreneur started, but it's only the beginning. The problem as they first perceive it may not at all represent the problem as they finally perceive it. Searching for facts about the new opportunity or problem is the second rocket stage, the bridge between the two perceptions. Only by opening their minds to as many potentially relevant facts as possible can entrepreneurs ensure that they will improve, expand, and enrich their final perception of the opportunity.

One helpful way of acquiring this new perception is turning to others who might have knowledge on the situation. Popular sentiment has entrepreneurs as self-driven people attached to their vision of success. However, in reality, successful entrepreneurs often take a more humble position and recognize that they don't have all the answers. They are open to considering what facts others can reveal to them in order to avoid making costly mistakes that could have been prevented, or better yet, to find opportunities others reveal to them. Therefore, it is incumbent on entrepreneurs to ask themselves, "In what other ways could others help me view my situation? Who else might have a useful but different perspective I could draw from?"

Use Several Viewpoints

Each of us sees "the facts" in a situation, or reality, through our own biases, filters, and acquired knowledge. Collaboration is a technique for overcoming this natural limitation we all face. Collaborative problem solving brings together a variety of viewpoints, which helps entrepreneurs obtain a better understanding of what they are actually facing. Group members in a problem-solving session will likely provoke each other to seek additional facts and to broaden the view of a problem.

Empathy is an important entrepreneurial skill. Being able to understand a situation from others' perspectives can educate the entrepreneur about obstacles and necessary actions as they move forward. How can entrepreneurs put themselves in someone else's shoes? If an organized problem-solving session is being conducted with a group of customers and related stakeholders, they can simply move around the room and "view" the problem from a different perspective. If they are at work and working on the problem, they can seek someone else inside the company to share the problem with. For example, if they have been thinking about the problem at their desk, they can get out of their chair and visit another department to get that area's perspective. Another way is to get outside of the building and talk about the problem with customers and industry experts who have experience with it firsthand. Any way you can view a situation from other viewpoints is beneficial.

Beware Unconscious Assumptions

Entrepreneurs are often confident people who make things happen because of their belief in their abilities and the opportunities before them. This in itself is good because it is this very feeling of certainty that encourages people to try new things in the world. We generally weigh the consequences of our future actions based on whether they will bring pleasure or pain into our lives. Each time someone gets excited about even the possibility of something good, their brain receives a burst of dopamine, the body's natural "feel good" chemical. Without this positive feeling, people would accept their current situation and only try new things when their survival depended on it. Neurologist Robert Burton[1] calls this sensation a "feeling of knowing" and recognizes it as a powerful force for bringing about change in the human condition. However, he also points out that it is often wrong because the sense of certainty emanating from this chemical reaction is not always based on the evidence of facts. Therefore, it is critical to take the time to gather facts and then make conscious and reasoned decisions to increase the chances of success.

Unfortunately, unconscious assumptions often hinder people from fact finding. All too often, assuming we know the nature of a particular problem, we may screen out apparently unrelated facts or take wrong information as fact.[2] Cognitive psychologists and behavioral economists suggest that irrationality based on incorrect assumptions can come from confirmation bias, availability bias, story bias, hindsight bias, and authority bias, among others.[3] Indeed, human decision-making is a complex endeavor, and more awareness of psychological faults prevents costly mistakes. The immense body of research literature devoted to this issue illustrates the importance of being careful in making big decisions. The research is so important that economist Daniel Kahneman won a Nobel Prize for overturning his field's notion of the Economic Rational Man. In fact, he evidenced that people are rarely rational in making the best decisions for themselves in the long run. But all is not lost. Kahneman states that better decisions can be made by turning to those who have addressed similar situations or problems in the past and learning from them. Again, fact finding betters our chances of success.

The attitude we take toward gathering facts is critical. We have to approach problems with an openness to new information that may challenge our preconceived perspective on it. As Zen master Shunryu Suzuki observed, "In the beginner's mind there are many possibilities, but in the expert's there are few."[4] Entrepreneurs should begin the search for facts as novices. By doing so, they can uncover the language, issues, critical success factors, and constraints inherent in the problem space. Many people believe they don't have the time to investigate a problem like this, that they have to deliver a solution before someone else does. This can be a major mistake, as missing relevant information to the problem can cause delays and waste resources later when the entrepreneur develops or sells their product.

Let's consider a story that illustrates the problem of relying on unfounded assumptions.[5] An engineering consultant was hired to solve a problem for a railroad company. He was asked to find ways to increase efficiency on a major rail service carrying automobiles across the United States. The automobiles were stacked two-high on each of the railroad cars. The engineer's first idea was to stack them three-high, increasing efficiency by half. Suggesting this idea to his client, he learned that it was hardly a novel one. He was told it was an impractical solution: numerous overpasses on the railroad system were so low that the company couldn't stack the cars three-high.

The engineer had two choices. He could simply accept this information and drop the idea, or he could do more fact finding. Rather than assume that the overpasses were too low, he viewed the responses themselves as a fact: "Several people say that many of the overpasses are too low." Investigating the company's specification manuals, he found that, among the thousands of overpasses throughout the system, only two were too low for three-high stacking. Armed with this new fact, he defined his problem as "How might we stack the cars three-high and make the two low overpasses compatible?" What had appeared as insurmountable facts turned out to be mostly assumptions. The real fact was that the engineering consultant's client had to overcome only minor roadblocks in order to realize a great gain. Fact finding led to a solution that brought him a steady stream of business from the company over the years.

Avoid a Negative Attitude toward "Problems"

If you automatically consider a problem a negative thing, then not only does your attitude lower your motivation to tackle it, but it also confines your fact finding: you start looking for only negative facts. Without a complete picture of the facts—negative and positive—your subsequent problem definition will be off the mark. No matter how formidable your initial perception of the problem, adopting a "can-do" attitude helps you open your mind to consider more information and viewpoints. The result might be a new viewpoint, direction, or definition that yields novel solutions.

Again, gathering these facts often requires interacting with a host of people who can shed more light on the problem. This open approach to observing and interacting with the members of a problem space will also help the entrepreneur gain trust with the observed in the process.[6] People appreciate being recognized for their knowledge on a subject. It brings subjects a sense of worthiness. As a result, the entrepreneur can gain credibility and build relationships with people that can be helpful later when future business activity takes place. All interactions are to be seen as opportunities to learn, adapt, and build relationships.

Share Information

In order to increase creativity and innovation through collaboration, entrepreneurs must embrace information sharing. An entrepreneur can't find and solve problems without the necessary information about their market and industry and their place in it. Lack of trust hinders fact finding. Unfortunately, entrepreneurs often avoid asking questions or volunteering information for fear of getting their ideas stolen or having that information broadcast out into the world. If the entrepreneur comes off as guarded or mistrusting, others may share misleading facts. They may give the entrepreneur incorrect information because they tell him what they think he wants to hear, or they twist the information to make themselves look better. Either way, the entrepreneur can avoid these pitfalls by coming across authentically with people they talk to, and this can only be attained by being open and sharing information as needed. While the entrepreneur risks putting their idea out into the world before it is ready, the consequences of misdirected fact finding leads to erroneous problem definitions later. What later appears to be an innovative product or service might turn out to be a huge failure because it was developed on poor information.

It should be noted that there are some industries where secrecy is more warranted. Defense contractors, major corporations with extensive R&D labs, and biotechnology companies build intellectual property fences to shield their ideas from the outside world. However, there are three reasons why most entrepreneurs are not justified in having such a guarded approach: (1) large companies already have immense resources and networks they can draw from in gathering the facts they need; (2) entrepreneurs who guard their ideas in overprotective ways come across as Gollum in the *Lord of the Rings* ("My precious!"), and no one will help a person who comes across as greedy or pathological; and (3) the idea that is shared in collaborative sessions will change into an entirely new idea when new facts are gathered. Essentially, the entrepreneur is protecting an idea that won't exist without further deliberation and experimentation. If an overly secretive entrepreneur goes into the market with such an idea, it is likely that the facts they overlooked will cause a change in direction anyway. Reality has a nasty habit of pointing out ignorance.

Say What You Think

In collaborative problem-solving sessions, it is important to say what you think. The rule is that there are no bad ideas during fact finding. If you offer information and ideas only to fit what you think the rest of the group wants to hear, you rob the session of your unique viewpoint. Similarly, if you are out in the field and asking questions, capture every fact you can from people you interview. Sometimes what seems to be the most off-the-wall observation is an indication of something important going on. With more investigation into the statement, other facts may emerge that are useful to understanding your problem.

Innovation occurs when new perspectives are embraced for further development. The person who sees things differently from the others is sometimes the one who sees them most clearly. However, the idea of seeing things differently makes some people uncomfortable. Many people second-guess themselves and believe that if no one else sees the problem as they do, then they must be wrong. In order to define problems accurately, you must overcome this discomfort and encourage everyone's open-minded input.

Evidence of the impact of new perspectives can be found in design firms every day. Companies pay top dollar to hire these firms to help them see their industries and markets in new ways. In design firms like IDEO, frog, and RKS, designers create new products and services for just about any potential client who walks through the front door, whether it is a large hospital chain or a toy company. One might ask why large companies would turn to much smaller enterprises for their economic future. The answer lies in the Innovator's Dilemma chronicled by Christensen.[7] Conditioned by past success and a local search bias, managers will often rely on past experience and honed mental models to guide future business decisions. After all, it would make sense to keep doing what has led to the organization becoming large in the first place. While rational, this approach often leads to disaster for the big company. Newer firms have fewer employee routines and customer expectations and thus have greater capacity to release innovative products into unsuspecting industries and markets. Therefore, beginning in a state of ignorance (or beginner's mind) can often be an advantage for new players developing innovative products and services. By having an outsider's perspective, entrepreneurs do not hold a local search bias and through the systematic application of effective, creative strategies, they can more easily generate ideas that are novel to an industry.[8,9,10,11] Enlightened executives who understand the perils of the Innovator's Dilemma and local search bias may not feel confident in their own company's ability to innovate and turn to design firms to suggest opportunities for growth. If a design firm can create new products and services on a daily basis for large clients, it is feasible that an entrepreneur devoting all their time and energy to a similar, context-independent approach can lead to the development of one good idea for a single business. Fact-finding skills properly applied within a creative process can give smaller firms an advantage in finding opportunities more established companies are overlooking.

Look for the Truth, Not Just Ways to Boost Your Ego

One major hindrance of good fact finding is a person's ego. When the focus of a person's involvement in a fact-finding session is to demonstrate how smart they are, problems are sure to arise. Team members must put their attention on the project at hand, not on their own feelings. Therefore, it is critical to separate a person's identity from an idea. The idea exists on its own and is to be treated that way. The attitude of everyone in a session should be that the purpose of the exercise is to uncover as many facts about a problem as possible. All ideas are welcome. Therefore, the entrepreneur must not take it personally if people offer differing perspectives that disrupt their current idea of the business. In fact, they should welcome it. The agreed upon goal of any fact-finding session should be to uncover information that can lead to better problem definition and solutions later. Therefore, the entrepreneur should focus the group on what is being said rather than on who is saying it. A defensive posture will hinder good fact finding. When an entrepreneur is less preoccupied with defending egos, people can more easily venture different points of view and different facts.

Six Fact-Finding Questions

To carry out these seven thinking process strategies, entrepreneurs can ask the follow questions to help uncover important facts about a fuzzy situation (Figure 2.2). Supplement these questions as you see fit by asking the five Ws (who, what, where, when, why) or with any other questions that come to mind. The purpose of fact finding is to have more clarity about the customer problem identified in Chapter 1.

What Do You Know, or Think You Know, about This Fuzzy Situation?

Because they hold preconceived ideas about the nature of a problem, people often downplay what they actually know. They may hesitate to offer facts if they

1	What do you know, or think you know, about this fuzzy situation?
2	What do you not know about this fuzzy situation (but you'd like to know)?
3	Why is this a problem for you?
4	What have you already thought of or tried?
5	If this problem were to be resolved, what would you have that you don't have now?
6	What might you be assuming that you don't have to assume?

FIGURE 2.2 Questions to Clarify a Fuzzy Situation

are less than 100 percent sure of them. In fact, people often know more than they think do. What seems obvious to one person may be unknown by another. It is important to include anything anyone thinks might be relevant. You should also be open to people seeing the fact another way and offering their perspective on it. Regardless of what is said, it is important to write it down. In later steps, you can select what you think are the most relevant facts to the customer problem.

Another important process skill when fact finding is to capture the facts in full sentences. Bullet points can make information gathering easier but lead to confusion later when interpreting the data. For example, if someone tells you that there is a communication issue between the typical salesperson and customer in the industry, you should not write, "communication issue." A better fact is "A communication issue exists between salespeople and customers." After such a fact is captured, you can ask a follow-up question, such as "What do you mean by 'communication issue'?" The respondent might answer, "The customer doesn't understand the technical lingo the salespeople use." You would write that down and perhaps follow with, "That's interesting. Tell me more about this problem." Answers to this request will uncover more facts for consideration later. Once you have covered that topic, you can then ask the rest of the group, "What else do we know about this fuzzy situation?" Repeat this process in this way until you and the group feel that you have exhausted all possible answers.

It is critically important to not rush fact finding because one uncovered fact that is buried in a hundred answers might be the one insight that a breakthrough solution is based on. After addressing what we know *about* the fuzzy situation, we can move onto the next question.

What Do You Not Know about This Fuzzy Situation That You'd Like to Find Out?

This question often produces even more revealing information than the first one and encourages thinking in new ways. What you don't know about a particular situation can often be the most pertinent fact. A good example of uncovering unknown facts comes from my product development experience at Procter & Gamble.

Procter & Gamble's fledgling Industrial Division had decided to go after a developing market for automatic car wash products in the early 1970s. In our product development department, a small team of chemists and engineers was rushing to fill out our existing product line. My boss asked me to take over the car wash section to speed up our product development efforts, especially in a floundering "hot wax" project.

Fortunately for me, I could hardly spell hot wax, let alone profess to be an expert on the product. I rarely took my own car through an automatic wash; as a young engineer, I saved money by washing my car by hand. Why 'fortunately'? Because I knew nothing about hot wax, I was free to display my ignorance, keep an open mind, and ask lots of questions to try to get a better handle on what needed to be done and why the project had been bogged down. Thus, my first question was a very simple one: "I don't know anything about hot wax. What is it?"

The team explained that hot wax was a relatively new but potentially profitable idea. It was a liquid spray applied as an optional service at the end of an automatic car wash. Automatic washes dispense all of their products in water-soluble form, and of course, wax doesn't dissolve in water. However, a small competing company had found a way to combine wax from the South American carnauba tree with certain solubilizing ingredients and water, yielding a stable fluid that could be sprayed onto cars. (Carnauba wax already had gained a reputation as the best wax for polishing shoes.) The competitor had received a patent for its product.

When I asked why our team had been bogged down for 18 months, the members explained that they couldn't come up with a combination of carnauba wax, solubilizers, and water sufficiently different from the competitor's to avoid violating its patent. The team had tried countless combinations and had even recruited a carnauba wax supplier to help, without success. What gradually became evident to my outsider's mind was that the team had focused its efforts on a specific challenge: "How might we develop a carnauba wax formula that does not violate the existing patent?"

Continuing my fact finding, I asked how well the competitor's product performed. To their response that it performed very well, I asked how they knew. They told me that, since the product was a hot seller, it was obviously doing a good job. When I asked what our test methods showed about the product's performance, they replied, "What test methods?" It turned out that because the team had been in such a headlong rush to enter the market, it had neglected to develop test methods. The team's understanding of the competing product's performance consisted of a single fact: a lot of people were buying it. I suggested that we quickly broaden our understanding.

Testing the competitor's product during lab simulations, we found no evidence that it adhered to car bodies. We got the same result when we tested the product in the automatic car wash. We had turned up a new fact: our team had been trying for 18 months to duplicate a product that didn't work.

As this story illustrates, inadequate fact finding had led the team to define its problem too narrowly. The team then redefined its problem to a broader challenge through more fact finding: "How might we develop a hot wax product for a spray-on water system that will adhere to car bodies and provide a worthwhile benefit?" This opened up many new approaches for the team, and a patentable solution resulted.[12]

Why Is This a Problem, Especially for the Customer?

Remember, we are addressing a customer problem, so we need to know why this is something we should devote our resources to. This question addresses why the situation is personally important to customers. What is their motive for wanting a solution to this problem? In entrepreneurship it is critical to pin down why the customer needs a solution to this problem. Entrepreneurs should solve problems that connect with customers in a personal way. The question also addresses what has been stopping entrepreneurs from resolving it. It helps you understand the problem on a concrete, gut level rather than in the abstract. By addressing this question, the entrepreneur also gathers information that can be useful in building marketing campaigns and a brand around the solution. Good solutions tied to problems customers care about are the foundation of good product development.

What Solutions Have You or Others Already Thought of or Tried?

This question aims to quickly provide as much background information as possible about the problem's current status. You're not interested in starting from scratch, as if the problem had never existed. If the problem exists, there are probably ways that customers deal with it and competitors try to solve it. It is unlikely that you'll be the first person to ever think about the problem; however, with a creative process you can be the first to develop a good solution to it.

Complexity expert W. Brian Arthur points out that recognizing what has been tried before can make problem solving much more efficient. You can learn from the past and others' mistakes. He provides jet technology as a metaphor for understanding this principle:

> If you open up a jet engine (or aircraft gas turbine power plant, to give it its professional name), you will find components inside—compressors, turbines, combustion engines. If you open up other technologies that existed before it, you find some of the same components. ... Technologies inherit parts from the technologies that preceded them, so putting such parts together—combining them—must have a great deal to do with how technologies come into being. This makes the abrupt appearance of radically novel technologies seem much less abrupt. Technologies somehow must come into being as fresh combinations of what already exists.[13]

Once an entrepreneur has chosen a customer problem to address, it is incumbent on them to study how other companies have approached the problem. How have competitors defined it? What solutions have they offered customers? What is good about those solutions? What parts of their solutions could be improved? How have customers responded to those solutions? Have customers even responded by creating their own homemade versions of solutions to address it? Much like how engineers design a new engine by building on previous technologies, entrepreneurs can create new businesses utilizing the best of others' approaches, improving shortcomings, and offering new twists never before seen. Rarely, if ever, is a new product or service entirely new. An engineer once told us that the only way to invent an entirely new product is to create it with a new chemical element that has never existed before; everything else is composed at least partly from already-existing solutions. However, recognizing new ways to understand a problem through fact finding can leave clues as to how to innovate in ways the industry has never seen before. Recombination with some new twists and additions is the most tried and true path to innovation.

If This Problem Were Resolved, What Would the Customer Have That They Don't Have Now?

In other words, what does the customer lack that they hope a solution will give them? In answering this fact-finding question, be extremely specific. Merely saying, "The customer needs a solution to this problem," gets your company nowhere, as you have not yet defined the problem. Answering this question with a clear, simple fact better helps define the problem. Only then can you identify what product or service would be helpful in satisfying the customer's need. If you're having difficulty answering this question, try to visualize a successful product or service that your company could deliver, then visualize how the customer would use it. In your mind's eye, imagine the customer experience. What actions are they taking? How are they responding to it? When do they use it? What occurred after they used it? Was anyone with them when they used it? What did they think of the product or service?

Your imagination can be your greatest tool for creating new possibilities. Use what you discover about the problem and its existing solutions to diverge and converge on possible scenarios you could deliver to the customer to make their lives better. Which ones would excite the customer? Which ones would you enjoy delivering? The role of the innovative entrepreneur is to make the world around them better. Use these questions to serve as prompts to creating that picture.

What Might You Be Assuming That Might or Might Not Be True?

Even without thinking about it, people often restrict their thinking by making unwarranted assumptions. Assuming, for example, that a product is too far out for customers to be interested in, an entrepreneur might not consider further exploration of the idea. Yet, many famous products were once considered crazy in their original formulation until some tweaking and modifications turned them into commercial successes. Crazy ideas can sometimes lead to crazy success. Consider Clarence Birdseye, the inventor of commercial frozen food. When Birdseye was a young man, he worked for the U.S. Biological Survey as a government field naturalist. His wilderness posts often afforded him the opportunity to take part in fur trading to make extra income on the side. During one long fur-trading adventure, he spent time with the Eskimos and observed how they kept caught fish preserved by allowing the frigid conditions to freeze their catch quickly.

He pondered whether the approach could work with other foods as well. Until this point, consumers had to either eat food quickly before it spoiled, preserve it with additives, or can it for future consumption. Birdseye offered a fourth option: applying the Eskimo method to vegetables, fruit, fish, and meat with his "Quick Freeze Machine." The innovation revolutionized the food industry, with the frozen food segment becoming a billion-dollar industry. Now customers could warm up the food and receive the same nutritional content it had before it was frozen. For a society that was moving away from the farms and into the cities and suburbs, Birdeye's innovation fit well into the industrial lifestyle of the twentieth century.

Process Considerations on the Six Fact-Finding Questions

There is nothing magical about the six fact-finding questions. They simply work well and prompt the entrepreneur and his or her team to uncover additional questions worth pursuing. You probably already use many fact-finding techniques, including industry reports, focus groups, and market research questionnaires, among others. Use these six questions to go beyond the information generated from these techniques and to weave that information into your creative process for mainstreaming innovation. The specific techniques you use are less important than the process you follow in getting as much unbiased information as you can about a fuzzy situation.

It is worth emphasizing again that how you document your answers to these questions is important. For each of these six fact-finding questions, state your answers in simple, complete sentences. For example, suppose the customer problem was "frustrating clinic visit" and the fact-finding question was "What do you know or think you know about this customer problem?" Simply saying "unhelpful desk staff" would be a far less useful answer than saying, "At checkout the receptionist can't answer my questions about my bill. They tell the customer to call their insurance company." Precision in your use of language permits an effective fact-finding process, leading to an insightful problem definition in Step 3, discussed in the next chapter of this book.

Furthermore, another process skill is to treat any reply to any fact-finding question as a fact, even if the reply is an opinion, perception, or belief. However, you can follow up an answer that seems like an opinion, perception, or belief by converting the assumption into a more accurate statement of fact. For example, the statement, "Mr. Jones does not believe he received adequate customer service from the clinic," is not actually a fact but simply someone's assumption. You can turn it into a more accurate statement of fact by stating, "Mr. Jones told me he called the clinic three times last week requesting information for his insurance claims and never received an answer." You could also capture other indicators of inadequate customer service as well. Use the more general answer to serve as a start to better defining the problem through follow-up questions.

Another critical skill during fact finding is to avoid using judgment while divergently gathering facts, for two reasons. First, you don't want to begin with a premature assumption about what facts are or are not important. Second, you don't want to make members apprehensive to give answers by making them worry about whether or not their "fact" is worth uttering because they can't decide whether it's an opinion, perception, or belief. What's important is to stimulate a flow of information. You'll have plenty of time later for sifting through and picking out the most relevant facts. For example, arguing over whether a patient is truly frustrated is a waste of time. It's far better to simply state, "Most patients are frustrated with the clinic's desk staff," or even better, "Most patients have to take care of their insurance issues on their own without help from the clinic." The latter are clear statements of fact finding about people's perceptions. A subsequent problem definition might become "How might the customer get help on legal and financial matters in a much more responsive way than clinics currently provide?"

Converging on the Most Pertinent Facts

So you have uncovered a wealth of information about the customer problem by diverging on answers to the six fact-finding questions. What do you do with all of this information? Now is the time to select (converge on) what you think are the most pertinent facts from this list that pertain to the customer problem you are trying to solve. In evaluating the facts you've obtained, the idea is to select the few that provide new insights. Sometimes such insights come from "old" facts that had been neglected or considered too simplistic. Sometimes they come from entirely new facts. Good judgment is important at this early stage in the creative entrepreneurial process: unwarranted assumptions or unimportant or irrelevant facts will lead to poor problem definition later, and eventually, off-target customer solutions.

As always, a collaborative approach is better in selecting key facts. Particularly during the startup stage of a company, whoever is responsible for the future success of the product or service must have the opportunity to take part in selecting the key facts in order to ensure not only accuracy but commitment. These stakeholders can include owners, investors, suppliers, distributors, future customers, and first employees, among others. If the group becomes quite large, good representatives from each category can be selected for converging on pertinent facts. For example, a few customers who represent the target profile well, a key supplier, the lead investor, and the founding team could be selected for the exercise. Once selected, the group should be instructed to select only the most relevant facts for further consideration. A good rule of thumb is to allow each member to select 10 percent of the facts from the list as most pertinent. So if there are 50 facts, each member chooses the 5 facts they think are most important in regards to the customer problem.

After each problem-solving member has chosen their key facts, the session facilitator addresses each selection. They clarify the fact by asking who chose it and why. After each person has discussed their choices, the group as a whole now considers which facts seem the most pertinent to the customer problem. Those facts are circled on the list and will be used again soon. Having the most relevant facts in hand provides the foundation for the next step of the process, problem definition.

You can never go wrong in collecting a lot of facts. Following are some real-world examples of inadequate fact finding leading to failed premature solutions.

Quick Fix Solutions Not Working!

An automobile manufacturer had been suffering heavy losses for several business quarters. The company was bound and determined to change the way it operated and had launched many initiatives. One of the most important was its decision to turn to its people, involving everyone in using their minds to improve quality and customer satisfaction and to increase innovation. The company had heard of my work at Procter & Gamble in involving managers in actually "managing the business" rather than just "doing my job." The company and its union had recently agreed in a letter of understanding to implement a joint program on Employee Involvement (EI) for its unionized employees. They jointly provided resources, including both unionized and salaried employees that would diagnose important training needs and create strategies and programs to meet those needs. Its first step was to form problem-solving groups in the plants guided by local and national joint steering committees. To build skills in problem solving, these groups had been taught standard analytical tools borrowed from statistical process control and total quality management programs (such as "cause-and-effect diagramming" and "cause-unknown diagnosis"). The company now wanted to expand Employee Involvement to include salaried employees and to develop problem-solving processes that were better suited for their jobs. It hoped that these employees and their managers would take more initiative in identifying opportunities for improvement and tackling them creatively.

During a preconsult, we agreed that the Simplexity process seemed highly appropriate for this purpose. This was confirmed during a preliminary training workshop designed to give several key employees some experience with the process and process skills. We agreed on a strategy to train a number of employees in applying the Simplexity process and in training others in the company. During this training, we had a chance to apply the process to a problem at a newly modernized plant that made a major component of the company's new front-wheel drive automobiles. The plant was setting new records for quality and low cost, but one department was struggling. Only about one-third of its output met the company's high quality standards, and employees had to work heavy overtime schedules in order to keep up with orders. The plant managers had tried several quick-fix solutions to resolve the production and quality problems, but none had worked. We established a cross-functional team of 15 plant managers and supervisors in order to apply the Simplexity creative problem-solving process to the problem. Along with one of the company's internal consultants whom I was training as a Simplexity facilitator and trainer, I conducted the application session with this team. We set aside about half a day for training in the Simplexity Thinking process and process skills and two-and-a-half days to apply the process to the team's fuzzy situation. During the training, we asked the team members to complete the Simplexity creative problem-solving profile. Remember, this instrument reveals individual differences in preferences for various phases of the creative problem-solving process.

The team discovered a very revealing insight. Of the 15 team members, 8 showed creative problem-solving styles heavily oriented toward quadrant 4, implementation. The other 7 showed styles heavily oriented toward quadrant 3, optimization. No members had creative problem-solving styles oriented toward quadrants 1 or 2, generation and conceptualization. In other words, the team was composed of people who preferred to jump quickly to action rather than first spending time in fact finding and problem defining. When we discussed these results, the team members were able to identify many instances in which they had mistakenly made assumptions about this particular problem, leading to one failed solution after another. Rather than take the time to define the problem accurately, they had simply jumped from the fuzzy situation to a solution time after time. They had spent all of their energy alternating between quadrants 3 and 4 and none in quadrants 1 or 2 (Figure 2.3).

These action-oriented individuals agreed to spend two days in quadrant-1 and -2 activity, gathering facts and defining problems (Figure 2.4)—even though the whole exercise was against their nature. Three specific problem definitions emerged from this exercise. On the third day, the group was able to create simple but specific solutions

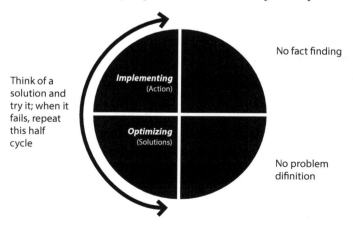

Only half of the creative process used.

FIGURE 2.3 The Results of Heavy Orientation Toward Quadrant 3 and Quadrant 4 Thinking Styles

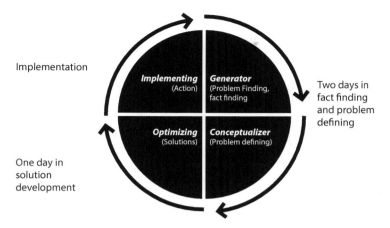

The entire creative process used.

FIGURE 2.4 Balancing Orientations Toward All Four Thinking Styles

that it could quickly implement to each defined problem. Within several months, most of the plant's production was high quality and was still improving.

STORY: Digging Out the Real Facts

Fear of being wrong causes other weaknesses in the creation of solutions. It prevents important facts and challenges from coming out, which can result in solutions that are not on target and lack commitment to implement. I was once asked to facilitate a team that had been struggling for over a year to improve the efficiency of its potato chip shipments. The problem was that, on average, the trucks were travelling half-full. Some key facts emerged during the fact-finding step of our process. One was that an outside vendor had proposed a new way of loading the trucks which would fill them completely and result in an annual savings of $12 million. Another fact was that the team had been conducting tests across the country to check if chip breakage would be negatively affected by the new method. When I inquired about the findings, the team said results were inconsistent: a little more breakage when shipped from Atlanta and Omaha, a little less from Los Angeles and Washington, and about the same from Buffalo and Dallas. They were now conducting additional tests from other locations. In addition, the Market Research department had stepped in to study (for the first time) if there might be an optimum level of chip breakage that users might prefer. They were also running tests in different cities and getting inconclusive results, which led them to run more tests. They seemed to be going around in circles and were in danger of running tests endlessly. To reduce my own frustration and to help the team focus and move forward, I engaged the members in using their creativity in problem definition using the "why-what's stopping" analysis (covered in more

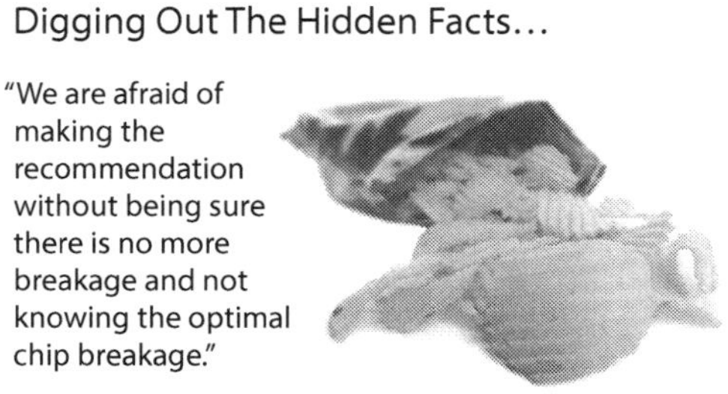

Digging Out The Hidden Facts...

"We are afraid of making the recommendation without being sure there is no more breakage and not knowing the optimal chip breakage."

FIGURE 2.5 Digging Out the Hidden Facts
Image licensed by Ingram Image

depth in Chapter 3). On a flipchart pad, I wrote the challenge "How might we write a recommendation to management by 3 PM today to approve the new loading technique?" The first answer to the "What might be stopping us?" question was that the breakage testing was not complete. The second answer was similar: they were not yet sure about the optimal chip-breakage level for consumers. I noted these two challenges, then asked the question a third time. (This is how the process works. In every step, we push divergently to expand our thinking.) We waited and waited. It was painful. Someone finally said, "I think we are afraid to make a recommendation without being completely sure. We do not want to be wrong." This new fact, which had been hidden, led to a new third challenge: "How might we write the challenge explaining the risk and asking management to take the risk with us?" (Figure 2.5). The team selected this challenge and wrote the recommendation well ahead of 3 PM. It was immediately approved the next morning, with $12 million to the bottom line. The team never thought that such an emotional fact would be legitimate to bring up in their work.

These examples serve to emphasize how crucial the fact-finding step of the creative problem-solving process is. Success in this stage often relies on our ability to overcome the habit of prematurely jumping to answers and solutions and sometimes requires us to dig up hidden facts or admit to challenges people are unaware of or fearful of saying. The transformative shift into a questioning mindset is a reverse shift from what most people have been taught in school and experienced in their daily lives. This art of asking the right questions underlies the empathy and simplicity skills required in every stage of this process. Following are real stories about the benefits of quality fact finding.

STORY: Speedy Fact Finding Averts Disaster and Triggers New Products

Flexibility depends on turning unexpected events, including crises, into opportunities, or at least restoring equilibrium quickly. Such opportunities may simply consist of achieving goodwill from the public or even inventing new ways to avoid such a crisis in the future. An excellent example is the Tylenol tragedy in Chicago several years ago, when several people suddenly died after consuming Tylenol pain-relieving tablets. Johnson & Johnson, the manufacturer, quickly removed all Tylenol products from store shelves, reassured the public, confined the danger to the local area, and discovered the root of the problem. Someone had deliberately injected a lethal poison into Tylenol capsules in some stores. The company proceeded to pioneer new, innovative, tamper-proof packaging that the rest of the industry has since adopted. The public was left with a very favorable image of Johnson & Johnson. The company demonstrated it was both expert about the products it manufactures and highly skilled in using its knowledge for innovative problem solving.

STORY: If You Don't Know, Why Not Just Ask?

Phil asked me to sit in on a meeting of his struggling product development team to observe and provide feedback on how they worked together. The conversation was quite random, bouncing from one topic to another. Everyone seemed to be talking about a different problem or issue. During their conversation, I heard the phrase, "I wonder what Andy really wants." Who was Andy? It was the team's manager, sitting just up the hall with his door wide open. Why wouldn't someone just go and ask him? Because it had been three months since Andy had handed the project to the team: "Come up with another liquid hard-surface cleaning product." The company was already successfully selling two such liquid cleaners, so the team began to sense it wasn't really sure what they were trying to do or why. Of course, no one wanted to appear stupid by telling Andy they had spent two months without making any progress. The team was facilitated through the creative problem-solving process, beginning with problem finding, which we also sometimes call the "fuzzy situation." In this first step, we are either looking for a new problem or we have found ourselves in a situation which is ill-structured, ambiguous, and undefined. Such a problem is sometimes found simply by being present or having a problem handed over. If we are creative, we know enough not to assume that we already know what the problem is. Instead, the process calls for us to defer judgment and put our effort into moving from a fuzzy situation to a clearly understood statement (or family of statements), beginning with the challenge, "How might we ...?" In this case, a key unknown fact that emerged was that Andy came to them after meeting with his own boss over lunch and gave them the third liquid cleaner project. What the group did not know was that at lunch Andy's boss had said, "We need to boost profits," and mused, "perhaps we should add another liquid cleaner to the two we already have." It turned out that the boss did not recall the casual conversation which Andy had taken as serious direction. When the team went through the "Why might we want to?" and "What's stopping us from?" analyses, they reformulated the challenge to "How might we create a new product that keeps households cleaner in a new way?" When shared with Andy, the new challenge was heartily accepted as a major move forward.

STORY: Finding Facts by Experiencing

Woody Allen once made this simple but profound statement: "80% of anything is just showing up." Once you take a break from reading and thinking about your problem and just "show up," you will likely experience unexpected events and new information to augment what you may already know or think you know. The Honda growth story is a case in point[14](Figure 2.6). In the fifties, Honda was a small Japanese company manufacturing small lawnmowers and scooters. They were interested in expanding their business beyond Japan and looked toward America. Believing the scooter would be inappropriate for the sustained speeds and long distances it would need to cover to be successful in America, they began developing a line of larger motor cycles called the Honda Dream. In 1959, they sent a small team of employees to California to figure out how to market their new product. To save expenses, the team shared a one-bedroom apartment and used scooters to run errands and make sales calls. They began to find out that these Honda Dream motorcycles were a tough sell, proving to be too fragile for the sustained speeds and long distances needed to cover to be successful in America. However, the small scooters roused unexpected interest! One day, so the story goes, one of the crew rolled into a Sears store on a scooter, parked it, and walked in ready to present the new Dream motorcycle. Before he could begin, the manager said, "What is that thing you drove up here with?"

"Well, it's a scooter."

"How quickly can you send me 200?"

All of a sudden, the team discovered there was a market for their small scooters! (Later the company progressed into making superior miniature motorcycles that they called the "Super Cub," which also became very successful.)

"80% of anything is just showing up."

FIGURE 2.6 Finding Facts by Experiencing

As an entrepreneur, if you choose to stay behind a computer and read and analyze market research, you will never have access to all of the facts you need. Be willing to step outside. When you're stuck, it's a great time to "get outside your box" somehow and experience your problem. Now how might this apply to you? We hope we have provided some helpful hints. For example, if you're with a large organization of many people just like you, how in the world are you going to stand out and be different than anybody else? There's an opportunity for you to distinguish yourself. Instead of doing the same work that everyone else is doing, ask, " How might I engage people in making change for the better?"

How an Entrepreneur Can Gather More Facts From the Field When Needed

A good fact-finding session is sometimes just a first step toward *more* fact finding. The session might also reveal that the entrepreneur still has some knowledge gaps that need to be addressed before moving into Step 3. Let's revisit the second fact-finding question, "What do you not know about the fuzzy situation that you'd like to find out?" If facts related to this question were selected as pertinent to the customer problem, we may need to go out into the field and search for answers. Additionally, answers to the other questions might also require further fact finding.

Follow-up Fact Finding

Generating a successful solution is preceded by good fact finding. A group fact finding session may reveal enough information to move forward in the creative entrepreneurial process. But it might also help the entrepreneur become aware of what they need to know more of too. A fluid and open approach to fact finding pays huge dividends later when a solution is brought to market. The entrepreneur can be confident that they have done their due diligence on their idea and are more aware of the challenges they will need to address for the company to be a success.

Investigation into addressing knowledge gaps can include reading, conversations with others who are knowledgeable on the particular issue, follow-up meetings with people you've already met, feedback from stakeholders like customers and suppliers, attendance at professional meetings and trade shows, and a general absorption of information relative to the problem or issue under study. Additional investigation in both related and unrelated fields is sometimes involved. This exploration provides the individual with a variety of perspectives on the problem, and it is particularly important for an entrepreneur, who needs a basic understanding of all aspects of the development of a new product or service. Entrepreneurs can search for additional background knowledge in a number of ways. Some of the most helpful are:

1. read in a variety of fields that might pertain to analogous issues;
2. join professional groups and associations to get direction on sources;

3. attend professional meetings and seminars that might have sessions on the topic;
4. travel to new places that might have different perspectives on the issue;
5. talk to anyone and everyone about your topic for possible leads to new information;
6. scan magazines, newspapers, and journals for articles related to the subject; and
7. develop a subject library for future reference.

Curiosity and Fact Finding

As you gather facts about the issue, you'll often come to the conclusion that you have much to learn to truly be knowledgeable on the topic. Don't let this situation dissuade you from moving forward. You can either work with what you have, turn away from the challenge, or embrace it. Those that let their curiosity drive them to find answers they feel they need to know become the innovators and drivers of progress in society. The greatest discoveries occur when someone seeks to get answers others are not willing to pursue. However, to get those answers, you must often admit your ignorance on something. Recognizing what we don't know is one of the hallmarks of an inquisitive and creative mind. A humble approach to turning to others for help in problem solving is one of the most important thinking characteristics you can have in creating breakthrough products and services. Management scholar Ed Schein calls this approach to problem solving "humble inquiry,"[15] *Good to Great* author Jim Collins calls it "Level 5 Leadership,"[16] and in *Give and Take,* Wharton professor Adam Grant credits information sharing as the foundation of creativity and productivity.[17] Whatever experts choose to call the process of asking questions and listening for new leads, it is clear that fact finding can drive innovation.

This mindset may seem contradictory to some driven people, but humility properly understood has worked well for some of the most successful entrepreneurs in the world. As Charles Koch, CEO of Koch Industries, told us recently,

> Humility doesn't mean looking down at your shoes and saying, "Aw shucks." It means knowing what you don't know and being willing to admit that to yourself and others. From that state of mind, you can get the answers you need to get things done.[18]

Brian Grazer, the producer of hit movies such as *A Beautiful Mind, Apollo 13,* and *Splash,* concurs with this sentiment.[19] He credits his success in a cutthroat industry to "curiosity conversations." These conversations are encounters he arranges with people outside the movie business that give him material for new storylines. He's always looking for inspiration to tell a story the general public might not be aware of or may have forgotten about. Whether it's the story of Nobel Prize economist John Nash's struggles with mental illness or NASA's crisis

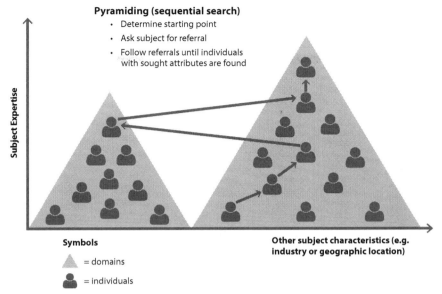

FIGURE 2.7 Pyramiding

management during the Apollo 13 mission, Grazer finds ways to make the audience more aware of issues in the human condition. He states,

> The entertainment business requires a huge amount of confidence. ... My confidence comes from curiosity. Yes, asking questions builds confidence in your own ideas. ... I use curiosity to pop the bubble, to keep complacency at bay.[20]

Grazer is persistent in arranging curiosity conversations, but he also benefits from his status as a celebrity and successful movie producer. How does an ordinary person without an extensive network at the top get these types of meetings? Is it asking too much for mere mortals to get answers to tough questions? Are the successful endowed with more gifts and resources that make fact finding easier? MIT professor Eric von Hippel believes the answer is no and that anyone can find answers to their questions if they employ a technique called "pyramiding"[21] (Figure 2.7).

Pyramiding

Pyramiding is a particularly effective method for learning from experts.[22,23] It is a search process based on the premise that "people with a strong interest in a topic or field tend to know people more expert than themselves."[24] Experts are anyone who may have extensive knowledge about the customer, problem, or existing solutions, but this definition can also be expanded to include external problem solvers from analogous domains who can offer novel solutions overlooked in the industry.[25,26] With some persistence, most entrepreneurs should be able to find an expert in a field to interview. The key is to find almost anyone who has a connection to the domain you are interested in. Because once this initial step of talking to someone connected to the field has been accomplished, the entrepreneur can initiate a "search on the fly" by concluding the interview by asking the expert, "Who in your organization or elsewhere do you think has more insight on this problem?"[27] This powerful question asked at the end of each interview creates a path to getting new answers to the inquiries you have.

When approaching a new lead, the entrepreneur should try to set up the next meeting by acknowledging the person who gave the lead. The purpose of the meeting should also be given. The referral and purpose of the interview respectfully delivered will open many doors for an entrepreneur. For example, an entrepreneur could say, "Miss Brown, I'd like to know more about supply chains in Malaysia. Tom Goldsby said you could be helpful to me on that matter. Could you spare twenty minutes to answer a few questions for me?".

It is amazing how quickly an entrepreneur can build a network using pyramiding. The ongoing use of the question requesting contact with someone who has more information on the subject can lead an entrepreneur to the top stakeholders in an industry. Once that level is reached, the experts may not be aware of anyone having more knowledge in their own domain, so they will often suggest an expert in an analogous field.[28] The movement from one domain pyramid to another offers divergent possibilities for new insights into the problem space, and in the process, the entrepreneur learns the vocabulary and perspectives of the experts. With a thorough immersion, an entrepreneur gains trust among relevant stakeholders by speaking their language. Engaging stakeholders in this way will later prove useful when the entrepreneur seeks resources and support for starting the business. After pyramiding, entrepreneurs will better understand who the customers are, the problems they have, and the solutions companies are currently providing in the industry. With good fact-finding skills and techniques, entrepreneurs need not start from scratch in generating solutions.

Summary

It is important to not overlook the importance of fact finding. Just recognizing a good problem to solve will not guarantee the creation of a good solution. Slowing down to really study the customer problem is an important step in creative entrepreneurship. Even the smartest entrepreneurs can make mistakes when they get sloppy and inattentive during any step of problem solving. In the previous chapter, we provided legendary entrepreneurs as exemplars of good problem finding, but four of them also provide cautionary tales for the importance of being good in all the steps of creativity. While Steve Jobs had an impressive string of hits, he also had a few misses in his career that might be accounted for by bad fact finding. In particular, the Apple Lisa was not embraced by the market because he denied the fact that most household customers would not pay $9,995 for the computer ($24,000 in 2015 dollars). He became too attached to the customer problem he was solving rather than taking a more objective view of his market's potential. The Polaroid company filed for Chapter 11 bankruptcy in 2001 because it would not accept the reality of digital picture taking during the previous decade. One reason Land left the company he founded was because he thought the company was not embracing new technology possibilities in the market. The Ford Motor Company is notorious for its production of the Edsel in 1958. Like the Lisa, the Edsel had many innovative features, but the price tag overwhelmed the target customer. The car never found a foothold in the auto industry. Walt Disney was not without his failures either. Some of his most ambitious projects also nearly bankrupted his company. *Fantasia,* for example, was a critical success but took a loss on the company's books because it required a new technology called Fantasound for full enjoyment in a theater. Only sixteen prints of the Fantasound were made available to theaters, which required the movie to travel between cities for viewing. The economics of the system did not hold up. This business failure, coupled with the loss from other experimental pictures during this period, put the company under financial strain. *Fantasia* is now considered a classic, but in its day it almost ruined the company.

As these stories evidence, removing a humble mindset and ignoring important facts can damage anyone's company. Ignoring reality is the ultimate form of arrogance in business, and it can happen to anyone. That legendary entrepreneurs can make this mistake should serve as warning to any of us that if we drop our guard, we can overlook important information. Creative entrepreneurship is a process that requires astute awareness of what you are doing and trying to achieve. When an entrepreneur diligently ask questions and seeks facts, they open up a world of possibilities for future products and services, and when they are stuck or in doubt, more fact finding will usually help ease the tension.

The one entrepreneur from the previous chapter who may have been the ultimate fact finder was Thomas Edison. Edison was a voracious experimenter and note taker. He surveyed every technology and trend he could come across, documented everything he learned, and expected the same from everyone in his Menlo Park laboratory. If lab employees didn't keep meticulous notebooks, he fired them. It may be his attention to fact finding that helped him amass 1,093 patents during his lifetime.

In this chapter, we discussed the importance of fact finding, provided six questions to prompt good fact finding, and offered techniques for following up on knowledge gaps that are identified during fact finding sessions. We also provided stories to demonstrate how good fact finding is accomplished. In the next chapter, we explain how to convert the converged facts into new problem statements. You will see how uncovering key facts can help an entrepreneur redefine the customer problem they intend to solve. Therefore, it is Step 3, problem definition, that helps an entrepreneur leap from solving an obvious problem to addressing a problem that no one has considered before.

Notes

1 Burton, R. (2008). *On Being Certain: Believing You Are Right Even When You're Not.* New York, NY: St. Martin's Press.

2 Kahneman, D. (2011). *Thinking Fast and Slow.* New York, NY: Farrar, Straus and Giroux.

3 Dobelli, R. (2013). *The Art of Thinking Clearly.* New York, NY: HarperCollins.

4 Suzuki, S. (1970). *Zen Mind, Beginner's Mind.* Boulder, CO: Weatherhill.

5 Basadur, M. S. (1995). *The Power of Innovation.* London, UK: Pitman Professional Publishing.

6 Emerson, R., Fretz, R., and Shaw, L. (2011). *Writing Ethnographic Fieldnotes,* 2nd ed. Chicago, IL: University of Chicago Press.

7 Christensen, C. (1997). *The Innovator's Dilemma: When New Technologies Cause Great Firms to Fail.* Boston, MA: Harvard Business Review Press.

8 Helfat, C. (1994). "Firm-Specificity in Corporate Applied R&D." *Organization Science,* 5, 173–84.

9 March, J. G. (1991). "Exploration and Exploitation in Organizational Learning." *Organization Science,* 2(1): 71–87.

10 Martin, X., and Mitchell, W. (1998). "The Influence of Local Search and Performance Heuristics on New Design Introduction in a New Product Market." *Research Policy,* 26(7,8): 759–71.

11 Von Hippel, E. (1994). "'Sticky Information' and the Locus of Problem Solving: Implications for Innovation." *Management Science,* 40(4): 429–39.

12 United States Patent 3,852,075: Hard Surface Rinse-Coating Composition and Method. Inventor: Marino Sidney Basadur, Evendale, Ohio. Assignee: The Procter & Gamble Company, Cincinnati, Ohio.

13 Arthur, W. B. (2009). *The Nature of Technology: What It Is and How It Evolves.* New York, NY: The Free Press and Penguin Books.

14 Sherman, D. (2009). "Fifty Years of Honda in America." *Automobile Magazine.* http://www.automobilemag.com/news/fifty-years-of-honda-history/.

15 Schein, E. H. (2013). *Humble Inquiry: The Gentle Art of Asking Instead of Telling.* San Francisco, CA: Berrett-Koehler Publishers.

16 Collins, J. C. (2001). *Good to Great: Why Some Companies Make the Leap … and Others Don't.* New York, NY: Random House.

17 Grant, A. (2013). *Give and Take: Why Helping Others Drives Our Success.* New York, NY: Penguin Books.

18 Goldsby, M. G. (2011). Personal communication, November 11.

19 Grazer, B. (2015). *A Curious Mind: The Secret to a Bigger Life.* New York, NY: Simon & Schuster.

20 Grazer, B. (2015). *A Curious Mind: The Secret to a Bigger Life.* New York, NY: Simon & Schuster, p. 33.

21 Von Hippel, E. (2005). "Democratizing Innovation: The Evolving Phenomenon of User Innovation." *Journal für Betriebswirtschaft,* 55(1): 63–78.

22 Von Hippel, E., Thomke, S., and Sonnack, M. (1999) "Creating Breakthroughs at 3M." *Harvard Business Review,* 77(5): 47–57.

23 Poetz, M. K., and Prügl, R. (2010). "Crossing Domain-Specific Boundaries in Search of Innovation: Exploring the Potential of Pyramiding." *Journal of Product Innovation Management,* 27(6): 897–914.

24 Von Hippel, E., Franke, N., and Prügl, R. (2009). "Pyramiding: Efficient Search for Rare Subjects." *Research Policy,* 38(9): 1397–406.

25 Rosenkopf, L., and Nerkar, A. (2001). "Beyond Local Search: Boundary-Spanning, Exploration, and Impact in the Optical Disk Industry." *Strategic Management Journal,* 22(4): 287–306.

26 Stuart, T. E., and Podolny, J. M. (1996). "Local Search and the Evolution of Technological Capabilities." *Strategic Management Journal,* 17(S1): 21–38.

27 Poetz, M. K., and Prügl, R. (2010). "Crossing Domain-Specific Boundaries in Search of Innovation: Exploring the Potential of Pyramiding." *Journal of Product Innovation Management,* 27(6): 897–914.

28 Von Hippel, E. (2005). "Democratizing Innovation: The Evolving Phenomenon of User Innovation." *Journal für Betriebswirtschaft,* 55(1): 63–78.

3
STEP 3: PROBLEM DEFINITION

Introduction

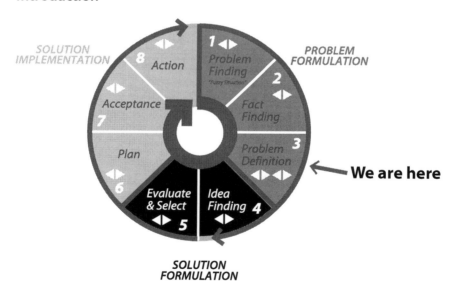

Legend has it that Albert Einstein once said, "If I had only one hour to save the world, I would spend fifty-five minutes defining the problem, and only five minutes finding the solution." This message implies that scientific advances come not so much from thinking up new solutions as from formulating problems in new ways or seeing them from different angles. With problems in the natural world, once you develop the formulation or angle, finding the solution becomes merely an exercise in mathematics or experimentation. When it comes to entrepreneurship, this emphasis on problem definition is equally important. Indeed, having a strong definition of the customer's problem is very helpful in creating a winning business solution. However, customer problems are typically not formulaic like scientific problems are. There are many factors that are continuously changing and interacting that make customer problems very complex, such as customer preferences, competitive dynamics, societal trends, and technology change, among others. Solving complex problems requires a different kind of thinking than programmed problems need.

Unfortunately, most people struggle with addressing complex problems because they feel stuck. They don't know where to start, which often leads to decision paralysis or kneejerk definitions of the problem. This is usually not a wise move. Due to the nature of complex problems, quick decision-making can cause a person to miss very important, but not obvious, factors in the situation. Solving complex problems requires slowing down and considering the different variables involved and how they interact. Most people, however, have no process for gaining this understanding. This chapter addresses that gap by discussing problem definition, Step 3 of our creative entrepreneurship process. Just as fact finding is the hinge between the fuzzy situation and a well-defined problem, so is problem defining the hinge between fact finding and solutions.

In problem definition, the entrepreneur uses the key facts selected from the previous step to generate definitions of the problem. These represent new directions or challenges for the entrepreneur to consider. It is a very organic approach where unexpected issues that bring new perspectives on the problem space can emerge. Rarely will there be a single "correct" problem. In fact, most problems are interrelated to a set of different and potentially useful challenges. Therefore, Step 3 helps the entrepreneur map the challenges to discover the key leverage points for designing pleasing business solutions.

Problem definition utilizes two tools for successfully capturing the customer problem space: challenge statements and challenge mapping. Let's first start with challenge statements.

Challenge Statements

Framing problems into challenge statements is one of the most important skills in problem definition.[1] The phrase "How might we?" (or "How might I?") is the powerful phrase that transforms converged facts from Step 2 into actionable challenges in Step 3. Every fact that was selected in Step 2 will be converted into a positively stated challenge that begins with this phrase. For example, a fact such as "the customer prefers to shop with others as a group experience" can be converted into the challenge statement "How might we make our store more inviting for groups to shop there?" However, that is just one possible way of wording the fact. Just as in Step 1 and Step 2, divergence is a critical practice in creative problem solving; therefore, we might also convert the fact into "How might we design the store layout to be more comfortable in dressing room areas?" or "How might we provide customer attention geared to groups and not just individual shoppers?" These are just three challenge statements derived from this fact. There are potentially many more. You would use this technique for each converged fact that was selected in Step 2.

Once you have generated a list of possible challenge statements, count the total number of suggestions given. Then take that total and multiply it by 10 percent. That number will provide the number of challenges to choose from your list. So, for example, if you generated 26 challenge statements, 10 percent of that total gives you 2.6. Rounding up, we would select the 3 key challenges that if solved would provide us great satisfaction. A survey of an industry will often reveal that the top innovators are those mavericks who are exceptionally good at reframing problems. As an example, let's look at the world of outdoor sports, a place where its practitioners are always pushing the edge of what's possible.

Problem Definition On the Edge

The ultimate test of a solution is when a person's life is at stake. For example, soldiers risk their lives on battlefields and problem solve their way to victory with great courage and ingenuity. Fortunately, most people will never go to war, but outdoor sports is an arena where regular people challenge their limits every day. Pioneers and legends in extreme activities often attain their lofty heights because of their stellar problem-solving abilities. In particular, they redefine their sports by tackling problems their contemporaries have overlooked. Let's look at three legendary outdoorsmen who transformed the sports world through ingenious problem definition.

Laird Hamilton

Laird Hamilton is a professional surfer who has conquered the biggest waves in the world. Wherever there is a wave that others fear, Hamilton makes camp and figures out how to surf it. Teahupo'o is such a wave. It was notorious for its size and ferocity, reaching heights of 70 feet and crashing into the shallow, rough barrier reefs of Tahiti. Anyone who attempted to surf it was risking their life. Unlike a normal wave in which a surfer could paddle into the swell and time a ride, the size of Teahupo'o made it nearly impossible to reach the apex. Why did Hamilton think he was capable of doing what other professionals thought was impossible? After all, other surfers in the world were just as physically gifted as Hamilton. The answer lies in how he thinks. His differentiation was his problem-solving ability.

While other surfers were trying to figure out how to surf Teahupo'o with traditional methods, Hamilton knew a new technique was needed. After much thought, he redefined the Teahupo'o challenge from "How might I surf the wave?" to "How might I get to the *top* of the wave so that I can surf it?" Hamilton knew if he could reach the pinnacle of the wave, he could then rely on his surfing skills to take over from there. From that problem definition, he developed the revolutionary method of tow-in surfing, in which another person on a jet ski pulls him into the cresting wave. Hamilton releases the rope when he's reached the apex of the wave while his partner on the Jet Ski rides down the backside to safety. From there, Hamilton can ride the wave. This technique eliminates paddling into the wave, which *is* an impossible task. The solution puts him in position to do what no other surfer had the opportunity to do: surf Teahupo'o! It is still extremely risky, but the technique has enabled him to come safely through some of the most death-defying rides in the sport's history. Hamilton's ingenuity is further demonstrated in some of his other innovations in the sport, such as the paddleboard and foil board. He's always looking for the next problem he can solve that will keep him on the forefront of the surfing world.

Yvon Chouinard

Now let's go from dangerous water sports to the equally risky world of rock climbing. Rock climbing is a particularly fitting pastime of expert problem solvers. Climbing a rock face requires nonstop decision making as to what route to take, where to find the next handhold, and what maneuver to make to propel the body upward. In fact, overcoming the ongoing challenges on a climb is why rock climbers call routes "problems." It is as mentally exhausting as it is physical.

Yvon Chouinard was an extremely good climber in the 1960s who, like Hamilton in surfing, was always looking for the next big challenge to conquer. He had climbed some of the world's most challenging rock faces, like the North America Wall in Yosemite National Park, but he realized that he could scale even greater mountains if he had better equipment. Ice climbing and mountain climbing require pitons for getting grip in the rock. Since Chouinard was climbing the toughest routes, he put his equipment through the toughest trials. Because his expectation for pitons was higher than the average climber's, he was faced with the problem "How might I find a piton that will withstand the trials I put it through?" Fact finding revealed there was there nothing on the market to meet his requirements, so he bought a secondhand coal-fired forge and began making his own hardened steel pitons. They worked very well, and other climbers began buying them from him. Chouinard was now not only a world class climber but an entrepreneur as well. He continued to improve equipment in the sport, and being the innovator he is, he turned his attention to new sets of problems in rock climbing. For example, unhappy with climbing gear and apparel, he formed the clothing company Patagonia and began selling rugged technical apparel with great success. Patagonia continues to grow today, but Chouinard now channels his problem solving genius on environmental issues so he can protect the mountains he loves.

John Collins

Not many people have heard of John Collins, but they have heard of the endurance challenge he created in 1978. The Ironman triathlon is an endurance event like no other. Athletes must swim 2.4 miles, bike 112 miles, and run a 26.2 mile marathon in under 17 hours in one day. It's quite a challenge. Most people probably wonder what type of crazy person would participate in such an event. Well, its people like John Collins. John Collins was a Navy commander who loved endurance competitions. As a member of the sports scene in Hawaii, he often heard cyclists, runners, and swimmers arguing over who the toughest athletes were. Was it the long-distance swimmer, the day-racing cyclist, or the marathoner? Collins had heard enough bickering and formulated a challenge to find out: "How might I create a race that determines once and for all who the best endurance athletes are?" On February 18, 1978, he organized a race that brought 15 athletes together to compete in the first Ironman triathlon. Before the race, each athlete was given a course description and instructions. On the last page of the booklet was the statement, "Swim 2.4 miles! Bike 112 miles! Run 26.2 miles! Brag for the rest of your life." Twelve men finished the race that day, and the winner was declared an Ironman.

The race was covered by *Sports Illustrated,* which spurred more entries in the event the following year. Collins eventually sold the race rights to two local Nautilus Fitness Center owners, and over the years ownership has transferred to different parties. The Ironman Company is now an international organization with thousands of competitors entering races all over the world. The one big difference between the first race and the current races is that anyone who completes the event in under 17 hours is considered an Ironman. You don't have to win the race to earn the title. However, the original distances still exist, and the challenge that Collins recognized in 1978 to determine who the toughest athletes on the planet are lives onto this day.

As these examples illustrate, framing problems in new ways can lead to revolutionary breakthroughs. It is indeed an important skill, and if someone wants to become more innovative, learning how to frame better challenges will help. However, there is another tool in problem definition that takes challenge statements a step further. The tool is called the "why-what's stopping" analysis, and it is a game changer when it comes to problem definition. Let's examine the next tool to use in creating good problem definition.

The "Why-What's Stopping" Analysis[2]

In order to better use the creative process, you must be able to broaden your point of view. Coming up with insightful "How might we?" challenges helps you do this. Further problem definition is attained by using the "why-what's stopping" analysis. This analysis often provides the greatest surprises and discoveries about how a problem is formulated.

1. Ask the complete question: 'Why...?' or 'What's stopping...?'
2. Answer in a complete, simple sentence.
3. Restate the answer to create a new "How might...?'

FIGURE 3.1 The "Why-What's Stopping" Analysis

Three Simple Steps

Using the "why-what's stopping" analysis effectively depends on your skill in asking two simple questions—"Why?" and "What's stopping me?"—and in employing a simple three-step process, as follows (Figure 3.1):

1. Ask the question "Why ...?" or "What's stopping ...?" of the perceived challenge.

   Let's use the earlier retail store example to see how this works. Assume the challenge we want to consider more is "How might we design the store layout to be more comfortable in dressing room areas?" Using the two simple questions, we could ask, "Why would we want to design the store layout to be more comfortable in dressing room areas?" or "What's stopping us from designing the store layout to be more comfortable in dressing room areas?"

2. State a specific answer to the question in a simple, complete sentence.

   So, "Why would we want to design the store layout to be more comfortable in dressing room areas?" An answer might be "So that groups will linger longer in the store." If the other question—"What's stopping us from designing the store layout to be more comfortable in dressing room areas?"—had been asked, an answer might be, "We haven't found room yet to put sofas and chairs near the dressing room."

3. Based on the answer, create a new challenge.

   Now we convert the answers into new "How might we ...?" statements. "So that groups will linger longer in the store" now could become "How might we entice groups to linger longer in the store?" and "We haven't found room yet to put sofas and chairs near the dressing room" now becomes "How might we find room for sofas and chairs near the dressing room?"

Asking "Why?" of a challenge, and then restating the answer into a new challenge, broadens your problem definition. For instance, suppose you're trying to help your teenage son think his way through a problem without solving it for him (Figure 3.2). If your son perceives his challenge as "How might I get tickets to the concert?" you ask him, "Why do you want to get tickets to the concert?" (In other words, "What is the intent?") His answer might be, "I want a date with Sue." You then help him turn that answer into a broader challenge: "How might I get a date with Sue?" There are many more solutions to this broader challenge than there are to the narrower challenge, "How might I get tickets to a concert?"

Similarly, asking your son the question, "What's stopping you from getting tickets to the concert?" helps him to narrow his challenge. Perhaps his answer is "the tickets have been sold out for weeks." You then help him turn that answer into a more focused challenge, such as "How might I find someone selling two tickets?" While there are fewer solutions to "How might I find someone selling two tickets?" than to "How might I get tickets to the concert?" perhaps this narrowed focus is exactly what he needs to come up with a solution. (Note that asking the question "Why?" of this more narrow challenge leads back to the original challenge: "How might I get tickets to the concert?" Hence the upward-pointing arrow in Figure 3.2 that links these two challenges.)

STORY: No More Green Stripes

Early in my career at Procter & Gamble, I was asked for help by a product development team that was formed at short notice in response to a competitor's new product. Colgate's green-striped Irish Spring was the first striped soap bar introduced to North America. With its aggressive advertising campaign emphasizing "refreshment," the soap was finding ready consumer acceptance. One of the rules at Procter & Gamble was that if we were the second entrant into a new market, a new product's competitive advantage had to be demonstrated prior to market testing. When I asked the team what was going wrong, they said that they had been unable to produce a green-striped bar that was preferred over Irish Spring in a consumer preference blind test. The team had experimented with several green-striped bars, all of which merely equaled Irish Spring in blind testing. It became evident to me that the team had chosen to define its problem as "How might we make a green-striped bar that consumers will prefer over Irish Spring?"

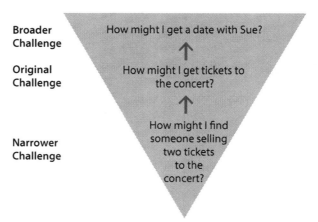

FIGURE 3.2 An Example of Using the "Why-What's Stopping" Analysis to Broaden and Narrow a Challenge

Applying the creative problem-solving process to the problem began with developing alternative ways to frame the challenge. By repeatedly asking, "Why might we want to make a green-striped bar that consumers would prefer over Irish Spring?" we generated many alternative "How might we?" challenges. The flash of inspiration came from the answer "we want to make people feel more refreshed." This led to the new challenge: "How might we better connote refreshment in a soap bar?" This less restrictive challenge, which included no mention of green stripes, gave us more room for creative solutions.

About 200 solution ideas for refreshment ideas were quickly diverged. On evaluation, two ideas stood out. One was an image of sitting on a white, sandy beach with blue sky, white clouds, and enjoying soothing, cooling breezes. The other was based on travel to the sea coast for refreshment. The eventual product result was a blue-and-white swirly bar with a unique odor and shape, which quickly won a blind test over Irish Spring, then soon achieved market success under the brand name Coast (Figure 3.3).

Solving this problem once it had been properly defined took the team mere hours. By leaping prematurely into solutions, the team had wasted almost 6 months before coming up with that problem definition. Many people and teams practice what we call "1 to 8" behavior. They skip the process and instead jump directly from problem to possible solution, over and over again.

Successful problem solving, however, requires people to begin the process with the recognition that they have a fuzzy situation and need to gather facts prior to defining the problem. Only after that is undertaken in a thorough fashion should they move on to exploring, evaluating, and selecting solution ideas; planning for implementation; and finally, taking action. The step-by-step process is detailed in Figure 3.4.

Coast

FIGURE 3.3 Coast
Image license by Ingram Image

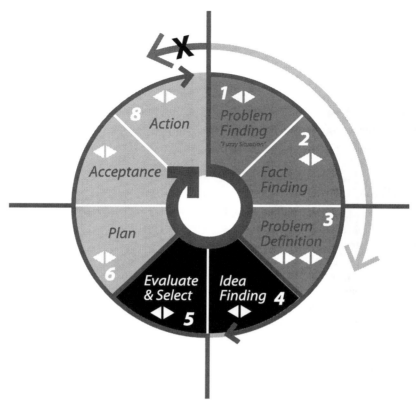

FIGURE 3.4 8-Step Process

As these examples illustrate, the first half of the creative problem-solving process is the *more* imaginative half. It's where what most people think of as design takes place. This is where questions and inquiry are raised, problems are surfaced, hidden facts are discovered, breakthrough challenges are defined, and innovative solution ideas are hatched. The back half of the process is where the solution ideas are analyzed against constraints, evaluated, and developed into practical solutions to be tested, perhaps including prototypes or drawings with step-by-step plans to gain acceptance by those impacted by the change. The final step involves putting a solution into play, which requires overcoming the natural fear that comes with unfamiliarity and lack of certainty. It's where naysayers will ask, "How do you know it will work?" For entrepreneurs, this is the stage where they do what is needed to take the concept to market. They're likely to make some mistakes in the process, but this stage is where the maverick entrepreneurs excel. The experience gained generates learning that launches a new round of innovation. Problems beget solutions, which lead to more problems, which lead to more solutions, ad infinitum. Their tenacity and ingenuity win people over to their ideas. They marshal the support and resources needed to get their business off the ground. The status quo is disrupted, and new opportunities arise in unexpected ways.

Breakthrough Collaboration

Another example of broadening the problem definition enabling "out of the box" thinking is illustrated by a consumer products company wanting to reduce the packaging costs of its potato chip products An interfunctional team had been formed to reduce costs and was now bogged down. The team's manufacturing members had identified a new packaging system that saved enormous amounts of time and money. The individual bags of potato chips were being packaged standing upright in larger boxes for delivery to customers. The new idea involved laying the bags on their sides in the boxes. The sales department team members were not at all satisfied with this solution because on delivery, customers open each box and count the bags before signing the receiving documents. Thus, the new idea would result in extra time and frustration for the customer and slow down the salesperson, which led to fewer sales calls per day. Obviously, an important challenge for sales was "How might we continue to make our required quota of sales calls per day?" By working together with the attitude of achieving full satisfaction for both sides, and by following the discipline of the Simplexity creative problem-solving process, a new problem definition was identified: "How might we lay the bags flat yet still allow the customer to quickly know how many bags are inside the box?"

Several solutions immediately became evident, including providing each customer with a weigh scale so that opening the box and counting was unnecessary. Rather than argue and disagree over solutions which appear to conflict because they address two different challenges, the creative process resulted in a new expanded challenge that encompassed both original challenges. In a union-management bargaining context this would be an example of making the pie bigger, where many more creative solutions could be generated to the expanded problem definition rather than simply moving up and down the zero-sum "we win, you lose" bargaining line. Some of these solutions would be capable of providing complete satisfaction to both parties.[3]

Broadening the Scope By Asking the "Else?" Question

There is usually more than one answer to the questions "Why?" or "What's stopping me?" Complex problems are rarely answered by getting a couple of answers. Further questions are usually required to draw out the richness of the problem space. Therefore, we often ask the questions repeatedly ("Why *else*?", "What *else* is stopping?") The continued search for more answers to the questions "Why?" and "What's stopping?" further broadens and narrows the problem scope.

Let's re-examine the clothing store scenario. The original question was "Why would we want to design the store layout to be more comfortable in dressing room areas?" Our first answer was "so that groups will linger longer in the store," which was converted into "How might we entice groups to linger longer in the store?" Now we could ask, "Why *else* would we want to design the store layout to be more comfortable in dressing room areas?" An answer might be "to attract shoppers back to the store for further visits," which can then be converted into "How might we attract shoppers back to the store for more visits?"

Using the "why-what's stopping" logic, we can now ask another narrowing question. The original question was "What's stopping us from designing the store layout to be more comfortable in dressing room areas?" Our first answer was "we haven't found room yet to put sofas and chairs near the dressing room," which was converted into "How might we find room for sofas and chairs near the dress-ing room?" Now we could ask, "What *else* is stopping us from designing the store layout to be more comfortable in dressing room areas?" An answer might be "we don't know what type of furniture to purchase for the remodel," which can then be converted into "How might we determine what furniture we should purchase for the new layout?"

Figure 3.5 demonstrates how a problem space can begin to emerge by repeat-ing the use of the "why-what's stopping" analysis. Each answer leads to at least one more fresh challenge that offers new insights. Furthermore, any of your subsequent challenges can become launching pads for repeating the three-step "why-what's stopping" analysis. As you map out the results of the "why-what's stopping" analy-sis, write each new challenge that you discover either above ("Why?") or below ("What's stopping?") the previous one. What results is a broadening hierarchy of challenges. Indicate the relationships between successive challenges by drawing upward-pointing arrows toward the top of the hierarchy. Place the challenges resulting from the "Else?" questions side by side.

The "why-what's stopping" analysis encapsulates the essence of good prob-lem definition, in that a complex problem is actually a field of connected broad and narrow problems. While most people intuitively think about different issues around a problem, without a process, they lack a coherent view of the big pic-ture. Two common outcomes often result: they stay stuck ruminating on what to do next because they are not sure if they really have a good understanding of what they are trying to solve, or they move too quickly latching onto a solution that will not have substantial impact on the problem. Neither scenario is good. Rumination prevents progress, and rash action leads to subpar outcomes that send a person back to the drawing board seeking another solution. A structured cre-ative process slows the person down momentarily to consider the facts around a problem, which supports better problem definition later. Once a problem is better defined, more successful solutions are possible. Thus, in the long run, a process approach to complex problem solving is both more effective and efficient than impulsive action.

Why?

How might we entice groups to linger longer in the store?

How might we attract shoppers back to the store for more visits?

How might we design the store layout to be more comfortable in the dressing room areas?

How might we find room for sofas and chairs near the dressing room?

How might we determine what furniture to purchase for the new layout?

What's Stopping?

FIGURE 3.5 Broadening the Scope

Challenge Mapping[4]

Now that we understand the mechanism behind the "why-what's stopping" analysis," we can capture the big picture of the problem space on paper. We call the visual outcome of the "why-what's stopping" analysis a "challenge *map*" because it provides a "lay of the land" of the problem we were originally trying to solve. It is essentially a map of connected problems. Challenge mapping enables us to get a 50,000-foot view of the problem space instead of being mired in one particular aspect of it. In crafting the challenge map, paper and Post-it notes are essential supplies for the exercise. If you are working on a problem alone, regular paper and mini Post-it notes will suffice. However, if more than one person is involved, easel paper, large Post-it notes, sticky dots, and markers are suggested.

You're now ready to map. Start with a converged challenge statement, as described earlier in this chapter, and write it on a Post-it note in the middle of the map. This is just a starting point for the mapping process. The "why-what's stopping" analysis will spread answers out around it as you go. Write the "How might we?" challenge statements on Post-it notes and stick them to their appropriate locations as you repeatedly apply the "why-what's stopping" methodology. Draw arrows connecting two challenges statements as soon as logical connections are made. Post-it notes are essential due to the fluid quality of the "why-what's stopping" analysis. As you answer the questions, you may find that another answer to a "Why else?" or "What else is stopping us?" question that sits alongside an earlier answer actually fits between the original and previous statements. When this insight occurs, simply move the Post-it notes to reflect the new connections, and then draw any new arrows needed to capture this. An example of this process is illustrated in Figure 3.6.

The map has an organic quality to it, in that the original "How might we?" question that started the map is now only one challenge among many. Unlike questioning methods like the 5 Why approach (asking "Why?" 5 times), the challenge maps

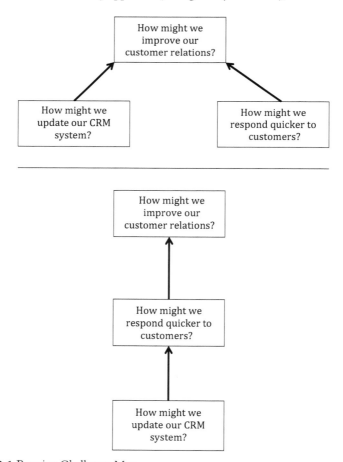

FIGURE 3.6 Practice Challenge Map

emerge in divergent fashion. There is no preconceived notion of how many challenges are to be identified. The final shape of the map, while usually being wider on the bottom, does not have a fixed shape either. More complex problems will naturally generate more challenges. Simpler problems can often be analyzed with just a few statements. Either way, a good challenge map is considered complete when participants can no longer generate answers to "why-what's stopping" questions.

When you have discovered sufficient new insights, it is time to select the most intriguing of the challenges for the next step: finding ideas for solutions to the selected challenges. As in the previous steps, once you have diverged and built a challenge map, it is time to converge on the key problems found on it. Ask each participant in the session to identify the top two or three "How might we?" statements on the map that if solved would bring great satisfaction. Participants then gather in front of the map, examine each card, and place a dot on the two or three cards they think are most pertinent to bringing progress to the situation at hand. In other words, the participants are to consider which challenge statements represent the most important obstacles to clear.

Looking at a large map and making these calls can sometimes be a bit overwhelming for some participants. A metaphor we like to use in making it easier for people to make their choices is to compare what they are doing to what lumberjacks do in the Pacific Northwest. In timber country, lumberjacks often drop cut logs into a river for transport downstream to wood processing plants. Often when there are a lot of logs in the water, the rivers become clogged and logjams occur. Experienced lumberjacks know the answer to this dilemma is to identify a few logs, that if pulled from the river, will unclog the logjam and get the logs flowing again. A problem space works much the same way in principle. Participants must recognize that some problems are more important than others and, if solved, will bring a lot of positive change to the situation.

Once each participant has made their selections, the facilitator follows the same clarifying approach as was applied in the fact finding step. The facilitator points to each Post-it note that was marked with a sticky dot and asks who marked it. Then, each person who marked the card explains (clarifies) why they did so. This approach is used until every marked card has received an explanation. After clarification is complete, the facilitator guides the group to choose the top 2 to 5 challenge statements to move forward into Step 4, solution generation. It should be noted that the selection with the most dots is not necessarily ordained to move forward into Step 4. Clarification often helps participants see the choices in a new light, so a selection that received only one dot may actually end up being chosen at the end of Step 3.

What Do You Do When You Don't Know What to Do Next?

Whatever the situation in which you find yourself, remember that you have a bullet-proof shield protecting you: The creative problem-solving process is always ready for launching. Whether you have found a problem—or a problem has found you—the trick is to realize that you are already in Step 1 of the process. So, now what? Just proceed to Step 2 and start fact finding; you never know what you're going to find when you start asking questions open mindedly. Gather information, talk to people, and visit with others. You will likely discover quite a few things you never knew. Some will be eye openers leading you into Step 3, where a new direction will begin forming with fresh challenges and a concrete strategy. Here's an example.

When the horrific September 11, 2001 disaster occurred, a global aerospace and airplane engineering company found itself especially hard hit. It had built a great reputation in the aerospace and aircraft field. There were 28 business units making all kinds of parts and systems for a variety of customers. Right after 9/11, the stock market went out from under them. The stock price dropped by half almost overnight. For a company that prided itself on using its stock price as a measure of its effectiveness, this posed quite a dilemma.

Rather than hunker down into a defensive shell, the company decided to deliberately use innovation to move forward and rebuild its business on its own terms. Here's how. In October, the top seven senior leaders met at their monthly roundtable meeting. The CEO and board chairman said to the others, "I don't know what to do next." This statement triggered the creative problem-solving process. The CEO was in the first step, "problem finding," recognizing that he was in a "fuzzy situation." The team had been trained in the creative problem-solving process and thus moved in turn to fact finding, then challenge finding, then challenge mapping. The challenge map, shown in Figure 3.7, became their strategic plan forward. They identified two higher level challenges as goals supported by four challenges that would drive their business for the next year or more and restore the price of their stock. The goals were "How might we increase our top line and earnings growth?" and "How might we get the Wall Street analysts excited about our future?" Below these goals were four supporting challenges which were more specific: (1) "How might we commercialize more new products every year?" (2) "How might we take advantage of the current low stock market prices (of other companies) to build up our own sales volume?" (3) "How might we change our business mix to improve consistency (there were gaps in their menu of offerings)?" and (4) "How might we increase cash flow to 100 percent of net income (up from the current 80 percent)?" They then engaged interfunctional and interdivisional teams across the company to begin solving these four key challenges. In net, by using the creative problem-solving process, they had created their own strategic plan to which they were strongly committed. The company became even stronger as a result of the crisis. The stock price was restored in less than two years, and the business continued to grow steadily for years to come.

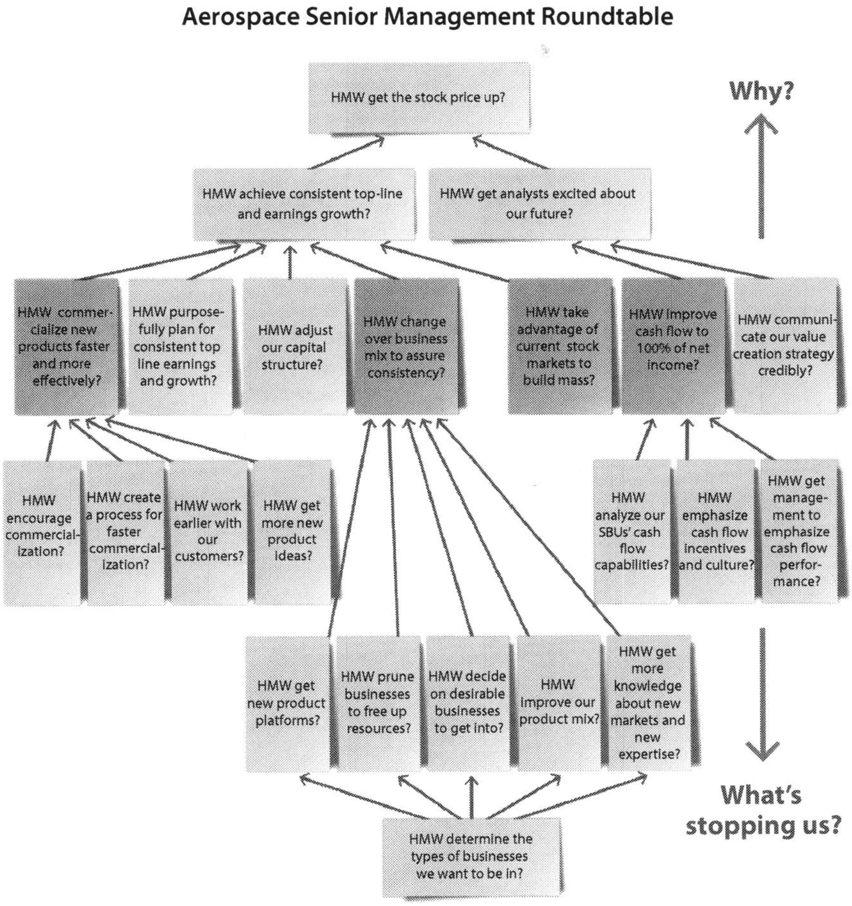

Aerospace Senior Management Roundtable

FIGURE 3.7 Aerospace Senior Management

Keep the "Why-What's Stopping" Analysis Simple

During the three-step "why-what's stopping" analysis, keep your answers to these two key questions simple, specific, and complete. Complicated, vague, or incomplete answers will lead to ambiguously stated challenges. Rather than successively broadening or narrowing a challenge, you may find yourself simply going around in circles.

For example, let's say you are addressing a production problem and were asked, "What's stopping us from decreasing our product defects?" If you reply that morale is low, you've provided an incomplete and vague response. If you really mean that people are not paying attention to quality, then the challenge that results from this much more specific answer is "How might we get our employees to pay more attention to product quality?" (This is more clear and more complete than "How might we improve morale?") Similarly, when you replied that morale is low in response to the question "Why would we want to reduce product defects?" perhaps what you really mean is "employees would feel better about their work." Then the challenge would be "How might we help employees feel better about their work?" Keeping the answers simple, specific, and complete gives you a logical hierarchy of more meaningful challenge statements, preventing you from going around in circles.

Is there a limit to the size of the problem-definition map created by the "why-what's stopping" analysis? The map's size is limited by three factors. At some point, broadening the problem further only makes it more esoteric ("How might I obtain happiness and bliss in life?") and impossible to answer concisely. Going in the other direction, you can continually narrow the problem into smaller and smaller chunks until the only thing that's stopping you is actually implementing an obvious solution. The third limitation is that you can spend only a finite amount of time on any particular problem. Eventually, you have to decide whether you've made your problem definition sufficiently complete and proceed toward solutions.

Challenge statements, the "why-what's stopping" analysis, and challenge mapping are incredibly powerful tools for problem definition. It cannot be emphasized enough that what we think is a huge problem may only be a piece of a much bigger problem space. Understanding what challenges are inherent in that problem space and their connections within helps a person make better decisions in where to allocate their time, energy, and other resources. This process can be somewhat difficult at first to use; however, once mastered, it fundamentally changes the way someone executes problem solving. For this reason, we offer the following story to help deepen your understanding of the fundamentals of problem definition.

STORY: The Handyperson's Challenge

Let's look at how the "why-what's stopping" analysis sorts out challenges of varying scope into a larger hierarchy. We'll use an adapted story from Sid Parnes, Ruth Noller, and Angelo Biondi's *Creative Action Guidebook*.[5] In this example, we'll ignore the "Else?" questions so that we can focus only on the idea of a hierarchy. We have added both the "Why?" and "What's stopping?" questions.

In a small chemical plant, a leaking metal float that had gradually lost its buoyancy had finally brought production to an abrupt halt. The plant's handyperson could hear water sloshing inside the float but couldn't detect the leak.

Considering these facts, if you were the handyperson using the creative problem-solving process we have covered in this book, you might readily think of several challenges, such as "How might I find the leak?"; "How might I make the leak more visible?"; "How might I restore buoyancy?"; and "How might I restore production?" Now how do you apply the "why-what's stopping" analysis in order to arrange these and other challenges in a simple hierarchy?

Suppose you arbitrarily start with the challenge "How might I find the leak?" Begin your three-step process by asking, "Why would I want to find the leak?" The answer might be "I'd like to repair the float." This answer leads to a broader challenge that sits higher in the hierarchy: "How might I repair the float?"

Suppose you decide to continue asking the "why" question. Asking "Why would I want to repair the float?" might yield the answer "we have lost buoyancy." This leads to the even broader challenge situated even higher in the hierarchy, "How might I restore buoyancy?" Asking "Why?" each time broadens the problem's scope. For example, there are more ways to restore buoyancy than there are ways to repair the float. Similarly, there are more ways to repair the float than there are ways to find the leak. Stated another way, while repairing the leak is one way to restore buoyancy, you might restore buoyancy without necessarily repairing the leak.

If you decide to continue asking the "Why?" question, you will discover new, broader challenges, such as "How might I get the machine running?" and even broader, "How might I get production going?" If at any point you decide to ask the "What's stopping?" question instead, you will discover narrower challenges. For example, asking "What's stopping me from finding the leak?" could lead to "the leak is so small that I can't see it." This could lead to a more focused challenge: "How might I make the leak more visible?" The hierarchy resulting to this point is shown in Figure 3.8.

If you were to continue asking "Why?" beyond the top of the hierarchy in Figure 3.8, you would enter the domain of the plant's management rather than that of the handyperson. However, the process continues to lead you to broader, more strategic challenges, like ever-larger waves from a stone dropped into a pond. Figure 3.9 shows nested hierarchies that illustrate how the company's strategic goals are linked to the day-to-day operations.

You could build the same hierarchical map in any number of ways. For example, suppose you start with a loftier goal such as "How might I keep myself and my employees in long-term jobs?" You could then ask the "What's stopping?" question successively to create the same hierarchy, this time from the top down. Eventually you would reach the challenge "What's stopping me from making the leak more visible?" or even more narrow challenges.

Four Boilers from Eight

Let's look at another example.[6] Using the "What's stopping?" question helped an industrial engineer who was trying to reduce the number of boilers providing energy to his plant's manufacturing processes (Figure 3.10). Having worked through fact finding, he had perceived his challenge as "How might I get the eight boilers reduced to four?"

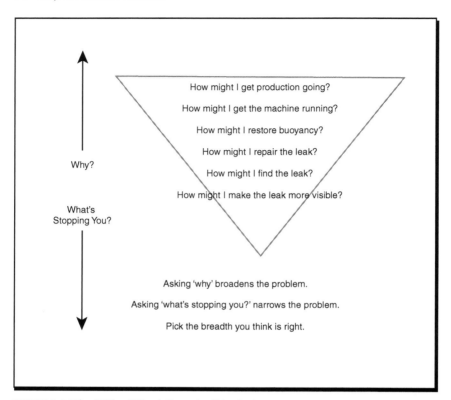

FIGURE 3.8 The "Why-What's Stopping" Analysis

Unable to meet this challenge on his own, he had asked a group of engineering colleagues for help. One of the group familiar with the "why-what's stopping" analysis asked him, "What's stopping you from getting the plant to use only four boilers rather eight?" His first answer was, "Nothing's stopping me; a similar plant in another region has already moved to four boilers from eight. Our plant could do the same."

His questioner knew enough about the analysis to probe further. He rephrased the question to ask, "If you already knew how to do it, then what's stopping you from getting the plant to use only four boilers rather eight?" After a great deal of thought and prompting from the rest of the group, the engineer said, "You know, what's really stopping me is that the plant manager is not interested in energy conservation, and the department managers are too busy to listen to my proposal." His challenge was then restated into "How might I get the plant manager to realize how important energy conservation is to attaining our goals, and how might I get the department managers to take the time to hear my proposal?"

To complete the "why-what's stopping" analysis, he was asked, "Why do you want to use only four boilers rather than eight?" His answer was "four boilers use

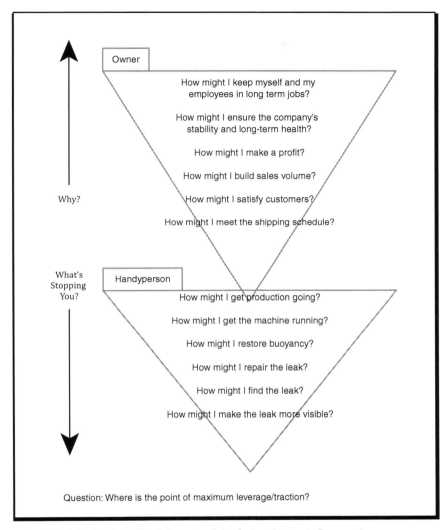

FIGURE 3.9 The "Why-What's Stopping" Analysis—Strategic Perspective

less energy than eight." The problem was then restated as "How might I reduce my plant's energy use?" Contemplating what was preventing him from using only four boilers gave the engineer a flash of insight. The key was not that he lacked the technical know-how but that his manager was not interested in energy conservation and that the department managers were too busy. Getting the managers' attention and convincing them turned out to be his key challenge. In this example, the owner of the problem obtained a new insight, a far better way to state his problem. This often results from repeated use of the "why-what's stopping" questioning process. The new challenges you create, whether broader or narrower,

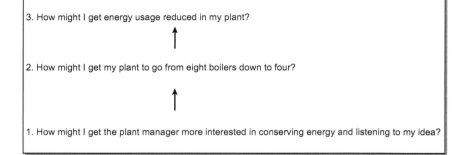

FIGURE 3.10 Four Boilers from Eight

are often better. This isn't always the case; sometimes the original challenge turns out to be the best of all, but this analysis helps you to consider other viewpoints, more broad and narrow, before you decide.

The "why-what's stopping" analysis we just described is very useful for general problem solving. If you recognize a problem, this technique can help you in better defining it, and better-defined problems are easier to solve. Once mastered, it is a game-changing skill that allows you to tackle almost any problem that comes your way. In Step 7, gaining acceptance, and Step 8, taking action, we will use the analysis again to help us overcome the roadblocks we might face in getting our idea off the ground. However, the technique can also be flexed to other purposes beyond specific problem solving. As you will also see in Chapter 6, the "why-what's stopping" analysis is a helpful tool for strategic planning.

Deep Thinking about Problems

Let's reflect a bit more on what a problem is. One way of looking at a problem is that it is a situation that requires some deep thinking to solve. If it weren't a problem, it wouldn't require any thinking. You would just go about your day using the solution that's been handy in similar situations. Problems range from the personal to the distant: "How might I lose 50 pounds this year?" "How might I help out that town that just got hit by a hurricane?" "How might I maintain a good relationship with my significant other?" Whenever a person feels anxious, concerned, or frustrated, it is likely that there is a problem lurking somewhere in the background waiting to be solved.

Entrepreneurs have their own set of problems: "How might I come up with my next great business idea?" "How might I get my first customers?" "How might I keep my customers happy?" A fundamental understanding and embrace of problems is crucial for entrepreneurial success. Essentially, delivering solutions to customers is the job of an entrepreneur. This is not easy. In contrast to traditional employees who execute existing solutions, an entrepreneur must define what problem will be solved and how. Dedicated effort, patience, and perseverance on the part of the entrepreneur to really address a problem from new angles separates him or her from the competition.

In this book, we have been examining problem solving within an entrepreneurial context. That is, you are recognizing a customer who has a problem that you offer a solution for. While problems are a negative situation for a customer, they are the source of opportunities for the entrepreneur. Therefore, if an entrepreneur wants to attain a powerful presence in their market, they should search for problems other companies can't solve. Good problem-definition skills reframe these challenges into more actionable forms where solutions are possible. In this section, we provide a modified version of challenge mapping to assist the entrepreneur in defining problems in ways competitors have missed.

Participants

Earlier in this chapter, we explained how to convert pertinent facts into diverged and then converged challenge statements. Once an entrepreneur has identified diverged and converged challenge statements, further problem definition can take place with customer challenge mapping. In building an insightful customer challenge map, it is helpful to have a diverse group of subject matter experts taking part in the exercise. A subject matter expert would be anyone who might have knowledge or a useful perspective on the customers and their problems. The entrepreneur should consider the entire ecosystem of stakeholders who affect the success of the future business. Participants could be customers, industry experts, potential suppliers and distributers, technology experts, key company members, potential investors, and experienced entrepreneur mentors, among others. Taking advantage of different people's expertise paints a clearer picture of where the company should compete. This approach is important because we often are conditioned to have a certain view of the world around us. Therefore, different perspectives can be helpful in triggering new ideas and possibilities. As Alexandra Horowitz states in *On Looking: A Walker's Guide to the Art of Observation*,

> There is a certain bias in everyone's perspective that has been named, by the French, *déformation professionelle:* the tendency to look at every context from the point of view of one's profession. The psychiatrist sees symptoms of diagnosable conditions in everyone from the grocery checkout cashier to his spouse; the economist views the simple buying of a cup of coffee as an example of a macroeconomic phenomenon.[7]

How do we determine who should be in the room? It's a judgment call. However, the more complex the problem space, the more likely you will need to have a more diverse range of eyes in the group. A group will typically be 3 to 10 people. However, we have found 7 participants to be the ideal number for a good session.

Therefore, if you desire to know the thoughts of a wide range of content experts, you might have to hold multiple sessions. When a large agricultural equipment manufacturer engaged in customer challenge mapping to determine how to design a product for the expanding Southeast Asian market, three days were devoted to the exercise. Several customer challenge mapping sessions were held with groups composed of different stakeholders. The objective was to uncover as many possible customer challenges as possible in order to find the golden nugget opportunities in the new market. Once the group achieved consensus on the top customer challenges, they were able to evaluate and select product specifications based on those challenges and move along in the process. Many companies in this situation would have simply pushed products they already had, but this organization decided to slow down and undergo a solid problem definition session before committing resources to the market.

Customer Challenge Mapping[8]

An application of the "why-what's stopping" analysis that is especially applicable to this chapter is a technique we call "customer challenge mapping." Customer challenge mapping applies the same three-step method previously covered in this chapter, but it has a small twist: instead of asking "Why might I / What's stopping me?" or "Why might we / What's stopping us?" we ask the question from the perspective of the customer. Thus, the challenge statements are written in the form of "How might the customer?" and the three-step questions are asked in the form of "Why might the customer?" and "What's stopping the customer?" Since the entrepreneur is seeking a solution to a customer problem, it is important to examine the problem space from the customer's perspective. Although there are likely other participants in the session besides customers, everyone is encouraged to provide answers to the questions.

Let's take an example. First consider ABC Company, which provides an online product to business owners of private practice medical clinics. Their product is unique and patent protected, and there is a feeling and evidence that their customer relationships have been deteriorating. After considerable market research, including surveys, interviews, and focus groups, the interfunctional team has come together and, based on these data and their own personal experience, converged on the following key facts:

1. Because of our incentive systems, we only invest selling time and support to our top customer resulting in lower support levels for low submitters; "Feed the strong, starve the weak."
2. Customers feel that customer and clinical support do not solve their issues to their satisfaction.
3. Customers feel they are getting clinically incorrect software product plans.
4. What's important to the customer should be of primary importance to sales and marketing and all of the company.

5. We want to be a customer-centric organization that enables our customers to effectively and efficiently provide outcomes that satisfy both customers and their end users.
6. Customers are not receiving the level of clinical and business support and mentoring they expect.
7. We have rules that create barriers to becoming a true partner with our customers.

The team then diverged on customer challenges and selected the following top customer challenges (HMTC means "how might the customer"):

1. HMTC get high quality clinical software product plans?
2. HMTC feel our sales approach is focused on their best interests?
3. HMTC feel a sense of commitment to them on their success rather than our own bottom-line?
4. HMTC treat his end users successfully?
5. HMTC believe that our treatment plan will be achieved predictably?
6. HMTC save time?
7. HMTC have a satisfying relationship regardless of his business volume?
8. HMTC get more support especially if they are low volume?
9. HMTC simplify the management of his practice?
10. HMTC improve his cash flow?
11. HMTC get immediate satisfactory answers to their questions?
12. HMTC feel confident they received the support they need?
13. HMTC get answers faster to his questions?
14. HMTC influence corporate culture?
15. HMTC provide his services without too many restrictive rules?
16. HMTC have a stress free work life?
17. HMTC treat patients without fear of things going wrong?

Then the team began to create a customer challenge map using the "why-what's stopping" analysis (Figure 3.11).

From the customer challenge map, the team selected seven final customer challenges (Figure 3.12).

As demonstrated in this example, customer challenge mapping is a very helpful tool for better defining what the customer's problem is. The "how might the customer" phrasing ensures that problems are pulled from the customer's perspective rather than assumed by the entrepreneur. Once a divergent customer challenge map is constructed, the same convergence methodology is applied as before. Each person selects the key two or three challenges on the map that they think hold the most opportunity for the company. The facilitator then addresses each selected challenge statement and allows each person who chose it to clarify why they did so. Once all selected statements have been discussed, the facilitator helps the group converge to the top two to four challenges to move forward into Step 4, idea finding.

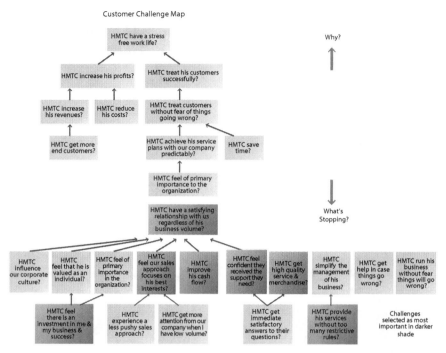

Customer Challenge Map

FIGURE 3.11 Customer Challenge Map

In design terminology, these customer challenge statements can now be translated into "project pillars." The "how might the customer" phrase is modified into a "how might we" challenge statement because now that we know what the customer wants, it is up to the entrepreneur to deliver the solution. Let's consider the Palm Pilot, a historic consumer electronics product that preceded the iPhone, for further understanding of how to perform preparatory work for idea finding. In a study of more than 700 product development teams, Gary S. Lynn and Richard R. Reilly[9] found that the most successful product launches came from a clear vision of what the team wanted to accomplish. Project pillars help focus the design efforts. For example, the project pillars for the Palm Pilot were (1) "How might we limit the size of the product to where it will fit in a pocket?" (2) "How might we synchronize the product seamlessly with a PC?" (3) "How might we ensure the product is fast and easy to use?" and (4) "How might we keep the price under $300?" Within those constraints, the Palm Computing Company was able to build the world's first successful personal digital assistant. Meeting those constraints required a lot of trial and error, but it provided targets to focus the team's creative energies.[10]

Customer challenge mapping provides informed decision-making as to what project pillars to move forward in creating a delightful business solution. Once

Using the Challenge Map
The group picked these final most important challenges facing customers:

1. How might the customer feel our sales approach focuses on his best interests?
2. How might the customer feel confident they received the support they need?
3. How might the customer get high quality clinical plans consistently?
4. How might the customer improve his cash flow
5. How might the customer have a satisfying partnership with us regardless of his business volume?
6. How might the customer provide his services without too many restrictive rules?
7. How might the customer feel there is an investment in me and my practice and success?

FIGURE 3.12 Using the Challenge Map

you have nailed the general design concept, this approach leads to more innovative outcomes than wandering aimlessly from one idea to another. However, customer challenge mapping does not guarantee that you will create a winning product or service, so you have to maintain an open mind to new facts that may arise as you create your solution. Overall though, our experiences applying this technique with entrepreneurs, companies, and students have been very positive. We have discovered that once people have a more clear understanding of the problem space they are addressing, they are more confident in designing solutions they believe their customers will appreciate. In the next chapter, we explain how to address the converged challenge statements to design successful products and services.

Summary

This chapter covered Step 3, problem definition, of the creative entrepreneurial process. Once you have formulated and selected a problem definition, creating specific solutions is easy. It's your use of creativity in defining the problem or in looking at it from new angles that gives you the edge. Too often, people rush into developing solutions without taking enough care to develop an effective problem definition.

Perhaps the single most powerful part of the entire creative entrepreneurial process is its emphasis on redefining problems before coming up with solutions. Many entrepreneurs put a solution on the market for a problem that customers have little concern with. Step 3, problem definition, requires you to re-examine your preconceived beliefs and assumptions, to become an innovator in defining problems as well as in solving them.

As an entrepreneur, even if you already have a business solution in mind, you might still want to step back and consider redefining the problem in new ways. In doing so, you might develop a new problem definition and solution that differs not only from your own preconceived notions, but also from those of your competitors. Better yet, if you involve customers and other stakeholders, you build legitimacy and credibility for your business. When you give people a chance to take part in formulating a problem, they develop a sense of ownership for its successful solution. They are emotionally invested and look forward to the solution coming to market, regardless of what their role is with the company. In the next chapter, we explain Step 4, developing a solution to the defined problem.

Notes

1 Basadur, M. S. (2013). "How Might We? Three Simple Words That Can Drive Economic Prosperity in Turbulent Times." *The American University in Cairo Business Review,* 1(2): 82–7.
2 Basadur, M. S. (2003). "Reducing Complexity in Conceptual Thinking Using Challenge Mapping." *Korean Journal of Thinking & Problem Solving,* 13(2): 5–27.
3 Basadur, M. S., Pringle, P. F., Speranzini, G. W., and Bacot, M. (2000). "Collaborative Problem Solving through Creativity in Problem Definition: Expanding the Pie." *Creativity and Innovation Management,* 9(1): 54–76.
4 Basadur, M. S., Potworowski, A., Pollice, N., and Fedorwicz, J. (2001). "Increasing Understanding of Technology Management through Challenge Mapping." *Creativity and Innovation Management,* 9(4): 245–58.
5 Parnes, S. J., Noller, R. B., and Biondi, A. M. (1977). *Guide to Creative Action.* New York, NY: Charles Scribner's Sons.
6 Basadur M. S., Ellspermann, S. J., and Evans, G. W. (1994). "A New Methodology for Formulating Ill-Structured Problems." *OMEGA: The International Journal of Management Science,* 22(6): 627–45.
7 Horowitz, A. (2013). *On Looking: A Walker's Guide to the Art of Observation.* New York, NY: Scribner.
8 Basadur, M. S. (1995). *The Power of Innovation.* London, UK: Pitman Professional Publishing, pp. 238–53.
9 Lynn, G. and Reilly, R. (2002). *Blockbusters: The Five Keys to Developing Great New Products.* New York, NY: HarperCollins.
10 Parnes, S. J., Noller, R. B., and Biondi, A. M. (1977). *Guide to Creative Action.* New York, NY: Charles Scribner's Sons.

4
STEP 4: IDEA FINDING

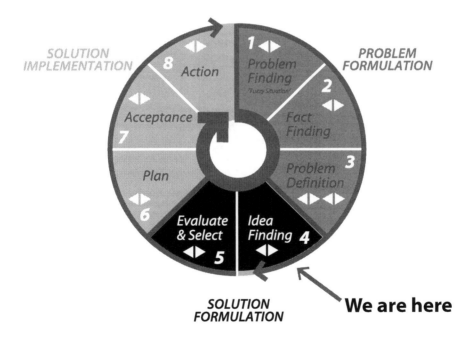

During the first three chapters of this book, we emphasized the importance of asking useful questions rather than simply giving useful answers. The goal of the last chapter was to come up with useful problem definitions. Now it's time to develop imaginative solutions. In the fourth step of the creative entrepreneurial process—idea finding—we move from discovering problems to discovering solutions. The idea-finding step is the hinge between a creative problem definition and the evaluation and selection of a promising solution.

Idea Finding

Imagine an archery target. In creative problem solving, the problem definition or challenge that you have selected from Step 3 becomes the target's bull's eye. The better defined the target, the easier it is to hit the mark. The process of idea finding means creating potential solutions and hurling them toward that bull's eye. How to fashion your arrows? If you have done a good job during the first three steps of creative problem solving, your targeted problem definition will probably be so well stated that one or two good solutions will leap out at you. In fact, you may find it difficult to resist simply grabbing one of these solutions and "running with it." However, as in each of the previous three steps, you must fight the temptation and instead generate as many potential solutions as you can without judging them. The more potential solutions you generate for a challenge, the more likely you are to find a superior solution, and it is much more efficient not to stop to analyze each idea as it is generated. Only a small fraction of the ideas will actually be worth further consideration anyway.

This step is a fifty-fifty proposition. It requires devoting half of our effort to aggressive nonjudgmental divergent thinking and half in careful judgmental convergent thinking. After both halves, a small number of best bets emerge and are taken forward to Step 5 of the process, evaluation and selection, for more formal scrutiny. (This step is described in the next chapter.)

Four Ideas for Generating Ideas

There are many specific techniques for generating ideas. Most are based on the principles of deferring judgment and extending effort to create many ideas.[1] They also require specific process skills to make them work, process skills that we'll examine in greater detail later.[2] For now, let's look at four excellent idea generation techniques that you can immediately use: brainstorming, blitzing, forcing connections, and deliberately building on radical ideas (Figure 4.1).

- Brainstorming
- Blitzing
- Forcing connections
- Deliberately building on radical ideas

FIGURE 4.1 Four Techniques for Generating Ideas

Brainstorming

One of the earliest, and still the most effective, techniques for generating solutions is called brainstorming.[3] You can do brainstorming alone or in a group. In either case, you come up with ideas for meeting your chosen problem while following these four important rules:

1. Do not criticize any idea.
2. Go for quantity of ideas (quantity breeds quality, so the more ideas the better).
3. Hitchhike—or piggyback one idea onto another—as much as you can.
4. Freewheel as much as possible (the wilder the idea the better—it is easier to tame a wild idea than to enliven a dull one).

It is inefficient to stop to criticize ideas as they are uttered as it slows the flow. Such criticism also prevents people from creating novel ideas, and they become reluctant to let their imaginations blossom. Remember that the point here is to offer new possibilities, not limit where the company can go.

Statistically speaking, you're more likely to find a good idea from a long list than from a short one. Moreover, scientific research backs this up.[4,5] And as more ideas are expressed, the opportunity to build additional ideas through hitchhiking increases. By piggybacking ideas onto one another, any idea or idea fragment becomes a building block for yet another. Don't waste time pondering what you dislike about an idea. Instead, select promising fragments and use your imagination and experience to build on them.

Some people find it difficult to accept or practice freewheeling. For many, it seems a waste of time to offer obviously silly, irrelevant, or wild ideas. But freewheeling helps people to break from their accustomed thought patterns, to see problems from new angles, and to provide leads to other solutions. It's a technique that many people must experience before they'll believe in it.[6]

Suppose you've defined a problem as "How might I better attract attention from potential buyers?" A freewheeling idea might be to take along an elephant (yes, a real one) to sales calls. While this is hardly a practical idea, it would almost certainly attract customers' attention. Now by visualizing the idea, you might find intriguing fragments to build on. Picturing the elephant's trunk, you might think about taking along a travel trunk filled with contest prizes or product samples. Thinking of the elephant's call, you might consider taking a trumpet to herald your arrival or an e-mail message with a link to a prerecorded message about your product. Building practicality into a radical thought often gives you feasible yet novel ideas and stimulates more imaginative ideas.

Blitzing

The second technique for generating possible solutions, called blitzing, means "blowing up" an idea into many and more specific ideas. Here, you focus on a single idea that suggests a broader theme. For example, a team working on the challenge "How might we improve our potato chip bags?" might have come up with the suggestion "to make them more useful when empty." In order to blitz this theme, the team creates a new problem definition: "How might we make our potato chip bags more useful when empty?" Brainstorming this new challenge leads to more specific ideas, like modifying the bags to be used as trash bags for a car once the chips have been eaten.

Forcing Connections

A third generation technique, forcing connections, requires you to use your imagination to force a fit between seemingly unrelated ideas or objects. For example, a product development engineer's challenge might be "What new household products might we introduce?" You could make two lists. One could be a list of objects you might find in a room of the house. The second could be a list of objects from somewhere else, say, the contents of your work desk. If you chose one object from each list at random, you might end up with a skylight and a pair of scissors. You could ask yourself, "How might I improve a pair of scissors by making them more like a skylight?" Ideas for solutions might include "put miniature lights on the scissors so you can use them in low light" or "equip the scissors with a magnifying glass for visually impaired people." You have forced a connection between two apparently unrelated things.

Deliberately Building Radical Ideas

A fourth idea generation technique is called deliberately building radical ideas. Here you select a preposterous idea from a list of possibilities and blitz it, focusing on its good aspects. For the problem definition "How might we generate publicity for our website?" a group might select the seemingly wild idea of using a cobra as a mascot for the company. Blitzing could lead to finding mascots from among other creatures that are less lethal but just as provocative. Or the group might use the cobra figuratively to jazz up the company's shirts and promotional material.

Using these kinds of techniques deliberately helps you to generate a surprising number of innovative yet practical ideas worth pursuing. Your success in applying them, like anything else, depends totally on your skill in executing them. (One does not learn to play second base without actually *playing* second base, over and over again). Your understanding and acceptance of them[7] and your skills in using them can also be developed[8] and measured.[9]

But often the real problem is that people are reluctant to move toward action. New ideas by nature cause discomfort. They require change of habit and, usually, hard work to make them succeed. When a team develops a promising new product, for example, it often decides to wait to show it to customers until the design is deemed perfect. This is actually a ploy to put off the risk of going to market. Quite often entrepreneurs will not know if the product is hitting the mark until it's in the hands of the customers. Inside larger organizations, managers may even hope to be transferred or promoted before launching a new product, leaving the risk to someone else. Instead, you must take calculated risks and accept that you can never be entirely sure of any decision. However, by utilizing the process in this book, you can make informed decisions that incorporate multiple perspectives and facts.

How many solution ideas are worth a closer look in the next step of the process? Remember that the goal of the creative process is to help you bring a solid business concept to market. Remember, it's better to build a business on one good idea than it is to accomplish nothing because you have too many good ideas to choose from. If none of your business ideas survives the subsequent evaluation step, then you can always return to the previous step to generate more. A good rule of thumb is to select five solution ideas to take to the subsequent evaluation step. Here are four useful guidelines for this selection process.

1. Pick concrete ideas. You should be able to visualize what the idea will look like when completed.
2. Pick ideas that are easy to understand. An uninitiated bystander should be able to understand your idea.
3. Make sure the selected ideas are on-target. They should address the selected problem definition challenge, rather than other related challenges.
4. Pick ideas for which an easy next step is obvious.

Following these four guidelines (Figure 4.2) helps you avoid ideas that appear noble but that are too esoteric and vague. If your challenge is "How might I reduce tension with my business partner?" for example, one idea might be "be friendlier." However, this is nowhere as useful an idea as "make time to meet my partner once a week at a coffee shop to discuss any issues we're having." The first one is a nice philosophy but not specific enough. The latter is much more likely

---

- **Concrete**
  Able to visualize what this idea will 'look' like when completed

- **Easy to understand**
  An innocent bystander should be able to read the ideas and know what it means

- **Targeted on solving your "How might" challenge**
  Remember, you are trying to solve the challenge(s) converged upon in Step 3, problem definition

- **An easy next step** is obvious

FIGURE 4.2 Guidelines for Converging on Best Ideas

to lead to actions that you can implement, the ultimate goal of creative problem solving. People often procrastinate because they don't have a clear idea of what they want to move forward. In the following sections, we explain how to better define what the idea is that you want to take to market. Once this concept is better understood, internal motivation will kick in to make it a reality.

STORY: Breaking through Patent Barriers

Some of the best ideas come from non-experts. Here is a real-world example. After solving the refreshment soap bar problem in the previous chapter, the team still was not finished and needed to conduct another round of innovative problem solving. Before it could sell the new soap formula, the company had to overcome a patent problem in the machinery design. There were already no fewer than six worldwide patents restricting how you could blend soap pastes of different colors. The team had to find a machine design to make their new product without infringing on anybody else's technique.

Visual sketches of the existing patents were lined up on the wall (Figure 4.3). Diverse points of view were assembled in a small team consisting of engineers, technicians, lawyers, and even a few people who were unfamiliar with soap technology. After this team had spent some time in fact finding, including discussing the visual sketches of the patented processes, a breakthrough solution soon

Breaking through patent barriers

After the idea for Coast was conceived – patent problem in the machinery design.
- The breakthrough solution soon came from a simple observation by the team member with the least technical knowledge and education.
- This person noted a small detail that the others had completely overlooked in their search for more complicated solutions.

The lesson: it's important to value the input of each member of a team, no matter their level of experience. Sometimes the best ideas come from people unencumbered by "too much" knowledge, people who can ask the simple questions that the so-called experts overlook.

FIGURE 4.3 Breaking Through Patent Barriers

came from a simple observation by the team member with the least technical knowledge and education. This person noted a small detail that the others had completely overlooked in their search for more complicated solutions. The lesson: it's important to value the input of each member of a team, no matter their level of experience. Sometimes the best ideas come from people unencumbered by "too much" knowledge, people who can ask the simple questions that the so-called experts overlook.

Customer Solutions

Now that we have learned the fundamentals of idea finding, let's apply it to an entrepreneurial context. In Step 3, problem definition, we identified key problems we'd like to address for our customers. In Step 4, we generate possible answers to the challenge statements. Let's say an agricultural company wants to expand sales of its equipment to new growth markets around the world, including Southeast Asia. The company has learned that one of the challenges for most Chinese farmers is that they are small operators and cannot afford the company's machinery. (How might the customer afford the machinery he needs to grow his business?) The company is ready to respond with ideas for its own challenge: "How might we provide more affordable machinery such as tractors to Chinese farmers?" It is now time to generate solutions. We now would bring subject matter experts into a group to be facilitated on these questions. We usually do not bring customers into these sessions because it is our job as entrepreneurs to provide solutions. Customers will be included again in Step 5, idea evaluation and selection.

We would post the challenge statement at the top of an empty easel pad and ask, "So, how might we provide more affordable equipment?" We would encourage a radically wild idea to get the process going. Someone might answer, "Give tractors away for free." We would write the answer down, no matter how outrageous. A wild idea eases the group into the problem solving, but it sometimes contains an element of possibility. The more intriguing features of a wild idea can sometimes be modified later into a feasible solution. For example, "give it away" could later turn into "help the Chinese government provide free equipment for small farmers." In this idea the government would buy tractors from the company and distribute them across the country to spur production. This idea isn't as wild as it seems when we consider the Homestead Act of 1862 that President Lincoln signed into existence to encourage economic development through free land grants. Let's look at what an easel pad might look like in addressing this challenge:

How might we provide a more affordable tractor?

1. Give it away.
2. Put a plow on the back of a Ford Fiesta.
3. Make a smaller version of an American tractor.

4. Provide a long term, low interest payment plan.
5. Make the tractor out of less durable metals.
6. Encourage tractor sharing.
7. Partner with the government to subsidize tractors.
8. Partner with the government in a campaign to help farmers increase the country's food supply.
9. Develop a reputation as a patriotic partner in reducing hunger in rural areas.
10. Design a tractor that is cheaper to operate.
11. Design a tractor that uses less fuel.
12. Et cetera.

After each challenge has been thoroughly addressed, the participants move into convergence. Each person in the group places one (or a few, depending on the length of the list of ideas) sticky dot on what they believe to be the best solution to each challenge statement. Just as in previous steps, once everyone has selected their choices, the facilitator takes each chosen answer and asks who picked it. Each person provides clarification for their selections. Once all selections have been covered, the facilitator guides the group to choose the top solutions for developing into a business concept.

Business Concept

A business concept is a more fully developed depiction of a customer, their problem, and the company's solution to that problem. It is at this stage that the entrepreneur creates a version of the concept. Working within the converged solutions from the previous section, the entrepreneur can craft different versions to show to customers and subject matter experts in Step 5 in order to ascertain which ideas have the most business potential. Ideas can be refined later. For now, it's important to get busy and start dreaming up what the solution could look like. Companies like Procter & Gamble and Disney often use storyboards and picture collages to get an idea going. The key point is that in the early stages of concept design, you don't have to get too technical. You're simply attempting to come up with ideas through the eyes of the customer. You're essentially asking yourself, "What solution to this problem would delight this customer?" Then, you're trying to convey what the idea could be through stories, pictures, and models.

We can imagine the agricultural manufacturer above drawing storyboards to show how their ideas would be employed in the field. They might even have collages of different sources of inspiration that will shape equipment design. They might write a business case describing the competitive situation, market opportunity, and their product concept, and if they're really creative, they'll build prototype versions of their machinery.

The design movement is popularizing prototyping as a way of developing concepts for more advanced feedback from customers and subject matter experts.

In the rest of this chapter, we provide substantial guidance on this popular design practice. Prototyping is not only the domain of designers and engineers; it is a practice anyone can use in shaping their ideas into executable form.

Prototyping

Burt Rutan, the American aerospace engineer who won the Ansari X Prize, believes that experimentation and exploration are important aspects of the human condition. He said, "I think we need to explore. I think if we stop exploring that we will run into mediocrity and we all will get bored."[10] Yet, how many entrepreneurs are mediocre because they launch products that don't challenge the status quo in the market? One key reason why entrepreneurs may hold back their best ideas is they're not quite sure how to make them real. Instead, they offer knockoff products and services that have a limited life in the marketplace. True innovation requires exploring the practical side of a market. What critical success factors are required for a product or service to work in this market? How do other companies address the problem we're solving? What part of their solutions can we incorporate? What can we do differently? What inspirations from outside fields can I design into my solution? Who do I need to help my company develop this solution?

Great accomplishments are possible when a dedicated team directs its attention to a well-defined problem. American history serves as testament to great problem solving. When national security is at stake, creative scientists, military personnel, government officials, and private enterprise channel their minds together in a common cause. The twentieth century was a time of unprecedented scientific and government achievement. In 1928, President Calvin Coolidge signed the bill approving the building of the Hoover Dam, which provided power and development to the western United States. In 1945, Robert Oppenheimer led a team of physicists to unlock the secrets of nuclear fission and bring about the end of World War II with the creation of the atomic bomb. In 1956, President Dwight D. Eisenhower authorized the Interstate Highway System, bringing all parts of the United States together by road. A generation later John F. Kennedy directed the nation's top scientists and American private industry to reach the moon before the Soviet Union, and the goal was accomplished in 1969. As of this writing, we can imagine even greater achievements, as NASA and private enterprise work together to solve the complex problems required to put a person on Mars. Great challenges inspire people to push the frontiers of human existence.

In previous chapters, we discussed how to identify who the real customer is and a major problem they have. Now we will provide direction on how to provide more depth to the business concept through prototyping. A prototype is a physical representation of an idea and is useful for attaining in-depth feedback from potential customers and subject matter experts. A model makes a concept more real. It's no longer just on paper and provides more information about what you are proposing to sell. It provides the respondent the opportunity to look at the concept from different angles. Therefore, a prototype is rich with details of what the entrepreneur is hoping to build. After all, visual communication is usually more informative than verbal communication. If a picture is worth a thousand words, a prototype is worth a million words. The next time you are discussing a business idea, show a prototype. Pictures and models intrigue people, and you're much more likely to hear people say, "Okay, I get it. Let me see more. Tell me how this works." A prototype can pique interest in seeing refined versions of the product or service later.

Prototyping In Five Stages

Most people avoid prototyping because they think it is too complicated or expensive. This need not be the case. Prototypes do vary in their sophistication and costs, but in the early stages of design, anyone can create inexpensive models made of simple materials like paper and tape to capture the most basic elements of an idea. As we display a prototype for feedback, we can modify the concept with another inexpensive model. Iteration is a key practice of good design. Feedback may tell us to go back to an earlier step like fact finding or problem definition. However, once enthusiastic support has been received for a simple prototype, we can build a more advanced conceptual prototype. A conceptual prototype is not necessarily polished or expensive, but it is more sophisticated than earlier rough prototypes. Conceptual prototypes are also known as surface prototypes because on the surface they start to take on the appearance of what the final product may look like.

You may have to create a few conceptual prototypes until you have a winning concept. When you are pleased with the conceptual prototype, you can begin building a working prototype. Although it doesn't necessarily have to be the case, it's likely that more costs will be incurred on this model because a working prototype has to actually *work*. It goes beyond merely looking like the final product. Working prototypes must demonstrate how the product functions. After a working prototype is found acceptable, some entrepreneurs build a presentation prototype to demonstrate a polished version of how the actual product will look and work. It doesn't have to be an exact replica of the real product, but it should appear to be. Sometimes companies substitute less costly materials that wouldn't be used in the actual product, but paint and final detailing is applied to give it a polished look. If the working prototype gets across enough information and garners support for follow-through, some entrepreneurs may bypass the presentation model and go straight to production with technical drawings, concepts, and working prototypes as guides for setting up the manufacturing processes.

Now that you have a basic understanding of what prototyping is and the various types of prototypes, you're now ready to learn how to actually build one. The following five techniques provide guidance on how to take your idea through the various stages of prototyping and ready your concept for production.

Stage 1: Drawing

Sketches

When you get an idea for a new product, service, or business, an easy early step for developing it is to draw a quick sketch of it and jot down notes. The sketch doesn't have to be particularly artistic or technical. It just needs to get a basic point across to someone else. This exercise doesn't require much in terms of materials or costs. A good pen and something to write on will get you going. Many great companies were founded by someone having an idea for a new business and writing it on the back of a napkin. For example, market leader Southwest Airlines was started this way. When Rollin King and Herb Kelleher met for dinner in 1967 at a San Antonio restaurant, they had an idea for a new airline. Grabbing a napkin, King drew a triangle representing flight routes between Dallas, Houston, and San Antonio. They would offer airline services that catered to frequent fliers who did business between the three cities. Southwest would later be innovative in its company culture and operations as well, but it all got started when King and Kelleher drew out the idea.

The napkin drawing of the three city connections was enough for King and Kelleher to get enthused about their idea. However, you may need to add more detail in your drawing to get an idea across. A wealth of popular resources is available for improving your drawing skills. Four very accessible books are *The Back of the Napkin: Solving Problems and Selling Ideas with Pictures, Drawing Ideas: A Hand-Drawn Approach for Better Design, The Sketchnote Handbook: The Illustrated Guide to Visual Note Taking*, and *The Doodle Revolution: Unlock the Power to Think Differently*.

The authors of these books—Dan Roam, Mark Baskinger and William Bardel, Mike Rhode, and Sunni Brown—all emphasize the power of adding visual language as a complement to numerical and verbal languages. Roam states

> Visual thinking means taking advantage of our innate ability to see—both with our eyes and with our mind's eye—in order to discover ideas that are otherwise invisible, develop those ideas quickly and intuitively, and then share those ideas with other people in a way that they can simply "get."[11]

Baskinger and Bardel offer a powerful explanation for the benefits of drawing:

> Your ability to draw is a fast, powerful means for thinking, reasoning, and visually exploring ideas—providing visual information for self-reflection and focused discussion with your colleagues, teams, and clients. Whether it is of a product, service, information, or system, a hand-drawn sketch communicates the essence of your idea and illustrates its potential. The simplicity of connection between mind, eyes, hand, and pencil shrugs off the layered burden that complex technology often adds.[12]

Rhode developed a method called "sketch notes" that focuses on capturing the essence of an idea through drawing. He encourages us to go back to our roots as children: "Kids draw to express ideas. They don't worry about how perfect their drawings are, as long as their ideas are conveyed. Ideas, not art!"[13] But while your drawings may appear childlike on the surface, they can still communicate some deep thought behind them. As Sunni Brown explains, "A doodler is engaging in deep and necessary information processing. A doodler is concentrating intently, sifting through information, conscious and otherwise, and—*much* more often than we realize—generating massive insights."[14] She further encourages the reader to "seriously elevate your skill in doodling: because you'll be elevating your skill in thinking and problem solving, too."

It's beyond the scope of this book to teach you how to draw; however, these books offer very accessible ways to develop this ability. As these examples illustrate, sketching is an effective way to document your ideas. Therefore, whenever you have an idea, draw it out and capture it. Notebooks are also important for writing as well as drawing. It is important to keep notes on the parameters, critical success factors, competitive conditions, possible issues, and new ideas in your notebook. Top entrepreneurs, engineers, designers, and inventors keep notebooks handy. They know that an idea is safe and won't be forgotten when it's captured in a notebook. Another benefit of keeping an active notebook is that it allows you to track changes in your concept. If someone suggests you do something you've already tried, you can pull out your notebook and show them what you did and explain why it didn't work. However, using creative problem solving, you can always be open to new ideas on how to tackle the issue. Drawings will help illicit more input for such changes.

Technical Drawing

As you progress with an idea, you may want the assistance of an engineer or draftsman to draw more technical sketches of the product. Drawings that capture the width, height, and depth along with measurements, parts, and components will communicate how an object should be made. Rudimentary skills in technical drawing can developed by taking art classes and mechanical drawing courses; however, open-source software, such as Google Sketch Up, can be used to craft digital three-dimensional drawings of your idea as well.

The best way to gain proficiency in drawing is to do it whenever you have an idea. Rest assured that if you don't see yourself as artistic, the more you draw the better you will get at it. You don't even have to always draw product concepts to develop artistic skills. Examine objects on your desk, such as a computer mouse, pens, and coffee cups, and examine with a designer's eye the shape, colors, and small details of the object. Try drawing them. Observe how the object reflects light. Take a guess at what it is made of. Try to figure out how it was put together. Think about the characteristics of objects as you draw them, and as you do you will develop a designer's eye. Ask yourself how the product could have been made better. What are its weaknesses? What are the good characteristics of the object? Why? What is interesting about the object? What do you think the entrepreneur was trying to achieve when the concept was developed? Was the objective achieved? How would you modify the object for a different market? Drawing the world around you with a critical eye will help you develop skills that will be helpful when you design your own products.

Stage 2: Model Building

Making It Real

A complement to drawing is model building. Designer Karl Aspelund describes a model as

> any kind of sample, mock-up, or attempt at physical representation of an idea, ranging from a standard architectural model to a sample garment on a mannequin. The creation of models and samples at this stage of any design is an attempt to bring the idea into the world and help us understand how the design will function there.[15]

Again, like drawing, model building can be an informal and relaxed method for capturing your idea, except now instead of being on paper it will be captured in 3D physical form. As Aspelund points out, "The model is real, but it's not the real thing."

If there's one phrase that best sums up prototyping, it's "build it." You may have had a good conversation with someone on a business idea and even drawn it on the back of a napkin, but if you want to really get across your idea, get some paper, cardboard, tape, and a pair of scissors, and start building a mockup. The same principles you utilized in drawing apply here. Use whatever is available that you can piece together to capture your idea. As Tom Kelley, general manager of IDEO, states, good designers "delight in how fast they take a concept from words to sketch, to model, and yes, to a successful new offering." In *The Ten Faces of Innovation,* he recalls how IDEO used modeling to develop a concept for a breakthrough medical instrument for nasal surgery. IDEO met with the medical advisory board of surgical tool company Gyrus ENT to discuss what surgeons wanted in the device. Ideas were flying around the meeting about what the instrument should look like, but the group was having a hard time grasping the general design of the product. Kelley recalls:

> Then one of our young engineers bolted from the room. Outside the conference room, seizing on the "found art" of materials lying around the office, he picked up a whiteboard marker, a black plastic Kodak film

canister, and a clothes-line clip. He taped the canister to the white board marker and attached the clip to the lid of the film canister. The result was an extremely crude model of the new surgical tool. He asked, "Are you thinking of something like *this*?" To which a surgeon replied, "Yes, something like *this*!" That initial crude prototype got the project rolling.[16]

Materials for Model Building

As the IDEO example demonstrates, you can make mockups with whatever is handy around you. However, if you want to be more adept at building models, you may want to invest a little money into a few basic tools and materials that can be found at any good art store or craft shop. Paper, illustration board, heavy cardboard, poster board, Bristol paper, chipboard, museum board, foam-core, canson paper, balsa wood, and basswood are good materials to have on hand. A utility knife, craft knife, a retractable blade knife, a handheld board cutter and beveler, dividers, a metal ruler, a T-square, a 30-degree by 60-degree triangle, a 45-degree triangle, and an ample supply of pencils, pens, markers, and charcoal are handy tools to design and shape the parts and frames of your prototype. Adhesives are important to hold your creation together. White glue, rubber cement, spray adhesive, balsa wood cement, and sticky tape can work wonders in building fairly stable prototypes.

Tips for Building Models

Building models comprises gathering materials, drawing out what you want to cut, cutting out the pieces, and gluing or fastening them together. Be sure to carefully measure your drawings on the materials so that you can ensure the parts fit together well. When you extract the parts out of the materials, slice against a metal straight edge such as a T-square to ensure an even cut, and put on a protective object underneath the material you are cutting so that you avoid damaging your table surface and dulling knife blades. It is also important to wear safety goggles. Just snipping a piece of metal can shoot a shard into the eye. Attentiveness during any cutting maneuver is essential. If you use glue to attach the parts, only apply as much as is necessary in order to avoid making messy models, and replace blades whenever they become dull.

The materials at this stage are inexpensive, so don't be afraid to make mistakes. That is the only way you can learn to develop prototyping skills. You will get better with time. If you are particularly adventurous and want to build a small model shop, you might consider purchasing some fairly inexpensive power tools and machines. A scroll saw and a chop saw are easy to use and very effective in working with wood and foam board to build slightly more realistic prototypes. Portable hand drills, a rotary shaft tool, a floor model drill press, and a hacksaw are worth considering as well. A shop vacuum cleaner and a draftsman table will complete your workshop. Clay and plaster are other materials you might also want to add to your supply shelf. You may find it worthwhile to build a small shop in your home to experiment with your ideas as well.

As you begin to build inexpensive prototypes, you will start looking differently at the world around you. You'll become curious as to how something was made, why it was made that way, and how it could have been made better. You might even find yourself picking up a copy of *Make* magazine or *Popular Mechanics* instead of your traditional business periodicals. Technology will no longer be a foreign concept to you. Also, as you iterate and build more models, you'll learn prototyping shortcuts and new ways to display the details of your ideas. As your prototyping skills improve, people will get a better idea of what is going on inside your head. You'll no longer have to struggle with trying to find the right words to get across your ideas. Your models will do the talking for you.

Stage 3: Conceptual Prototyping

The Purpose of a Conceptual Prototype

A conceptual prototype advances the best elements of your previous rough prototype. The rough prototype should have given you a general idea of what the product might end up being, but the conceptual prototype starts to take on more detail of the form, fit, and function of the final design. This does not mean that you have to invest significant amounts of money into prototyping yet. In fact, it doesn't necessarily have to have all the working parts of what you envision the final version being. However, it should start to at least resemble what you think it might become. That's why a conceptual prototype is sometimes called a surface prototype—because on the surface the observer can get a better idea of what the product will look like. When the PalmPilot was being developed at Handspring Inc., company co-founder Jeff Hawkins carried a conceptual prototype of it in his shirt pocket for weeks to see how it felt. He whittled the prototype out of wood. The dimensions of the wooden PalmPilot were very similar to the version that went onto the market.[17] Capturing the anticipated look of the product can be further attained by putting together a more realistic version of the product through adding vinyl overlays, paint for the overall appearance, and buttons and accoutrements from other products.

Rapid Prototyping Techniques

For centuries, prototypes have been carefully built using hand tools and machine tools, a process that requires much skill and time. However, there are many technologies available for rapid prototyping that allow a three-dimensional prototype to be constructed in considerably less time and without requiring that same high level of skill with hand tools and machine tools. The design information for rapid prototyping is typically created using a computer-aided drafting (CAD) program, often in one that allows the user to create virtual spheres, rectangular prisms, and other solids. These are repositioned and scaled, duplicated and arrayed, squashed, twisted, or folded. Sometimes they are joined together, and sometimes they are subtracted from one another. The resulting digital object is then saved in a format that can be used by the prototyping technology.

Rapid prototyping (RP) technologies can be classified as either subtractive, where we cut away unwanted material, or additive, where we build a model, typically by stacking up different layers of materials, each a horizontal cross section. One additive process is laminated object manufacturing (LOM), where one layer of a material is placed on top of another; these may be paper or paperboard with glue on one surface, for instance, each piece the exact shape of a horizontal cross section at a different elevation within the object. This same "slicing" is used for most other additive RP technologies. Stereolithography (SLA refers to stereo-lithography apparatus) is a process where photo-curable plastic resin is drawn from a vat to selectively place a thin layer of the liquid down where it is cured by a laser beam, one layer at a time; this polymerizes and solidifies the part, growing it from the bottom up. Another RP additive technology is fused deposition modeling (FDM), where a spaghetti-like strand of material is heated and extruded onto a platform to build the first layer of a product; a second layer is extruded on the first, and so on until the entire object has been built. Solid object printing (SOP) is a technique where print heads are used to selectively place material. In some instances, we can use a plaster-like powder and have a colored or clear binder agent printed on a thin layer of the powder, on which is wiped the next layer of the powder until the entire part is built. In other instances, we can have the build material itself, sometimes a wax, placed down by the same mechanism seen in some paper printers. Selective laser sintering (SLS) uses a laser to make certain areas of powder, often plastic or metal powder, stick together. Each of these (and other technologies not mentioned) has specific advantages and disadvantages. In general, while the specialized materials are somewhat costly, prices for rapid prototyping machines have decreased over the years even as the technology advances.

In addition to three-dimensional additive RP technologies, there are subtractive technologies. Some of these are primarily two dimensional, while others are three dimensional. Two-dimensional subtractive technologies cut out wanted areas from sheet stock according to digital information. These include lasers, plasma arc cutters, electrical discharge machining, routers, milling machines, water jets, and more. For some systems, a programming language known as G-code is used to tell a computer numerically controlled (CNC) machine to turn on, where to cut, and how fast to cut. In other instances, specialized computer interfaces are used, and some of these are as easy as sending data to a printer. Cutting out parts from a flat sheet is generally a two-axis system. Full movement to cut shapes through all axes is possible on a three-axis system, and it is even possible to have a four-axis system (where it is possible not only to machine along paths for curves generated in the x, y, and z axes, but to add a different motion, such as a turntable, which is considered a different degree of freedom, even though the object really only exists in three-dimensional space) or a five-axis one. Lathes are also used to create parts with circular cross sections.

CNC machines build prototypes from images captured with computer-assisted design (CAD) programs or machine languages such as G-code. A G-code program may appear intimidating to the untrained eye, but with a little training the fundamentals of the language can be quickly picked up. Although there is a bit of a learning curve to the programs, the technology is becoming increasingly easy to use. There are computer-aided manufacturing (CAM) systems that let you generate a complex G-Code program by starting with a CAD drawing and using the features of that drawing to create tool paths. If you are interested in learning machine languages and running rapid prototyping equipment, visit your local university or community college. They likely provide courses on how to write milling programs and run the machinery. A short programming course consisting of 10 hours of lab time along with 25 hours of training in a machine shop can make one proficient enough to start building prototypes. You will need to devote an additional 5 hours per week at home writing programs to run in the shop. A helpful feature of modern prototyping software is that you can write the program in Microsoft Word and save it to a flash drive that you can bring later to a programming lab. You can then verify that you wrote a good program to build your prototype by testing it in a virtual milling machine on the computer screen. The screen will show a digital version of your part and the tool that will be used to cut out shapes for your prototype. When you activate the program, you will see how the cutting tool would operate in the real world on your object. The verifying program lets you know if your program will be successful in the machine shop. Fortunately for the novice prototyper, the programming is becoming much easier as CNC code is increasingly generated by using CAM systems.

Even if you do not learn how to do rapid prototyping yourself, a basic understanding of the process may help you to get a prototype made. Knowing the different processes and machines will enable you to approach the appropriate technology experts who can build your prototype. You will also have a better idea as to the costs and time involved in the process. Still, if you wish to advance your design skills, we encourage you to learn rapid prototyping. As the rapid prototyping technologies become more available and easy to use and as design becomes a more common business practice, entrepreneurs may use prototyping machines in the future like they do LaserJet printers today. Like any technology movement, the spoils will go to those who adopt the new ways sooner.

The Three Dimensions of a Good Prototype

Now that you have a more refined prototype, you will be able to receive even better feedback on whether your idea is hitting the mark and how it might really work. Be open to the feedback and make changes as needed. Even though you're much further along in the design process, it's okay to continue making changes. Use simulations when you can, but also build a prototype at an intermediary phase of your design if it is helpful. Often, the purpose of many prototypes is not to present the design to others, but to facilitate gaining knowledge. As A.G. Laffley, chairman and CEO of Procter & Gamble, tells his employees,

> The essence of prototyping is to try and try again, iterate and reiterate. The key is not to seek perfection at any single step, but, through trial and error, to get a little improvement all along the way. Learn; get closer; learn more; get a little closer. And continually build on the insights of the user."[18]

He adds,

> Prototyping is the process of finding mistakes, and of adding value, so don't worry about perfection. ... [T]he key is to get the ideas out there in tangible form; the more people are comfortable with this show-and-tell, the more ideas that will be generated, which is the point.[19]

As you build more advanced prototypes, you will be judged on higher standards of quality. The three criteria that determine the quality of a prototype are functionality, expressivity, and credibility. Functionality is met if the product is able to do what the customer expects of it. The product "must be able to function as a useful, effective and also perhaps a desirable object."[20] For example, carabiners are very useful tools for rock climbers to hook their ropes through. They trust that the carabiner will not break if they fall off the side of a mountain. Expressivity means that the product looks like what the customer expects. It can be original, but it must not be too far away from the norm or else customers may be confused by its appearance. If a customer has to ask, "What is it?" you're probably missing the mark in your design. Regarding the carabiner example, a climber wants to know that their equipment meets traditional standards. With their lives depending on their ropes, harnesses, and carabiners, they do not want to take a chance on using equipment that looks too experimental or unreliable. Credibility means there is a seamless interaction between the product and the customer. The product is reliable, and the user can get to the point where they use it without thinking. When a skilled climber reaches a point where they want to secure the rope, they can subconsciously reach down for a carabiner and attach it to bolts in the side of the rock. If a climbing aficionado wanted to design a new carabiner, they would want to take functionality, expressivity, and credibility into account. You will want to take the same approach as you design your prototype.

Manufacturability

Manufacturability of the product is also worth exploring. The best design is a collaborative process between the designer, manufacturers, and technicians. Materials and production processes are very important elements of manufacturability. Material requirements include hardness, which is the material's resistance to surface penetration (or local plastic deformation); toughness, which is the material's ability to absorb energy without breaking; elasticity, which is the ability of a material to spring back to its original shape after being subjected to force; plasticity, which is the ability to permanently take on a new shape after being subjected to a force; brittleness, which is the likeliness a material will break; ductility, which is the ability of a material to bend, stretch, or twist without breaking; strength, which is the ability to withstand a force without changing shape or breaking; tension, which is the pulling force a material can withstand from both ends; compression, which is how much a material can withstand pushing or squeezing; torsion, which is the degree of twisting the material utilizes; and shear, which is the amount of force that splits a material.[21] Manufacturing considerations include the volume of production that can be undertaken in a batch, material costs, the speed of production, and the manufacturing applications that will be utilized to build the product.[22] Information on materials to be used and manufacturing processes to be applied will give you a better idea about the costs and requirements that need to be met to build your product.

Stage 4: Working Prototype

The Purpose of a Working Prototype

Now that you have decided what the product will look like and what its function is, it's time to build a working version of it. Depending on the complexity of the product and your experience, you may need to enlist help from engineers and craftsmen to help you develop a working model of your idea. The working prototype is probably not the final version of the idea, but it is very close to what will go into production, so it's a good idea to collaborate with technical experts in its design. While a working prototype doesn't necessarily have to look like the final version, it does have to successfully demonstrate the principle of the product.[23] Most of the bugs need to be worked out, and it needs to be easy to use.

Building a Working Prototype

Although a working prototype will be more sophisticated than a conceptual prototype, it doesn't have to cost a lot of money to build. *Wired Magazine* provided its favorite examples of iconic working prototypes of famous products. They aren't the most polished objects, but they worked. Examples included the Super

Soaker squirt gun and the Apple I computer. The Super Soaker was built with an air pump, a series of check valves, PVC pipes, plastic tubing, and a two-liter soda bottle. The Apple I consisted of a motherboard and keyboard attached to plywood.[24] The concepts worked. The Super Soaker tallied over $200 million in sales, and the Apple I provided the technical foundation for Steve Jobs and Steve Wozniak to revolutionize the computer industry. As these iconic models demonstrate, the main focus of the working prototype is demonstrating how the product gets the job done.

You may find toys in your attic that can be helpful in building prototypes. K'Nex, Legos, and Erector sets are easy, inexpensive materials that have been used by many inventors and engineers to address design issues. If you've been to the EPCOT theme park at Walt Disney World, you've probably ridden the extremely popular ride Soarin' Over California. The ride lifts guests' seats into the air and gives them the sensation of flying by placing them in front of an IMAX-sized screen. Wind blows through your hair and the smell of pine needles wafts through the air to add to the effect. The ride runs at 100 percent capacity from the moment the park opens to the minute it closes. EPCOT sometimes even opens a half-hour early to allow guests the chance to get in the line queues early to get a ticket for the ride. What you probably didn't know was that an Erector set is responsible for overcoming its design challenges. While IMAX theatres exist in most major cities, the moviegoer always remains seated on the ground. But not at a Disney park. Walt Disney Imagineering had to devise a way to create the sensation of flying. Imagineer Mark Sumner figured it out. He used an Erector set to design the basic seat and lift mechanism. A cantilever system hoists the guests off the floor and into the air. Guests "ooh" and "ah" as they sail over California's landmarks. It's one of Disney's most popular rides, but it never would have been built if Sumner had not pulled out his Erector set and experimented with the ride mechanics.

Machine Principles

A basic understanding of machines may come in handy as you develop prototypes. The Naval Education and Training Program Development Center defines a machine as "any device that helps you to do the work. We use machines to transform energy. Another use is to multiply force. Machines may also be used to multiply speed. There are only six simple machines: lever, block, wheel, axle, inclined plane, screw, and gear. When you are familiar with the principles of these simple machines, you can work on better understanding the operation of complex machines. Complex machines are merely combinations of two or more simple machines."[25] A little understanding of technology, machinery, and power can provide you with a toolkit to better move an idea further. Of course, you will want to work with technical experts, and you will have a better interaction with them if you understand some basics about machinery.

Presentation Prototyping

After you build a successful working prototype, you may decide to produce a presentation prototype that you can show to attract your first customers. A presentation prototype is a selling tool to show potential customers what the product will look like and how it will function. It may not be entirely the same as the product sold, but it will be a close facsimile. When Altair Product Design conceived a bus that would revolutionize public transportation, it decided it had to make a believable prototype to convince government officials that the bus was worth purchasing. The company imagined building a bus that would be to public transformation what a Frank Gehry building is to architecture. The company utilized CAD drawings for demonstrating how the innovative hybrid powertrain system would work inside a novel bus frame. Altair received positive response from a few potential customers, but company chairman James R. Scapa decided that because of the extreme innovativeness of the product, it would need to be experienced firsthand to win more customers over to the new concept. He told his engineering team to "get physical and get physical fast."[26] So instead of going to customers with CAD drawings and 1:10 scale models, Altair built a bus around an inexpensive aluminum bus frame. Transit buses are made out of stainless steel to endure the wear and tear accumulated over an average 20-year life span, but building the demonstration bus out of steel would have been prohibitively costly. Also, by actually building a less costly version of the bus, Altair was able to more easily identify potential structural flaws in the design. Altair would not sell the aluminum bus on the market, but it proved helpful in selling the product concept to venture capitalists and government officials.

Now that we've covered prototyping, the next step is to manufacture the product. Manufacturing is included as a step in prototyping because it should always be considered in the design process. Keeping the manufacturing end in mind will help you as you design your prototype. The next section will provide an overview of common manufacturing techniques. There are many techniques available, but some of the most common techniques utilized in going from prototype to sellable product are covered.

Stage 5: Manufacturing Processes

Manufacturing Preparations

Once the prototype has been approved, it's time to manufacture it. Contract manufacturers (or your own machine operators) are given guidance on what is to be built. Working drawings are provided to show all the details a particular part must embody so that it can be properly manufactured. Shape, dimensions and sizes, locations of holes and bends, and special details are provided in the drawings. Special instructions on materials and surface finish may be included in the detailed drawing as well. Assembly drawings show where the parts go and how they fit together. The picture looks like the object has been photographed a millisecond after exploding. All the parts of the product are separate in the drawing but very close to each other. This depiction of the product allows you to see every part on its own while also having an idea where it fits into the design. If electrical and hydraulic systems are used, schematic drawings may be used as well. It is important that the contract manufacturer or machine shop have detailed drawings so that they can plan the most efficient production run of the product.[27]

Tooling Up

If your product has a unique shape, tools and equipment may need to be prepared to manufacture the object. This process is called "tooling up." A common practice is to make a mold of the final prototype. Silicone (or sometimes wax) is wrapped around the object to attain its shape. Then, the silicone is pulled away from the object and used to create a mold. Injection molding can now take place as plastic pellets are melted into liquid form and injected into the mold under pressure. Sometimes production of approximately twenty units is run to determine if it looks good enough to move forward with a full run. With this inexpensive mold, changes can still be made before investing in a full run. If the results are satisfactory, a metal mold is typically produced to make a full run of the object. Metal molds are more costly but also stronger and can hold up for repeatable, long production runs. A strong metal mold can stamp out a large number of products during a milling cycle. Another popular method is known as blow molding, in which plastic is blown into a mold and expanded to match the mold's shape. Hollow containers, such as shampoo bottles, are commonly made in this fashion. There are many other production techniques, but these two are very common in machine shops that specialize in designing unique products.[28] For further guidance on manufacturing issues, consult experts in manufacturing technology, production operations, and management science.

Deeper Considerations for Prototyping

Most entrepreneurs do not have a process for creating products and services, instead favoring an intuitive approach of hit-and-miss experimentation. If you've gotten to this point in the book, you can see that a structured creative process can guide an entrepreneur to systematically developing a unique business concept. The entrepreneur must be open to where the process takes them. This approach may intimidate some entrepreneurs because it may force them to enter new domains they have little experience in. However, by following the steps in this book, entrepreneurs will get the answers they need to reduce the ambiguity of previously unseen opportunities. The creative process helps you gain subject matter expertise on your industry and target market by following the steps of problem identification, fact finding, problem definition, and idea finding. Including a diverse group of potential customers and subject matter experts in a facilitated dialogue brings clarity to the entrepreneur. If the entrepreneur wants to go a step further to gain a deeper understanding of their business concept, they can consider addressing the following product issues:

Consideration 1: What's Already Out There?

Once you have an idea for addressing the customers' needs, you can ask yourself, "Am I currently capable of making this happen? What is currently possible for me?" You'll need to know what you can accomplish within your industry's dynamics. Answering the following questions can help you find out:

- Do I have the capability to do this?
- Do other people have the capability to help me do this?
- Is there intellectual property on the market I have to be aware of?
- What are the technological needs of the product?
- Will I have to invent technology for the product or use someone else's?
- If I need to use someone else's technology, can I get access to it?
- Will I have to license or buy it from another company?
- Can I partner with a company somehow with a win-win arrangement?
- Is the supply chain accessible?
- Do I have the knowledge to pull this off?
- Can I hire people or bring them on my management team to make this happen?
- Can I contract with someone to help bring me the knowledge requirements I need for this product?

These are just a few of the questions you might ask yourself as you assess your capability to bring the product to market. You can get answers to these questions, but it's going to take a lot of hustle talking to people from many different disciplines and industries. It can be done; rarely do you need to invent a product from scratch. There are people out there whom you can bring on board your company, contract with, or partner with.

As you do this, you need to focus on how you can be different and better than your competition. Remember, companies are always making design decisions as to what their product can do, how it can look, how long it will last, and how much it will cost. There are a lot of possibilities for what a product can be, so chances are that current companies have missed things some customers might want.

Let's consider an example of how you might work through this. One of our student teams is working on an audio product for cars. We won't give the details of the product (to protect their idea). We told them to seek answers to these questions:

- What audio equipment is already out there?
- What cars are using this equipment?
- What are the features of these cars? What's their size? What type of cars?
- Can all cars use your audio equipment? Or will only certain types of cars have it?
- What's the age group of the customers who usually buy this equipment?
- Is this product "after market," or does it come with the purchase of the car?
- Is it a do-it-yourself (DIY) product, or does a professional have to install it?
- Is it sold directly to the consumer (B2C) or is it a business-to-business (B2B) product?

Consideration 2: How Close Is This Product to Getting to Market?

Okay, so let's say you've gotten answers to a lot of those questions, and you're moving forward with the product. Is everything going to be great now? Probably not, but that's alright. The product may not be perfect, but it will probably be refined once it's on the market. However, you do want to make sure that any glaring problems are addressed before launching. This is where engineers come in.

If possible, to avoid making any catastrophic mistakes, you most likely will need to bring on board, contract, or seek the advice of the following experts:

1. Someone with expertise in technical specifications: Engineers really appreciate looking at diagrams and descriptions that capture what the product is. It's one of the key tools that helps them think through your product.
2. A marketing specialist who knows how to bring the product to market.
3. Financial experts that understand the reality of bringing a product and company like yours into existence.
4. A project manager who can work with the different groups and move the project forward. Chapter 7 will provide more ways you can be the project manager inside your company.
5. A human factors expert for tweaking the technical specifications to address how a person actually uses the product.

So, how do you find these subject matter experts? Well, it's not easy, and it's this consideration that often separates the serious entrepreneur from the person with just a good idea. You'll have to put some miles on your shoes, car, and frequent flyer membership. You have to go where these types of experts meet. That would be places like clubs, trade shows, and hangouts like cafés and coffee shops. You want to seek out different people with different backgrounds and inputs.

Now if you're willing to do this, you'll be surprised how much people will help you. Go-getters are impressed by other go-getters. Just go up to them and start talking to them. People love to share their ideas and advice. Tell them what you need help with. A good way to say this is "I need help with x. Do you know anyone who can help me with this?" And then follow the trail. You'll be amazed at how things come together when you do this.

For more help, here are more resources for doing these steps:

1. MS Visio—for flowcharts and basic project management processing.
2. Arduino Chipset—integrates with various platforms and can be expanded as needed, limited only by your creativity.
3. Raspberry Pi—pocket-friendly mini computer.
4. WBS–work Breakdown Structure.
5. Kickstarter—website used to seek funding for startup projects, great for farming ideas and seeing patterns.
6. Uspto.gov—US Patent and Trademark Office website, use to search for patents.
7. Scholar.google.com—Google Scholar Search: use to search for research about technology and R&D.
8. First Develop India (FDI)—a Make In India website.
9. IEEE.org—a good source of extensive technology news.

Summary

Chapters 1, 2, and 3 helped us identify an important customer problem to address. This chapter provided guidance on how to design a solution for that problem. Four techniques were given for generating these ideas: brainstorming, blitzing, forcing connections, and deliberately building on radical ideas. Promising ideas can be shaped into more detailed possible solutions for the customer. Prototyping is a practice that can help the entrepreneur think through their ideas in more detail. Prototypes reveal problems with designs that verbal descriptions might miss. Once problems are identified, prototypes can be reworked through iterations until a good design is ready for customer feedback. Five stages of prototyping help the entrepreneur further an idea: drawing, model building, conceptual prototype, working prototype, and manufacturing processes. Two considerations that advance an idea are (1) "What's already out there?" and (2) "How close is this product to getting to market?" Knowing what's already on the market can serve as source material for designing a product or service. After all, everything on the market has a connection to something that's already in existence, and recognizing what milestones are ahead for getting to market assists the entrepreneur in identifying what areas of expertise might be needed to make the product or service possible. If the techniques are followed in this chapter, the entrepreneur should have a few good ideas to consider taking to market. The next chapter explains how to generate selection criteria to determine which design to actually take to market.

Notes

1 Parnes, S. J., and Meadow, A. (1959). "Effects of Brainstorming Instructions on Creative Problem Solving by Trained and Untrained Subjects." *Journal of Educational Psychology,* 50(4): 171–6.
2 Basadur, M. S., and Basadur, T. M. (2010). "How Creativity Relevant Attitudes Trigger Behaviors, Skills and Performance." Presented at Society for Industrial and Organizational Psychology (SIOP) 2010 Annual Conference, April 8–10, Atlanta, GA.
3 Osborn, A. F. (1953). *Applied Imagination: Principles and Procedures of Creative Problem-Solving.* New York, NY: Charles Scribner's Sons.
4 Basadur, M. S., and Thompson, R. (1986). "Usefulness of the Ideation Principle of Extended Effort in Real World Professional and Managerial Problem Solving." *Journal of Creative Behavior,* 20(1): 23–34.
5 Parnes, S. J. (1961). "Effects of Extended Effort in Creative Problem Solving." *Journal of Educational Psychology,* 52(3), 117–22.
6 Basadur, M. S., Graen, G. B., and Scandura, T. A. (1986). "Training Effects on Attitudes toward Divergent Thinking among Manufacturing Engineers." *Journal of Applied Psychology,* 71(4): 612–17.
7 Basadur, M. S., and Basadur, T. M. (2011). "Attitudes and Creativity." *Encyclopedia of Creativity,* 1(2): 85–95. San Diego, CA: Academic Press.
8 Basadur, M. S., Graen, G. B. and Green, S. G. (1982). "Training in Creative Problem Solving: Effects on Ideation and Problem Finding in an Applied Research Organization." *Organizational Behavior and Human Performance,* 30: 41–70.
9 Basadur, M. S. and Finkbeiner, C. T. (1985). "Measuring Preference for Ideation in Creative Problem Solving Training." *Journal of Applied Behavioral Science,* 21(1): 37–49.
10 Griffin, M. (2007). "The Real Reasons We Explore Space." *Air and Space Smithsonian,* 22(2): 48.
11 Roam, D. (2013). *The Back of the Napkin (Expanded Edition): Solving Problems and Selling Ideas with Pictures.* New York, NY: Penguin Books.
12 Baskinger, M., and Bardel, W. (2013). *Drawing Ideas: A Hand-Drawn Approach for Better Design.* New York, NY: Watson-Guptill Publications.
13 Rhode, M. (2012). *The Sketchnote Handbook.* Berkeley, CA: Peachpit Press, p. 15.
14 Brown, S. (2014). *The Doodle Revolution: Unlock the Power to Think Differently.* New York, NY: Penguin Books.
15 Aspelund, K. (2014). *The Design Process.* 3rd edition. New York, NY: Fairchild Books.
16 Brown, S. (2014). *The Doodle Revolution: Unlock the Power to Think Differently.* London, UK: Penguin, pp. xiii, 4.
17 Lynn, G. S., and Reilly, R. R. (2002). *Blockbusters: The Five Keys to Developing Great New Products.* New York, NY: HarperCollins Publishers.
18 Lafley, A. G., and Charan, R. (2008). *The Game Changer: How You Can Drive Revenue and Profit Growth with Innovation.* New York, NY: Random House.
19 Ibid.
20 Rusten, G., and Bryson, J. (2010). *Industrial Design, Competition, and Globalization.* New York, NY: Palgrave Macmillan.
21 Rogers, G., Wright, M., and Yates, B. (2010). *Gateway to Engineering.* Clifton Park, NY: Delmar, Cengage Learning.
22 Central Saint Martin's College of Art & Design (2007). *Making It.* London, UK: Laurence King Publishing Ltd.

23 Kivenson, G. (1977). *The Art and Science of Inventing.* New York, NY: Van Nostrand Reinhold Company.
24 Leckart, S. (2010). "Original Models: A Look at Iconic Tech Prototypes." *Wired Magazine* (August 11).
25 Naval Education and Training Program (2008). "Basic Machines and How They Work." www.bnpublishing.net.
26 Vasilash, G. S. (2010). "Developing a Better Bus." *Time Compression Magazine,* (August 26): 12.
27 Brusic, S. A., Fales, J. F., and Kuetemeyer, V. F. (1999). *Technology: Today and Tomorrow.* New York, NY: Glencoe McGraw-Hill.
28 Rogers, G., Wright, M., and Yates, B. (2010). *Gateway to Engineering.* Clifton Park, NY: Delmar, Cengage Learning.

5
STEP 5: EVALUATE AND SELECT

Introduction

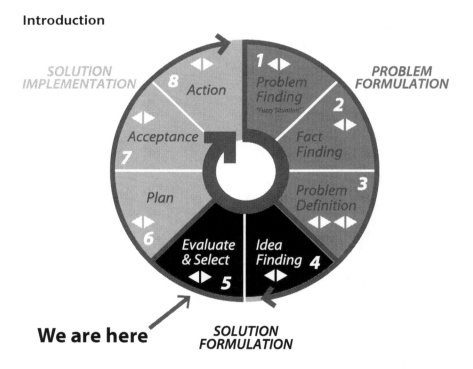

All too often business ideas are shot down for lack of imagination. Just as it takes an open mind to effectively develop new ideas, so it takes an open mind to effectively evaluate new ideas. Once you've selected a small number of business concepts in Step 4, your next step in the creative entrepreneurship process is to evaluate their potential for taking them to market. You want to choose at least one idea as a useful solution around which you can develop a practical business.

This evaluation process can be relatively simple or relatively complex, for a number of reasons. Determining which of three franchises to open, for example, requires nothing more complicated than talking to existing franchisees and doing some background market research. A more challenging task is to evaluate, say, a new form of healthcare. It's more difficult to make these decisions when we lack a single, simple yardstick or scale to measure the relative worth of the choices. Franchises have proven track records that can be compared relatively easily, whereas a new healthcare business will have to address numerous legal, technical, and economic factors. Usually the more innovative the business idea, the more thought that will be needed in determining how to evaluate its potential. You have to use more than a single criterion in choosing.

Think about buying the right car from among a few models. You wouldn't base your decision on only one criterion. While price may or may not be important to you, so might gas mileage, roominess, style, and array of colors available. Your final choice will be based on several of these yardsticks. Selecting the appropriate "yardsticks" or criteria themselves is an important and often tough job.

Similarly, you can't often evaluate possible solutions to a customer problem by using only one criterion. It would be a mistake to evaluate an idea based on cost alone, for example, and ignore other criteria such as aesthetics, ease of use, and durability.

Choosing criteria can be equally complicated whether you're evaluating options alone or as part of a group. When you are making your evaluation on your own, it is sometimes easy to leap based on one obvious criterion. When you belong to a team making the evaluation, it can be difficult to agree on which criteria to use. What's important to one person might be less important to another.

Your first step in evaluation is to create a list of potential criteria for measuring your selected ideas. As you do so, suspend judgment and logic and extend effort. You'll find that some of the best criteria will come to you further down your list. Only after creating this list should you exercise judgment to select the most important few criteria, perhaps through discussions with other people, such as potential customers, subject matter experts, the founding team, and other company stakeholders. In any case, taking the time to develop and select useful, comprehensive criteria is a must. Just as in the idea-finding step, it's hard to say just how many criteria are the right number. Having too many can be as counterproductive as having too few. An entrepreneur must give great thought to what will really determine the future success of the new product or service and then make business decisions based on those criteria. It is an important exercise, but one often overlooked by entrepreneurs. No matter the number of criteria you use, the idea is to carefully and open-mindedly examine each of your selected customer solutions.

Let's return to the ABC Company example. The company was attempting to improve its customer experience performance in the face of a pending major

What criteria might we use to evaluate and select the very best ideas?

- Speed of implementation
- Difficulty to copy
- Cost/financial impact, cost of resources; quarterly expectations
- Impact on our customers' current productivity
- Availability of resources
- Feasibility
- Scalability
- Impact on customer loyalty
- Impact on revenue
- Reliability

- Regulatory impact
- Newness
- Impact on sales reps
- Impact on customer's users
- Impact on employee morale
- Impact on costs
- Acceptance across tiers
- Acceptance across channels
- Acceptance by sales
- Impact on growth

FIGURE 5.1 What Criteria Might Be Used to Evaluate?

increase in competition. The team had identified seven key customer challenges and had created several good ideas as possible solutions ready for further evaluation. Following is a list of potential criteria the team diverged before converging on the most important (Figure 5.1).

Then they discussed the list and created the following top criteria to select their very best ideas (Figure 5.2). Some of the final criteria were made up of combinations of the original list after thorough discussion.

Converging by Consensus Skills

No matter which step in our process, a team must demonstrate certain converging skills to ensure a high quality innovative result. They are summarized in Figure 5.3. Consensus is vital when it comes to evaluation in a team. Without it, implementation is in jeopardy because there will be a drop in commitment. Some members will begin to feel like outsiders. Achieving consensus is a learnable skill. For example, one of the skills is understanding that differences in perception is a good thing, not a bad thing. If five different people have expressed five different facts about the same issue (some even apparently conflicting), this is not an obstacle to slow us down, but an opportunity to *get smarter*. Let's clarify what we know and what we don't know and move on. Don't worry about small differences; just build on the big things you agree on. Evolve some words that satisfy everyone. Say, "By the end of the week," instead of arguing over "which is better, Thursday or Friday." Listening carefully to other people not only builds clarity and understanding but also builds trust. Remember, we are here to solve a problem, not to debate. Building a deeper understanding underpinning what people are trying to say also requires the ability to use simple language. You never really

Selecting our very best ideas…

Final criteria to evaluate and select the very best ideas:

1. Impact on loyalty
2. Feasibility
3. Speed of implementation
4. Competitive advantage & can't be copied easily
5. Financial impact – reflecting the cost of resources as well as the quarterly reporting reality – Wall Street expectations

These criteria were used to further evaluate and pick the very best ideas from the list of best ideas initially generated from 7 customer challenges.

FIGURE 5.2 Selecting the Most Important Criteria

Converging by Consensus Skills

- View differences in perception as constructive.
- Listen carefully to what others say about an option.
- Explain exactly what the words within an option mean to you.
- Build on points of agreement. Evolve words that bridge small differences.
- Give unusual options a good hearing.
- Focus on making good selections, not protecting turf.
- Work towards full group participation.
- Say what you think.
- Don't let higher status or more vocal people swing the group.

FIGURE 5.3 Converging by Consensus

Integrating and building on many good ideas often leads into one really comprehensive great idea!

- Defer judgment as you evaluate – keep an open mind!

- Complex problems often require a system solution – many ideas get joined together so the sum is larger than the parts.

FIGURE 5.4 Integrating and Building

know what the words mean unless they're really simple. It is also important to not shy away from unusual options. Try to avoid playing it safe. Someone needs to step up and say, "Why aren't we considering this option over here? Let's talk about it to see if we might take the riskiness out." Good teams are also able to get beyond protecting their own personal interests and work for the overall organization's benefit. Good teams work at getting everyone involved and saying what's on their mind. Unfortunately, some people will shrink into the woodwork when it's time to start choosing. What if there are seven people in the room and you've got something to say, but the other people are going in a very different direction? What you must avoid thinking is, "Well, there's something obviously wrong with me; I'll go along with them and not say anything." You might as well not be on the team because you may be the only one with an insight that is a game changer. Do not contribute to what is known as "groupthink." The team must also work hard at not letting higher status people swing the group. If you happen to be the boss, your special skill is not to act like one. You must be extra good at being one of the team.

Sometimes this evaluation process does not even lead directly to the implementation phase. Instead, it often points you in new directions. For example, the entrepreneur might suddenly decide to try modifying a product or service that they like but that falls short against a particular criterion. This spontaneous surge of idea building can lead to a much different and better business opportunity (Figure 5.4).

STORY: Evaluating with an Open Mind

A grocery products company was looking for a way to help consumers better handle their household trash. The company felt it could improve upon the polyethylene bags that most people used. A product development team was assigned to the challenge "How might we improve the handling of household trash?"

One of several interesting and imaginative solutions that the team had developed was a cardboard product that resembled a pizza box. Pushing its top made the box telescope into a free-standing trash container with several polyethylene bags nested inside. This stand-alone device eliminated many of the disadvantages of single polyethylene bags. It hid the trash beneath a hinged cardboard top and was convenient and decorative to boot. When one of the bags was filled, you simply pulled a cord to tie its top and took it out of the box, leaving the next bag ready to use. The team members appeared excited about the possibilities of this idea and were eager to move into evaluation. Even though this was a very unusual idea, the evaluation was performed using a standard company screening technique for new product ideas: the market research department had written a single-paragraph description of the idea and presented it along with several others to a group of consumers. The department had included in its description the fact that the new product would add about 10 cents to the cost of each bag. Asked for comments, consumers said the product sounded like a good idea but that they would probably balk at paying the 10-cent premium for it. Without further consideration, the group abandoned the idea.

After putting considerable effort into generating ideas, the group had devoted little time to an appropriate evaluation process. For example, they could have stopped to consider that in the past when paper grocery bags cost nothing, if consumers were simply asked whether they would buy a new kind of bag for 10 cents each, most would probably have said no. Under that scenario, we might never have seen polyethylene bags at all. However, given the chance to experience the advantages of polyethylene bags rather than just read about them, consumers might have given a very different answer. If the market researchers had been as creative in evaluating this radical idea as the team had been in developing it, they might have discovered that people were willing to pay the extra cost and perhaps more.

This story demonstrates the importance of keeping an open mind not only when conceptualizing new ideas but also when evaluating them. Here, the first stages of the innovation process had been successfully executed to produce a unique product idea; however, because the latter stages were poorly executed, the overall thinking process was still incomplete. Possibly, the team members had been almost afraid of their own idea and were relieved to find a reason not to proceed with it.

Once you have selected the appropriate criteria, you can apply them to your selected possible solutions from Step 4. As in the other steps of this book, what specific technique you use to evaluate ideas is not as important as the process itself. Two useful techniques for evaluating ideas are the criteria grid method and paired comparison analysis.

Criteria of Choice: The Criteria Grid Method

The criteria grid method[1] helps you to judge your selected possible solutions against each of a few selected criteria. We must first ask the question "By what criteria might we evaluate our selected ideas?" Then select the most important and construct the grid in Figure 5.5. The criteria grid is an organized approach to prioritizing or selecting the best one of several "top contender" ideas for solutions. To use the grid in Figure 5.5, follow these steps:

1. Generate a list of possible criteria. Select the key criteria, and word them carefully.
2. Select an arbitrary scale (e.g., 0–3) to rate the criteria, and fill in the chart.
3. Proceed down with one criterion, not across the criteria.
4. Examine possible ways to weight the criterion after filling in the chart.

This chart does not tell you what choice to make, but it does help you understand why you select an alternative.

Let's use the car purchase example to illustrate this method. Suppose you have narrowed your list to four car models and three criteria: initial cost, gas mileage, access to service and reliability. List the four models vertically on the left and the four criteria horizontally across the top of the grid.

Now evaluate each of the four models against each criterion in turn. Start by evaluating all four models for their initial cost. Then evaluate all four for gas mileage. Then evaluate all four for access to service. Keep in mind that you are not *ranking* the models against one another. The point of this exercise is not to pick the best of a bad lot, or conversely, to discard several good options. Perhaps none of the models will turn out to be suitable, all of them are suitable, or only some will be suitable. That's something you will determine later during your selection decision. For now, your goal is simply to understand the worth of each model option.

That's why it's important to rate each model separately from the other models against each criterion in turn. Furthermore, make your ratings against each criterion separately from the other criteria. Don't evaluate a single model, or a single idea, against all the criteria at once. By rating each idea in turn against one criterion at a time, you avoid the "halo error." This occurs when a rating against one criterion biases your evaluation on subsequent criteria.

Excellent=3 Good=2 Fair=1 Poor=0	Initial Cost	Gas Mileage	Access to Service	Reliability
Car 1	3	3	0	0
Car 2	2	2	3	3
Car 3	1	1	3	3
Car 4	2	2	3	3

FIGURE 5.5 Evaluation of Car Options Using the Criteria Grid Method

All you do now is choose an arbitrary scale to make your ratings. You might use a four-point scale of letters, say, E for excellent, G for good, F for fair, and P for poor. Or use numerals, such as 3 for excellent, 2 for good, 1 for fair, and 0 for poor. It doesn't matter whether you use letters or numerals. Neither does it matter how much latitude your scale has. As a rule of thumb, a four-point numerical scale is easy to understand and provides a handy picture.

After you have filled in the grid, you might want to weight the criteria if you think they carry significantly different importance or impact. Avoid weighting until after you've graded the ideas. If you try to weight the criteria before evaluation, you may be tempted to base your decisions on weights rather than simply on the criteria themselves.

Be careful, especially if you use numerical ratings, not to get carried away with the numbers. The criteria grid method is not designed as a purely analytical procedure. It is difficult to account for all of the relevant criteria, and you can't possibly have all of the knowledge at your fingertips to accurately rate each option or to weight each criterion. While this method permits you to apply judgment and logic to the options, its main purpose is to help you understand the strengths and deficiencies of each idea. Because the method generates a lot of discussion within a group, it ensures a more complete understanding of the options and a better consensus on what to do next. It is important not to rush to judgment. The bottom line is it is the quality of the conversation that counts, not the numbers themselves. To illustrate this point, let's remember our telescoping method of evaluating from Chapter 1. Scientific evidence[2] supports our in-depth experience that this three-step disciplined method helps minds to stay open and increases skill in both idea evaluation as well as idea generation. Shown in Figure 5.6, the telescoping method not only enables groups to more skillfully evaluate ideas that they have generated, it also enables the evaluation step to contribute more to the creative process than would be attained from simply selecting from among a list of solutions. Performed skillfully by emphasizing the clarification step, evaluation significantly improves the quality of the ideas being evaluated *while they are being evaluated*. As a result, brand new high-quality ideas often emerge through telescoping.

STORY: Reducing 65 Down to 13 in a Hurry

A product development team was hard at work generating ideas for a brand new product and had developed no fewer than 65 exciting possibilities. With a clear deadline facing them, the members had to choose one and launch a project in time for a test market. During discussions about evaluation criteria, one overarching criterion surfaced: The project had to be completed in nine months. The 65 options were screened against this criterion and only 13 survived the test. The team was then able to select a number of more stringent criteria to evaluate the smaller number of ideas in much less time (Figure 5.7).

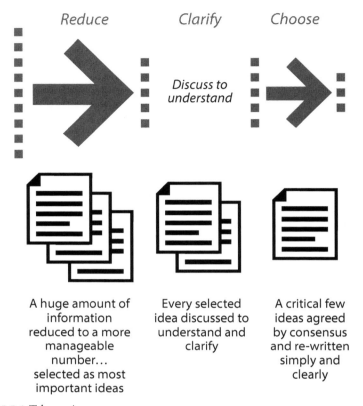

Reduce *Clarify* *Choose*

Discuss to understand

A huge amount of information reduced to a more manageable number... selected as most important ideas

Every selected idea discussed to understand and clarify

A critical few ideas agreed by consensus and re-written simply and clearly

FIGURE 5.6 Telescoping

Too many ideas?

They are all pretty good!

How might we make the list more manageable?

Is there an overarching criterion we can all agree on?

An Example

65 new product development project candidates.

Overarching criterion: how many can be executed in 9 months?

Only 13 could be achieved.

They could be then be evaluated using additional criteria.

FIGURE 5.7 Too Many Ideas?

STORY: Choosing between Two Great Options (Breaking a Two-Year Log Jam)

A process facilitator recounted the story summarized in Figure 5.8 as follows:

> Here's how I recall the story behind that two day workshop. It was hard work, but the group was very pleased and indicated we had broken a significant logjam! The group gathered at their headquarters working on selecting a new machine for the Eastern European and Asian market. The challenge the group had encountered was in deciding how they could evaluate and by consensus, pick the best of two available options to go to market. This market opportunity was significant with potential sales of upwards of 20,000 units per year. Prior to this workshop, the team had met and discussed the various specifications and customer requirements. We facilitated the group to converge on what they thought were the 7 biggest challenges facing the new customers.
>
> Once these were selected, we created a criteria grid to compare two machines—each was already being built and sold in other regions of the world. The group spent two days in Step 5 of the creative problem-solving process and used the criteria grid to compare the two options. The seven

Do we go with option A or option B?
Picking the best solution when you have 2 distinct options…

How?

1. Diverge on customer challenges (HMTC) to frame these as the customer needs.
2. Converge on the list using dots to prioritize the most important customer needs.
3. Discuss (telescoping) to gain alignment around the customer needs and agree on priority HMTC (musts/wants).
4. Create a grid & rank each option with each customer 'must'/'want' – 'is a must' vs. 'is a want'.
5. Identify the gaps – rate the work effort required to fill the gap for each option.
6. Create the ideal specification.
7. Select the best option and move towards implementation.

FIGURE 5.8 Which Option?

customer challenges became the criteria against which to evaluate the two options. They deepened their discussion by identifying each criterion as either a "Customer Must" or a "Customer Want" and comparing how much technical effort might be required to fill any gaps to ready the options for market. The team finally reached consensus on the better of the two and created a detailed blueprint on what the final go-to-market product would look like. They could then begin vetting this new product offering in the concept stage with customer feedback and make further modifications before going to market. The two-day workshop resulted in breaking a two-year logjam that had stymied the team from moving forward.

Blended Criteria: Paired Comparison Analysis

The second evaluation method, paired comparison analysis (PCA), forces you to blend all the criteria together, rather than separate them as in the criteria grid method. PCA is a method of evaluating several options by a head-to-head comparison of all pairs of options taken in turn. In each head-to-head evaluation, you consider two questions: Which of these two options is the best or most important? How much better or more important is it? Let's use this method in another example to evaluate the relative importance of several pressing problems.

Suppose you're a manager pondering five trends that affect your business: (A) increasing foreign competition, (B) growing economic uncertainty, (C) rapidly changing technology, (D) rapidly changing consumer tastes, and (E) a growing shortage of skilled employees. You are trying to decide in which order to address these trends. Using PCA, you place the trends both vertically and horizontally on a grid, as in Figure 5.9.

You begin the analysis by comparing A on the vertical axis with B on the horizontal axis. Suppose you feel that growing economic certainty (B) is a more important trend than increasing foreign competition (A). If so, you place a B in the A-B box. Next, you must judge whether the difference in importance is only slight (1), moderate (2), or great (3). If you decide slight, you mark the number 1 beside the letter B in the same box (B-1).

Your second comparison is between B on the vertical axis and C on the horizontal axis. Deciding that growing economic uncertainty (B) is a much more important trend than rapidly changing technology (C), you mark B-3 in this box. Next, you compare C on the vertical axis with D on the horizontal axis, then D on the vertical axis with E on the horizontal axis, and so on. In effect, you are descending the "stairs" formed by the shaded boxes.

When you have reached the foot of the stairs, you return to the top and descend the second set of stairs, comparing A-C, B-D, and C-E. Don't forget to place a number beside each letter to reflect each trend's relative importance. If you truly believe that two options are equally important, use a zero. However, do your best to avoid zeros. The whole idea of PCA is to differentiate between options.

Example: Completed Paired Comparison Analysis

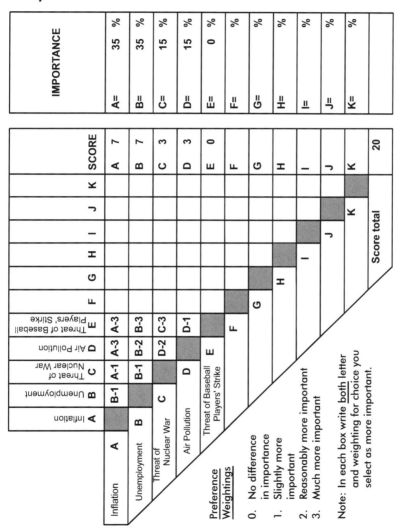

FIGURE 5.9 Paired Comparison Analysis

On the third descent, you compare A-D and B-E. The final descent consists of only one comparison, A-E. "Going down the stairs" is a simple way to avoid making comparisons of one option repeatedly, such as comparing A with B, C, D, and E in succession. It's a way of mixing the choices so that none is favored. The idea is to make as unbiased a comparison as possible for each pair of options.

After you've made all the descents, score the results by adding the numbers beside each letter, no matter where in the grid it appears. Then mark the five totals under the Score heading. Thus, your scores in the example are 7 for A, 9 for B, 3 for C, 1 for D, and 0 for E, totaling 20.

Your final step is to calculate the weight that you have assigned to represent the importance of each of the five trends. Divide the score for each of the five options by the total score of 20, then multiply the result by 100 to obtain a percentage figure. Thus, the relative importance of increasing foreign competition (A) is 7/20 x 100 = 35 percent. The relative importance of growing economic uncertainty (B) is 45 percent, the relative importance of rapidly changing technology (C) is 15 percent, the relative importance of rapidly changing consumer tastes (D) is 5 percent, and the relative importance of a growing shortage of skilled employees (E) is zero. Thus, not only have you ordered the options according to their priority, but you have assigned weights to their relative importance. You believe, for example, that growing economic uncertainty (B) is the most important trend of the five and is about 3 times as important as rapidly changing technology (C). Under PCA, the option judged least important frequently earns a weight of zero. This does not mean that the option is unimportant, but only that it's the least important of the group.

Paired comparison analysis in group decision-making is a powerful method of promoting give-and-take and consensus-building. Group members discover that they have different ideas about which criteria are important. They also find that their teammates have different values and knowledge that, taken together, help everyone better understand the options. The more skilled the members are in listening open-mindedly to each other and in valuing others' knowledge and points of view, the better their understanding of the options and the better their evaluation.

Remember that the solution or combination of solutions that you pick may not have scored highest on a numerical scale. The solution you consider the most valuable might have received a lower score not because it's a poor one but because it will be the one most difficult to gain acceptance for and the most time-consuming to implement. Successful entrepreneurship depends on solid execution as much as innovative business concepts. Even the greatest idea can fail if it's too difficult to implement. Therefore, the entrepreneur must balance great design with practical follow through. If a product or service idea can satisfy customers and quickly find a foothold in the market, then you may select it over a higher-scoring option. Whatever your decision, what lies ahead is the implementation phase of the creative problem-solving process. You must creatively plan for bringing your product or service to market, for gaining acceptance of the innovation, and for taking action to overcome the sticking points that might prevent successfully cementing your company in the industry.

Confirming the Selection

After converging on a solution with one of the two previous methods, an entrepreneur could confirm the choice by following top design firm IDEO's criteria for evaluating a winning product or service. Tim Brown, the company's CEO, advises that the best-designed products and services are desired by their customers (human desirability), can be reasonably built (technical feasibility), and make economic sense (business viability). As we have emphasized in this book, the combination is attained by designing the product with the customer in mind. The entrepreneur observes, researches, and interacts with customers to attain a good idea of what they like and respond positively to. Aesthetics that the customer will find pleasing and interesting are taken into consideration. Pleasing aesthetics may vary for different customers in different market niches and regions. The products should be reliable and easy to use for the intended customer. The products must also be feasible for the company to manufacture. If the product is too complicated or intricate to be produced in great numbers, the entrepreneur will have to strongly consider whether it should be produced. Thus, a major aspect of commercializing a product is deciding what materials, components, and fabrication techniques make the most sense for manufacturing. And finally, the business viability of the product must be considered. The product might be interesting and well received, but if it doesn't make business sense to produce it, it may need to be modified or dropped. Brown points out that an entrepreneur should bring these three constraints into a harmonious balance.

In the previous sections, we explained how to use the criteria grid and PCA method to evaluate solutions for selected customer problems. Now let's look at how we can apply IDEO's design criteria in a similar way. Using easel paper, we can write the following questions at the top of separate sheets of paper:

1. What would make a solution *desirable* to this customer?
2. What would help make a solution *technically feasible* for us to produce and deliver?
3. What would be required for a solution to be *economically viable* for us to produce and deliver?

Once the participants have diverged and provided answers to these questions, the group converges on the top two or three choices from each category. The facilitator addresses each selected criteria and asks the people who marked it to discuss their choice. After clarification of the selections has taken place, the facilitator marks the criteria that the group believes best captures human desirability, business viability, and technical feasibility for this particular customer solution. The group now discusses whether the product or service passes the test of IDEO's three design requirements.

Another method that can be used to confirm the innovativeness of a product or service was provided by Jackson and Messick.[3] These researchers examined creative output and developed the following four criteria for assessing the creativity of a product or service.

1. Unusualness—the product or service is surprising.
2. Appropriateness—the product or service also makes sense.
3. Transformation—the product or service makes me look at the world in a new way.
4. Appreciation (technically known as "condensation")—every time I use it I savor the experience, still find something new, and deepen my enjoyment.

If the group believes the concept clears the grid criteria or PCA method and it follows up with the IDEO criteria or Jackson and Messick assessment, we are confident an idea is well developed. It can now be tested with relevant audiences, including customers, to gauge potential interest in the new product. Focus groups, interviews, and surveys are often used to do this. Feedback does not need to be this formal though. If you are kicking around an idea and building a cheap prototype to examine the realities of the idea, you can ask a group of trusted colleagues, experts, customers, and suppliers to give you feedback on the idea. Companies like Procter & Gamble, for example, often invite 10 customers for in-depth individual interviews on their thoughts about the concept. They believe if they have selected a good representative group of customers, sufficient feedback has occurred that warrants whether the idea is to be pursued, modified, or dropped.

These sessions test the concept with market reality. You'll find out if you have anticipated your customers' needs well at this point. A short pitch is given to anyone who might have insight to what you are working on. Thus, physical representation of the business idea, whether it be a prototype, feasibility study, business plan, or venture, provides the ultimate feedback on the validity of the idea. The entrepreneur must be very open to feedback at this stage. This is where the entrepreneur's conception of what will be accepted in the outside world is tested for realistic assumptions of that reality. Many novice entrepreneurs seek confirmation of their concepts in this stage, but they should be open to complaints and criticisms subject matter experts and customers may have with the product or service.

If necessary, the entrepreneur may need to consider going back to an empty slate if initial runs of the display prove negative. Humbling yourself to the realities of your target market's expectations is difficult, but should be considered. This is also where the gamble of design occurs, for it may be that the market will respond favorably to the product once it grasps the concept of what you are trying to sell. This may take time. Thus, calculated risk taking is one of the most important skills an entrepreneur must develop. You must venture into new territory to make a creative contribution while also avoiding overly risky moves. In the end it is your call. Ideally, though, if you have taken an intellectually honest approach with others, you will have spent the appropriate time and effort in examining your idea from many different perspectives. If you've gotten this far in the process, it is likely you will just need to refine the concept and go forth with the business.

This is also a good starting point for meeting with subject matter experts because having a product idea of substance for the group to work with provides a focal point to guide development. The business idea gives them a frame of reference to which they can apply their knowledge. Sawyer[4] found that ideas are more creative with some degree of structure to guide the group's thinking because structure offers clear thought around possible issues. Based on the work of psychologists Robert Weisberg and Joseph Alba,[5] Sawyer explains that all solutions are derived from past experiences:

> [P]ast experience is always the way you solve problems—even insight problems ... these were difficult not because you're blocked by prior experience but because you don't have enough of the right kind of prior experience. ...[6]

If done properly, the meeting will be an improvisational give and take between the entrepreneur and the group. In using the advice of subject matter experts, the entrepreneur might:

1. go back and rework major areas of the concept where they feel it falls short;
2. search for another market for the idea and adapt it by doing research on the new domain;
3. scrap the idea and pursue new ideas to explore;
4. scrap the idea and focus on other solutions from Step 4; or
5. shore up any minor areas that the experts think need refinement and move forward into the next stage of development.

The entrepreneur should be reminded that if one of the first four options is taken, the hard work was not done in vain. New skills were gained and, additionally, major losses of investment may have been prevented. Entrepreneurs will cycle through these practices—playing with an idea, displaying it to others for feedback, and taking the advice and refining the concept for showing again—over and over through the entrepreneurial process.

When organizing a short presentation, explain your idea and show a prototype if you have one. Ask the group what they think of it. Simple questions like the following can unearth a wealth of valuable information:

- "Do you think this has potential?"
- "Do you care about the problem this product is trying to solve?"
- "Do you think this product will solve a problem for you? If so, what problem is it solving for you?"
- "If this were in the market, would you like to buy one?"
- "Would you like us to build a more polished prototype of this for you to see?"

- "What do you think are the strengths of this idea?"
- "What do you think are the weaknesses of the idea?"
- "Do you think I'm reaching the right market?"
- "What if the product was to do 'this,' would you like it more?"
- "What concerns or barriers do you think I'll face?"
- "Can you suggest others who can help me with this idea?"

A helpful tool for capturing all the suggestions is to use a video camera to record the session. This allows you to focus on what the group is telling you and allows for more lively interaction than spending time writing down the comments. You can play the video later and use the comments to refine your concept. Additionally, if the respondent provides an answer you're unclear about, be sure and follow up with a clarifying question, such as "When you say 'the product is ugly,' what do you mean by that? What do you mean by 'ugly?'" This is an ideal time for dialogue to gain a better understanding of your customer and what product or service might truly satisfy them.

These sessions are invaluable for evaluating your product or service. At the end of this chapter we provide forms for capturing key insights from these sessions. Figure 5.10 provides a Customer Feedback Form for Product/Service Concept, Figure 5.11 provides an Expert Feedback Form for Product/Service Concept, and Figure 5.12 provides a Refined Product/Service Concept Form. We have included completed forms by a former student who did an excellent job in collecting insights. Irina Mueller is a doctoral student in music who is minoring in entrepreneurship and is a world-class violinist. After exploring problems for her fellow violinists, she discovered that the cases they carry their instruments in are problematic. Specifically, all the violinists she talked to were overwhelmingly dissatisfied with the storage options in cases. Carrying sheet music was especially frustrating. As a result of stuffing accessories and sheet music into their cases, the zippers often broke, which led to problems with their violins in transport. Additionally, the cases did not distribute weight well. Irina recognized that cases are often as important as the instrument itself because of what is carried in them. These insights helped Irina design a case that worked more as an organizing system rather than just a storage unit. Details of her design can be found in her Refined Product/Service Concept Form. As her example demonstrates, a good collection of interviews about the concept revealed new insights and patterns that her early intuition on the idea did not reveal. You will notice that Irina provided excellent detail in her answers, which helped her later explore key opportunities for improving her product concept.

At this point in the process, Irina has only invested minimal time and money in developing the concept, but the return on this small investment is high. It seems she is right on track and can proceed into producing a manufactured version of her product. The next steps will require much more capital and sweat to bring the product to market; however, she can approach this effort with confidence because of the preliminary work she has accomplished on it. In fact, that is where Irina is at today, as she is seeking quotes on advanced design and manufacturing. However, if she had learned that there were too many problems with her idea, she could have dropped back to a previous step to modify the concept. This is an important point because many people think new product design is composed of expensive, time-intensive explorations, but that doesn't necessarily need to be the case. If the idea is picked up for more serious prototyping and development, as Irina is currently pursuing, costs and time commitments will go up. But the conceptual stage of our process should be relatively low cost if fundamental creativity principles are followed. Major mistakes are averted by systematically trusting the process. In the next section, we provide more detail on iteration, an important practice in gaining proof of concept of your business idea.

Iterations: The Key to a Good Proof of Concept

This chapter has covered Step 5, evaluation and selection. After showing an idea to others, it's likely there will be areas that need improvement. Good design is rarely achieved in one try. We must work with an idea and tinker with it until we think we have come upon something that is worth bringing to market. It requires the entrepreneur to be playful and to work with many possible combinations until something feels right. When the entrepreneur likes what they have, they show it again to others for their feedback. After the entrepreneur displays their idea, he or she asks for feedback from the group for suggestions on how they could have made it better. The entrepreneur takes this feedback and goes back to the drawing board to address it. After playing with the new information, they redesign their idea, and when they feel they have answers to the concerns, they present the idea to a group again. The group could be the same group, or it could be another group that might bring a different perspective. The entrepreneur will continue this process until it appears that they are receiving consensus of interest and approval from others. When an idea seems solid, proof of concept is attained. Implementation of the idea can now take place.

Although some entrepreneurs may have been lucky enough to have had success with an instant insight into the market, it is more likely that most learned from trial and error and playful contemplation in developing an idea. However, while play is a natural behavior, it is unfortunately often conditioned out of people over time, especially inside large organizations. Thus, it is imperative that entrepreneurs regain a playfulness to working with business ideas. To gain a perspective of playfulness, the entrepreneur must see the business idea as one open to evolutionary development. They must avoid being locked into protecting the idea and instead see it as something to be played with. The entrepreneur must set aside their ego and work with different variations of the idea in different contexts until they are sure they have a possible winning combination.

Entrepreneurs should also set high aspirations for their ideas. Sawyer[7] has found that people come up with more creative combinations when they set expectations for having ideas that are unique and valuable. If the combination does not pass that test, then they should continue playing with different combinations until they feel they've developed an idea with excellence. In business, "unique" means something new to a market or something that is better than rival products or services. "Valuable" means that value is attained when the customer feels the derived benefits from the product or service exceed the costs of purchasing it. If the value of an idea is low, then the entrepreneur can work on ways to provide more benefits, for example, with more features, better customer service, or ease of use, or they can lower the costs to the consumer in purchasing the product or service, for example, by lowering price, increasing the ease of adoption, or lowering any switching costs.

Playing with various combinations of inputs to find a true entrepreneurial insight into the market takes a tremendous amount of genuine passion and love of the business idea. Passion and love will sustain the entrepreneur through the most difficult times in developing a true market insight. As Steve Jobs once observed, if people don't love their idea, they'll give up. A sane person wouldn't want to do the work it takes to get an innovative product to market. It takes heightened commitment that goes beyond standard goal pursuits. To find that right combination of business inputs requires a "stick to it" and "never give up" attitude and the good health required for the entrepreneur to work a demanding schedule. Things the entrepreneur can do to strengthen this resolve are to be sure that they have chosen a business idea that they know they'll absolutely love to do and to avoid choosing a business idea solely because they think it will be financially successful. As Guy Kawasaki says in the *Art of the Start*, "If you want to get an investment, show that you will build a business. Make meaning. Make a difference. Don't do it for the money. Do it because you want to make the world a better place."[8]

Summary

This chapter covered Step 5, evaluation and selection. The criteria grid and PCA methods were provided as ways to select a business solution to move to market. Methods from IDEO and Jackson and Messick[9] were also covered as confirmatory selection mechanisms. Besides bringing good selection, these exercises will be particularly useful in building cohesion inside a new company. They assist entrepreneurs with mindfully considering what is important to the customer and the business. Informed, deliberate dialogue helps build a more unified front when the company approaches customers and investors. The movie *Startup.com* provides an excellent example of what happens when a founding team isn't on the same page as to what features should be in a product. Kaliel Isaza Tuzman and Tom Herman, co-CEOs of govWorks.com, squabble throughout the movie, even in front of customers, as to what their website will do for municipalities. They eventually burn through all of their cash before they can identify what they are truly selling. Both were smart and hardworking entrepreneurs, but those good qualities couldn't overcome the lack of focus they had in creating their product design.

Even a solo entrepreneur can benefit from these exercises by including subject matter experts and company stakeholders into the problem-solving sessions. While entrepreneurship is a risky endeavor, risk can be mitigated by making more informed decisions from the input of others. With a technique like the criteria grid method, PCA, or the modified IDEO proof-of-concept approach, you can evaluate the solution options you created during the first four steps of the creative problem-solving process. To proceed toward implementation in Steps 6, 7, and 8, you now must select at least one solution that you believe will make a valuable contribution to the life of your customer. If none of your solutions appears good enough, you must move back in the process to create better solutions for fresh consideration. You might need to research your market more to uncover some facts you overlooked. Having gotten this far into the process, you might have new knowledge that will help you uncover some issues you weren't aware of when you started working on the concept. Or maybe you need to go back to the drawing board and come up with a different solution. Perhaps you weren't working on the right problems and further problem definition would be helpful. In doing so, you might decide you have to go all the way back around the wheel and start over with a different target customer and set of problems to consider. If this occurs, it is important to maintain confidence and carry on. Time was not wasted. Bigger mistakes were averted before additional resources were invested. Therefore, good stewardship and deliberate problem solving through the use of selection criteria supports the entrepreneur in making smart calls that investors and other stakeholders will appreciate. The next chapter covers how to implement a solution that did meet selected criteria.

1. Customer's name _____

2. Customer's address_____

3. Place of interview _____

4. Date of interview_____

5. Why did you choose to interview this customer?

6. Describe this customer.

7. What did the customer like about your product/service concept?

8. What did the customer not like about your product/service concept?

9. How did the information you gathered modify your idea?

10. What one word or phrase best describes what the customer is looking for in a business?

11. What one word or phrase best describes the customer's reaction to your product/service concept?

FIGURE 5.10 Customer Feedback Form for Product/Service Concept

Customer Feedback Form for Product/Service Concept 1/5

1. **Customer's name**: Natasha
2. **Customer's address**: Muncie
3. **Place of interview**: BSU orchestra library
4. **Date of interview**: 11/22/13
5. **Why did you choose to interview this customer?**
   I initially spoke with Natasha when I was just beginning to gather ideas for my business in general and had not spoken to her specifically about my case. She was in the orchestra library while I was copying some music, and she asked about my business class, so I thought I would take advantage by showing her my sketch.
6. **Describe this customer.**
   Natasha is a doctoral student in violin performance, from Russia. She is very focused on playing the violin and works extremely hard. She is not afraid to offer her opinions (in general), so I value her input. She is very curious about my business concept and the idea of "business" in general, although I do not think she would actually want to have anything to do with business.
7. **What did the customer like about your product/service concept?**
   Natasha really likes that you could personalize and attach whichever portion she would need. She especially liked having a concert clothes, large music, and laptop portion. She liked the idea of being able to roll everything when it got too heavy to carry. She liked the idea in general very much and would definitely like to be one of the first to try out a prototype!
8. **What did the customer not like about your product/service concept?**
   This was not necessarily what she did not like but what she wanted to make sure my idea would be able to do. She would want her violin case itself to be easily accessible and easily attachable. She would want to be able to move compartments around easily—in other words, have the wheels also attach to the case if she does not need the suitcase portion, or only the laptop portion. She asked how heavy everything would be and was somewhat skeptical that I will be able to make it light enough in general. It should also not be bulky and easily maneuverable when all possible compartments are attached.
   Natasha also suggested trying to make a more minimalist, cleaner design on the computer somehow, so it would be easier to visualize the concept.
9. **How did the information you gathered modify your idea?**
   I think a third key design element (1. Wheels, 2. Attachability of all compartments) will be that the violin is easily accessible, even when there are things attached on top of it. I also need to do some serious brainstorming and research into what light and durable materials will be possible to make this work. I am struggling with the drawing aspect—I need to find some digital program that I can figure out to make my idea look better.
10. **What one word or phrase best describes what the customer is looking for in a business?**
    Practical neat design that works—reliability of business.
11. **What one word or phrase best describes the customer's reaction to your product/service concept?**
    Wow! It looks complicated. (But she really liked it once she figured out my drawing.)

Customer Feedback Form for Product/Service Concept 2/5

1. **Customer's name**: violist (undergrad in BSSO)
2. **Customer's address**: Muncie
3. **Place of interview**: BSU Sursa Performance Hall
4. **Date of interview**: 11/22/13
5. **Why did you choose to interview this customer?**
   She was available during break in rehearsal, and she has been using an oxygen roller for her viola case.

6. **Describe this customer.**

   This undergrad violist has serious back problems and has been ordered by her doctor not to carry her case. So she has been strapping it precariously to a set of wheels that are usually used for people who need oxygen tanks. She seems somewhat shy but was happy to talk about her experience with her case and hear and see my idea.

7. **What did the customer like about your product/service concept?**

   She really liked that it would enable the case to be securely attached to the wheels. She liked the idea of being able to add additional compartments also. She liked that it would be light and compact.

8. **What did the customer not like about your product/service concept?**

   Nothing, really.

9. **How did the information you gathered modify your idea?**

   She did give me some ideas based on her own experience. Security would be really important. She liked that her own contraption folded into itself and became relatively small, so I would definitely want to make sure that my wheel/handle part can get really small when not being used. She also mentioned that hers is pretty hard to maneuver and suggested that I think about wheels that were very flexible and turnable, so the whole thing was easy to pull around corners and pull in general. She thought she could use a longer handle than what she currently had. In general she wasn't concerned about pulling the instrument over bumps but did like the idea of having more bounce in the wheels (hers are completely rigid).

10. **What one word or phrase best describes what the customer is looking for in a business?**

    Something that makes her life easier and less painful. Innovative solution.

11. **What one word or phrase best describes the customer's reaction to your product/ service concept?**

Awesome—she would buy one immediately!

Customer Feedback Form for Product/Service Concept 3/5

1. **Customer's name:** Alex
2. **Customer's address:** Muncie
3. **Place of interview:** BSU Practice Room
4. **Date of interview:** 11/22/13
5. **Why did you choose to interview this customer?**

   Alex was not completely convinced of my original idea, so I was curious to see his reaction of my first sketch.

6. **Describe this customer.**

   Alex is an undergrad violin major at BSU. He seems to have trouble setting goals and being motivated, although he clearly has the potential to be a great violinist. I have been giving him additional lessons, and it made me wonder if he is reserved about giving me feedback since usually I am the "expert" offering *him* feedback.

7. **What did the customer like about your product/service concept?**

   He seemed to like the different options for what he could add, as well as the wheel idea in general.

8. **What did the customer not like about your product/service concept?**

   Alex still seems skeptical that (a) this would work or that (b) he would be interested in something like this. After suggesting that it might make his future gigging life easier, he seemed to be more interested. I wonder if he just doesn't see a need for it for himself. He did say that it would probably really help traveling soloists.

9. **How did the information you gathered modify your idea?**

   I still need to work on making the idea more concrete, although it keeps getting more defined.

10. **What one word or phrase best describes what the customer is looking for in a business?**

    Something of immediate value and practical application.

11. **What one word or phrase best describes the customer's reaction to your product/ service concept?**

    Mmmm—nice.

Customer Feedback Form for Product/Service Concept 4/5

1. **Customer's name**: Asia
2. **Customer's address**: Muncie
3. **Place of interview**: BSU practice room
4. **Date of interview**: 11/22/13
5. **Why did you choose to interview this customer?**
    Asia had not seen my design yet, and she is always carrying around her shoulder rest because it doesn't fit into her case.
6. **Describe this customer.**
    Asia is a new undergrad at BSU—she is playing violin, however she is not a violin major. I believe her major at the moment is music and media. Asia seems to be working very hard (taking additional lessons with me every week) and has a great positive attitude.
7. **What did the customer like about your product/service concept?**
    She really liked the practical aspect of having a compartment to fit her oversized shoulder rest, so it would be integrated into her case. She thought it was a cool idea in general and seemed very interested in seeing what the next step was. I could really tell she was thinking, "Man, this would really help me if I had one."
8. **What did the customer not like about your product/service concept?**
    She liked what she saw and had some more ideas, such as a keyring for keys on the outside, a small place for a phone, offering several different strap options for the backpack version, including having a front strap like serious mountaineering backpacks.
9. **How did the information you gathered modify your idea?**
    I had forgotten that I had at some point considered the front strap for the backpack, and I think I need to reinvest some more time studying straps—I had been focusing more on the wheels than the backpack idea. I think it's possible to have both versions. I think the keyring convenience would be an easy option to add, and it actually made me think of another idea for attaching all the components; possibly rather than using zippers, I could have some sort of ring-and-hook system to attach everything. I'm not sure if this would be as secure; however, I don't want to rule it out yet as an alternative, especially if I am able to go more minimalist and lightweight.
10. **What one word or phrase best describes what the customer is looking for in a business?**
    Fun and practical solutions.
11. **What one word or phrase best describes the customer's reaction to your product/ service concept?**
    Awesome! That would be really great!

Customer Feedback Form for Product/Service Concept 5/5

1. **Customer's name**: Lindzy
2. **Customer's address**: Muncie
3. **Place of interview**: church in Marion
4. **Date of interview**: 11/24/13
5. **Why did you choose to interview this customer?**
    Lindzy was one of the first people I interviewed when I was trying to come up with an idea (she's the one that was also unhappy with the backpack she and I both have), and I hadn't talked to her in a while. We both played a church gig together, and I took advantage of the opportunity afterwards to show her my sketches.
6. **Describe this customer.**
    Lindzy is very calm and very focused on her violin.
7. **What did the customer like about your product/service concept?**
    Lindzy was extremely excited by what she saw. She thought it would be absolutely amazing to have this to travel with and make things easier to pack and carry. She really liked all the options

and really lit up with the idea that there might be an alternative out there to what she presently has in the near future. Her excitement meant a great deal to me, especially since she is generally pretty calm and soft-spoken.

8. **What did the customer not like about your product/service concept?**
She mentioned I should be sure to have wheels that can turn in all directions to make it even easier to maneuver.

9. **How did the information you gathered modify your idea?**
Somehow after talking to Lindzy the idea became much more concrete in my own mind—I could see my ultralight, ultra-practical case rolling around an airport and being easily stowed in the airplane. Although I still don't know exactly how this will work, I can start to see exactly what I want it to be able to accomplish for musicians.

10. **What one word or phrase best describes what the customer is looking for in a business?**
Something practical and innovative.

11. **What one word or phrase best describes the customer's reaction to your product/ service concept?**
Wow!

---

1. Expert's name_____

2. Expert's position_____

3. Place of interview_____

4. Date of interview_____

5. Why did you choose to interview this expert?

6. Describe this expert.

7. What did the expert like about your product/service concept?

8. What did the expert not like about your product/service concept?

9. How did the information you gathered modify your idea?

10. What does the expert think makes a business successful in this industry?

11. What one word or phrase best describes the expert's reaction to your product/ service concept?

FIGURE 5.11 Expert Feedback Form for Product/Service Concept

Expert Feedback Form for Product/Service Concept 1/2

1. **Expert's name**: Dr. Keely (name changed for book)
2. **Expert's address**: Muncie
3. **Place of interview**: BSU
4. **Date of interview**: 11/23/13

5. **Why did you choose to interview this expert?**
   I hadn't thought to speak with Dr. Keely until after my committee meeting, when she talked about the new shoulder rest design and the Kickstarter program she'd been involved with. I felt her experience with Kickstarter and active professional musicians in multiple areas made her feedback at this stage of my design qualify her as an expert.

6. **Describe this expert.**
   Dr. Keely is the newly appointed viola professor at BSU. She seems very serious and committed to doing well here.

7. **What did the expert like about your product/service concept?**
   Dr. Keely thought this is a fantastic idea, and she loved the name as well. She was a freelancer for several years before coming to Muncie, and she resonates with feeling like a "pack mule" when she has full days of gigs, carrying her viola, another bag with clothes, another bag with food, purse, coffee mug, etc. She seems very excited at this convenient solution and is curious to see where it goes from here.

8. **What did the expert not like about your product/service concept?**
   She encouraged me to look into ultralight, ultra-durable material, such as tents, which would also be waterproof (I'd been thinking only of actual backpacks for backpacking). Her main concern is that this will get heavy very quickly if I don't address the material issue, and I agree completely. She also had a great idea, which was to make the compartments so they could collapse into a very small space, so you could always take all of the compartments with you on a trip and interchange things as you need them, rather than leaving some at home if the material was thicker and stiffer. This seems like a really great idea to me and actually helped open my mind up to some perhaps even better solutions for making this work. A minimal issue she mentioned was to perhaps flip the location of the laptop with the accessories bag, which would likely distribute weight better. Honestly I'd been thinking they would be interchangeable anyway, but I think it would be good to have the design drawing set up this way regardless.

9. **How did the information you gathered modify your idea?**
   The collapsible idea actually really made me think of other options. I started to think of stuff-sacks and waterproof bags that we use for camping, and I think this might actually help to become a solution to where I could make this without redesigning the case. If I make the compartments more flexible and have the attachment system so that it could be adjusted with cross-bands or those flexible pull-tie things (for closing off the opening to sleeping bag stuff sacks), then that would make the compartments adjustable to the case the customer already has. I'm thinking I could make compartments with zippers to open them, and then the adjustable bands on the ends where the attachment is—perhaps with a small and secure hook system. The instrument itself would be covered with a large version of this—with a zipper for easy access to the instrument, and pull-chords on the ends to fit the instrument. With this kind of a system I think the option to actually carry the whole thing seems much more realistic.

10. **What does the expert think makes a business successful in this industry?**
    Innovative idea, energy to make it real, practical solution for everyday use.

11. **What one word or phrase best describes the expert's reaction to your product/service concept?**
    What a great idea!

Expert Feedback Form for Product/Service Concept 2/2

1. **Expert's name:** Prof. Manner
2. **Expert's address:** Muncie
3. **Place of interview:** BSU violin studio
4. **Date of interview:** 11/23/13
5. **Why did you choose to interview this expert?**
   I wanted to get further input on my design at this stage since Prof. Manner travels and performs frequently.

Entrepreneur's name_____

Business name_____

Original Concept

1. Describe the customer:

2. Describe their problem:

3. Describe your solution:

Modified Concept

4. Describe the customer:

5. Describe their problem:

6. Describe your solution:

Process Reflection

7. How did the concept change from the original solution to the modified solution? Describe each version of the concept you created as well.

8. What key insights brought about these changes?

9. What were the most helpful/influential ideas provided by the customers for changing the concept?

10. What did your customers like most about the concept?

11. What did your customers like least about the concept?

12. What were the most helpful/influential ideas provided by the experts for changing the concept?

13. What did your experts like most about the concept?

14. What did the experts like least about the concept?

Process Debrief

15. What went well during this assignment?

16. What didn't go so well or could have gone better during this assignment?

17. What did you learn that you didn't know before you did this assignment?

Next Steps

18. What are your biggest sticking points/issues right now regarding your project?

19. What are the next steps you need to take to move forward with your project

FIGURE 5.12 Refined Product/Service Concept Form

6. **Describe this expert.**
   Prof. Manner is the violin professor at BSU and travels to perform with her trio frequently, usually involving air travel. She thinks very practically.

7. **What did the expert like about your product/service concept?**
   She really liked where the design had gone from when we originally talked about my vague idea weeks ago. She liked the many options, especially for concert clothes, music, and laptop.

8. **What did the expert not like about your product/service concept?**
   Prof. Manner was concerned that the practicality of fitting this concept into the overhead in an airplane would be an issue. I assured her that I would figure out an easy solution so that this aspect of my design would be beneficial rather than annoying.

9. **How did the information you gathered modify your idea?**
   I need to be sure that the compartments come apart easily so that everything can be quickly stowed in an airplane. The top portions must be easy to take off and be compact to fit under a seat, as well as the larger lower suitcase portion. I need to find airline specifications.

10. **What does the expert think makes a business successful in this industry?**
    Solution that works easily.

11. **What one word or phrase best describes the expert's reaction to your product/service concept?**
    Nice progress—keep making it even more refined and more practical.

Refined Product/Service Concept Form
Entrepreneur's name: Irina Mueller
Business name: Chameleon Case
Original Concept

1. **Describe the customer:**
   My original customers were musicians in general, which I quickly narrowed down to string players, specifically violinists. These customers ranged in level of professionalism from freshman college students, through amateur adult musicians and professionals with full-time performing or teaching careers.

2. **Describe their problem:**
   Across all levels, violinists were unhappy with their instrument cases for a number of reasons. The most common problem was lack of storage space, including for essential accessories, reasonable amounts of music, oversized music, laptop, and extra items when traveling. Another issue was travel in general, with the complaint that it is hard to carry multiple items, and also the one backpack on the market is too heavy, bulky, and impractical for what it is designed to do. A related issue was the lack of quality hardware, especially in regards to the zipper for the (too-small) music storage space on most cases.

3. **Describe your solution:**
   My solution was a violin case idea with multiple attachable storage compartments that were interchangeable depending on the musician's needs. An additional aspect of the case was wheels, so that when all of the compartments and items were attached to the case, it could be pulled if it was too heavy to carry. At this stage I was trying to avoid rebuilding the actual violin case itself and make the system somehow attachable to a customer's current case. I was thinking some sort of case cover, with zippers that would attach the additional compartments, and lightweight, although formed compartments. I was going to have a larger suitcase style compartment underneath the case (for clothing, concert shoes, heavier bulky items), an extra-large oversized music compartment between the suitcase and case itself, then on top have compartments for large accessories, laptop, regular-sized music, and personal items.

   The wheels were going to be attachable to the instrument case itself as well without the suitcase portion and have a compact pull-out handle. Exactly how this was all going to work was not very clearly defined at this point.

Modified Concept

4. **Describe the customer**:
    My design will still be available to any violinist; however, I will be targeting very serious, busy college music students and busy, traveling professionals. The flexibility of my design will also make the product available to violists as well.

5. **Describe their problem**:
    These customers are very busy and are often away from home all day or for several days at a time. They need to take larger amounts of items (music/instrument related, and also personal items, laptop/clothing/food) with them. They travel frequently, either by bus, carpool, or airplane, and need to think compactly for the items they take with them. Taking several bags is usually necessary; however, this can lead to forgetting a bag, and it is uncomfortable at best to carry everything.

6. **Describe your solution**:
    My case concept will be flexible to fit a customer's existing instrument case. Compartments will be able to be bought separately or as a complete set, so the customers can choose which compartment they normally need on a regular basis. All compartments will work individually or together and be easily interchangeable.
    The "attachment" component will be available in two versions:

    1. Complete case cover—ultralight, strong, and insulating material to protect the instrument from temperature changes (this is a big issue with most cases)—this would be zipped around the case, and then fit to the actual case shape by pulling on drawstrings at both ends. The case cover will have a series of hooks placed strategically, to which additional compartments can be attached. Backpack straps or a shoulder strap will be able to be attached to this portion.

    2. Minimalist straps—(see drawings)—ultralight, strong straps will be attached to the instrument case with secure clips. One strap will go around the case lengthwise, the other two across the middle—four adjustable clips will hold the straps to the case. All straps will be one unit and have pull straps to fit the case securely. The straps will have the same series of hooks as the case cover for attaching the compartments. If this system is used, the customer could still use their current backpack and shoulder straps since this option should not interfere with this aspect of their instrument case.

Compartments: These will be made of ultralight, flexible, strong material. (I'm still researching, although there seem to be lots of options. I want to use the most advanced material possible that will still enable a reasonable cost.) The concept I want to pursue will have the compartments be made so they can be condensed—I'm thinking sort of along the lines of a stuff sack from backpacking. When in use, the compartment would expand to the size needed, be hooked to the case attachment, and then have drawstrings which would make the compartment as compact as possible. When not in use, any compartments could be folded up into a very small space and still be taken along on a trip in case they were unexpectedly needed. The compartments will have well-designed, flexible zippers lengthwise so items inside can be easily accessed when the compartment is hooked to the case. The material will be waterproof. Larger compartments may have some netting inside to serve as dividers within the compartment to help keep things organized. If all the compartments need to be taken off (for instance when stowing the instrument in airplane overhead bins, they can remain clipped together, and a strap could be clipped to the entire unit. With the complete case cover, this could also be turned into an extra bag if necessary.

Wheels: These will be on a "to-be-found" or "to-be-invented" flexible spring system to serve as suspension for the safety of the instrument. Wheels will have to be rotatable in all directions to make the case concept easy to maneuver. There will be a pull-out handle—possibly flexible or rigid, depending on prototype experiments. Materials and design research is still necessary for me in this area, including if the clip system will work to attach to the case and/or suitcase portion.

Suitcase portion: This will likely have to be more rigid since when in use it will be underneath the case and the wheels would be attached, and also so that concert clothes do not get wrinkled. I still want to retain the minimalist lightweight material if possible, perhaps coming up with a frame that could be collapsed inward or snap into place when pulled apart. Dividers or nets of some sort should be incorporated into this.

Process Reflection

7. **How did the concept change from the original solution to the modified solution? Describe each version of the concept you created as well.**
    Please see Question 6 above for detail on my current version. As I tried to come up with a way to make this idea work, I originally could not think of a way to attach everything to an existing case. I started out thinking more like a backpack; however, that seems too similar to the Shar Joey (https://www.sharmusic.com/Shop-Shar/New/Joey-Violin-Case-Carrier. axd#sthash.IGUEFXT1.Q4SaHVRF.dpbs), and I felt too limited by this idea. From the beginning I wanted to have interchangeable detachable compartments to make the case customizable for the particular needs of the customer's day or trip. I originally envisioned more rigid compartments that would be zipped together. However, this idea seems complicated, rigid, and limiting in terms of flexibility for fitting to any case. The idea of clips makes more sense, and the idea of very compactable and size-adjustable compartments is opening up more possibilities to keep the entire design as compact and lightweight as possible.

    The wheel idea came about relatively early in the process and seems a logical solution to the aspect of weight; regardless of the material I use, the entire unit will necessarily get heavy when all the items are placed inside the compartments, and the option to pull everything like a carryon luggage bag makes sense at this point. As I invested time into trying to figure out wheels, I thought a small, luggage-style compartment on the bottom would make sense as well. This distracted me from the backpack idea for a bit. However, the lightweight, compact stuff-sack concept for the compartments is making me reconsider the ability to keep marketing the system as a carryable item as well.

    My design started to get bulky for a while as I added more compartments, which was frustrating. The recent idea of the stuff-sack compartments sparked some new energy and many more ideas about getting back to a more trendy, minimalist, compact, and practical solution.

8. **What key insights brought about these changes?**
    The initial wheel idea came from Prof. Manner, coinciding with the realization that the items themselves would be heavy. Speaking with Dr. Manner gave me the idea of the stuff-sack compartment because she suggested making all the compartments compactable so that you could take them all with you easily on a trip in case you needed them. Just looking at a stuff sack made me think about using clips instead of zippers and pull-strings, which would make everything more easily adjustable.

    The complete case cover came as a realization that separate case covers already exist in large quantities (usually super heavy for extreme weather protection), and I'm sure a lightweight option is possible to which all of the compartments can be attached. The minimalist strap idea came from brainstorming with Nick from his suggestion about making everything simpler.

9. **What were the most helpful/influential ideas provided by the customers for changing the concept?**
    Many insights from customers about what they like to have with them, or what they already take and have to have extra bags for, was helpful in deciding which compartments to start with. The need for a suspension system and fully rotational wheels was brought up by many as well.

10. **What did your customers like most about the concept?**
    Having space for all their items in one place! Many like the wheel aspect as well. The most excitement seems to come from the interchangeable aspect of the compartments.

11. **What did your customers like least about the concept?**
    For a while the entire unit looked and seemed like it would get quite bulky, which caused some concern, as well as "How are you going to make it work?" As my idea gets more refined, this concern is going away, and I think the stuff-sack idea, which few have seen so far, will get an even better response.

12. **What were the most helpful/influential ideas provided by the experts for changing the concept?**

    I think the most dramatic change, or clarity-bringing idea was for the collapsible compartments, leading to a flexible, lightweight solution.

    The most helpful feedback to me was the fact that experts agree that this is a need that isn't addressed by anything on the market except perhaps the Shar Joey, and this product does a poor job.

13. **What did your experts like most about the concept?**

    The idea in general as a product that would make musicians' lives easier.

14. **What did the experts like least about the concept?**

    The lack of clarity in the design.

Process Debrief

15. **What went well during this assignment?**

    My idea gained much more clarity and seems much more real and realistic after the stuff-sack compartment idea came about. I continued to get really interested and excited feedback from potential customers, which is highly encouraging. Many have said they would want to be among the first to buy my design once it's out there, which is very motivating. I am getting the sense that this a very real issue to musicians, and the idea that someone is making something to help them is getting much more intense positive feedback than I expected.

16. **What didn't go so well or could have gone better during this assignment?**

    I honestly felt pretty stuck for a while at the beginning of this assignment. I didn't know how to get to the next step of making a design that I felt might actually work without being bulky. Instead of going out and talking to more people, I withdrew and tried to figure it out on my own. When I finally did take the step to talk to people again, the solution materialized very quickly, and I need to remember this the next time I run into a problem with the design. I also felt the design concept was getting beyond my own personal possibilities, which I realized after speaking with Dr. Goldsby should not be a concern at this point. Once I realized I should be focusing on *what* I wanted the design to do, rather than getting stuck on *how* I wanted to do it, I got back on track with generating ideas and talking to customers.

    This isn't necessarily something that didn't go well; however, I am finding that I'm struggling to come up with words to describe the various aspects of the case since this doesn't really exist yet. Likely the terms I use will become more precise and clear as the concept solidifies.

    Drawing my idea is a challenge; however, I'm working at this. It is helpful to be talking with someone and to show the drawing and explain it and answer their questions referring to the drawing.

17. **What did you learn that you didn't know before you did this assignment?**

    I have been learning throughout that it really is not difficult to go out and talk to people. This has been a personal issue I'm working on, and I have been surprising myself that I am fully capable of presenting myself and my business concept confidently and professionally and that people are very eager to respond. This has perhaps been the most significant thing for me personally. In terms of the product, it appears there really is no other alternative than the Shar Joey that attempts to address this musician issue. This is highly encouraging because clearly musicians would love to have something like this, and I know from personal experience and other customer feedback that the Shar Joey is not a successful solution.

Next Steps

18. **What are your biggest sticking points/issues right now regarding your project?**

    I need to find out exactly what I can and cannot do similarly to the Shar Joey. A concern to me is that they also use clips to attach the backpack to the case; however, this is in the form of a very rigid semi-enclosing unit. This will largely influence the design of the attachment component.

I need to do whatever is necessary to make my drawings more clear and convincing so that as I show them to more experts and possible designers my idea will be clear.

I need to make some choices and start defining materials to start getting some cost projections.

19. **What are the next steps you need to take to move forward with your project?**

I need to find out what materials are possible and realistic (in terms of quality, durability, weight, and *price*) for the compartments. My parameters are as lightweight as possible, as strong and tear-resistant as possible, waterproof, condensable, and price realistic for a serious college student and professional musician.

I need to decide if I want to do some experimenting on my own, which I feel I could do with the current design, or if I need to, I can enlist the help of a separate design consultant. I feel like I could come up with some things to try on my own case to get a sense for the practical aspect of accessing the instrument with the various compartments attached. While I'm not sure I would want to test the strength of my stitching, I could get some rough compartments made and clipped on to see how this could work.

I need to continue to research clip options (I've started looking in the mountain climbing industry, since the strength, safety, and reliability in this area are likely industry leaders, and I could see the size options working with my design).

Notes

1 Parnes, S. J., Noller, R. B., and Biondi, A. M. (1977). *Guide to Creative Action*. New York, NY: Scribner.

2 Basadur, M. S., Basadur, T. M., and Beuk, F. (2014). "Facilitating High Quality Idea Evaluation Using Telescoping." *Wirtschaftspsychologie (Business Creativity)*, 16(2): 59–71.

3 Jackson, P. W., and Messick, S. (1965). "The Person, the Product, and the Response: Conceptual Problems in the Assessment of Creativity." *Journal of Personality,* 33: 309–29.

4 Sawyer, K. (2008). *Explaining Creativity: The Science of Human Innovation*. New York, NY: Oxford University Press.

5 Weisberg, R. W., and Alba, J. W. (1981). "An Examination of the Alleged Role of Fixation in the Solution of Several 'Insight' Problems." *Journal of Experimental Psychology: General,* 110(2): 169–92.

6 Sawyer, K. (2008). *Explaining Creativity: The Science of Human Innovation*. New York, NY: Oxford University Press, p. 88.

7 Ibid.

8 Kawasaki, G. (2004). *The Art of the Start: The Time-Tested, Battle-Hardened Guide for Anyone Starting Anything*. New York, NY: Penguin Books, p. 132.

9 Weisberg, R. W., and Alba, J. W. (1981). "An Examination of the Alleged Role of Fixation in the Solution of Several 'Insight' Problems." *Journal of Experimental Psychology: General,* 110(2): 169–92.

6
STEPS 6, 7, AND 8: SOLUTION IMPLEMENTATION

Introduction

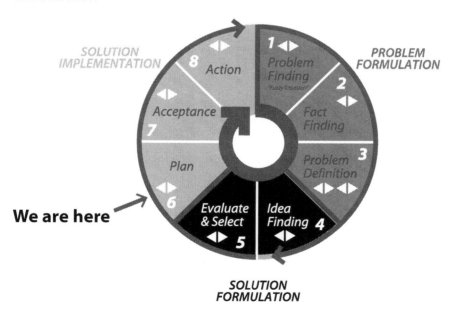

In the previous chapters of this book, we progressed from uncovering customer problems to selecting a business solution. These first five steps are the design component of creative entrepreneurship. This book focuses on this design aspect by extensively covering how to identify and solve important customer problems, an important but overlooked topic in the entrepreneurship literature. However, a design is useless if it is not implemented. Therefore, in this last chapter we provide guidance based on our experiences coaching clients and students in getting their solutions to market. Successful implementation includes three steps. You need to create a plan of specific actions you will take to implement the solution, gain acceptance for the solution, and take the plunge to carry out the specific actions in your plan.

Step 6: Action Planning

Let's take a moment to understand the psychology behind what you are about to do. In effect, you are about to create change. Austrian economist Joseph Schumpeter called this entrepreneurial phenomenon "creative destruction." You are about to challenge the status quo of your industry. If you covered the first five steps of this book well, you are about to launch an innovative product or service into the market. It would seem that success is almost guaranteed. But if only it were that simple. The biggest challenge to successful execution isn't always our competition; it's ourselves. Entrepreneurship is an exercise in grit and perseverance. It's accepting the challenge of handling the details of execution and committing the time and effort to do the important, but hidden, tasks that make the vision real. Many nascent entrepreneurs love talking about the big idea behind their business but procrastinate on putting in the countless hours needed to build the foundation of the business.

Worse yet, when obstacles appear on the way to market, they may procrastinate further as fear of making the wrong decision or being turned down leads to startup immobility. Overcoming the sticking points that hinder an idea from reaching the customer is often the difference between a "wanna be" and a full-fledged entrepreneur. Pushing yourself and your team to bring a product or service to market is one of the most discomforting things we can do. You'll have to practice a bit of amateur psychology on yourself and on whomever your change will affect. It's one thing to have a good solution, but it's an entirely different thing to encourage yourself and others to overcome the obstacles and resistance to turn a new business concept into a sustainable source of revenue. That's why you must give as much attention to the steps involved in implementation as you do to problem formulation and solution generation.

Personal Action Planning

In order to understand the importance of Steps 6 and 7 in the process (action planning and gaining acceptance), consider the psychology behind Step 8, taking action. Taking action on a new idea means heading into unfamiliar territory. Discomfort is natural. Think of how you felt before you plunged off a diving board for the first time. In the same way, it's easy to back away from taking the plunge to implement a new solution and think about doing it later. You'll need to use your ingenuity to overcome this urge to procrastinate.

Psychological Roadblocks to Action

Let's look more closely at several psychological roadblocks that impede action (Figure 6.1).

Fear of Failure

Failure is a common experience for many legendary entrepreneurs. For example, Henry Ford's early automobile businesses, Detroit Automobile Company and the Henry Ford Company, had short lives, as did Steve Jobs's second computer company, NeXT. However, both persevered to find the right formulas for success in their respective industries. As Walt Disney, an entrepreneur who also filed bankruptcy as a young man, once said,

> I think it's important to have a good hard failure when you're young. I learned a lot out of that. Because it makes you kind of aware of what can happen to you. Because of it I've never had any fear in my whole life when we've been near collapse and all of that. I've never been afraid. I've never had the feeling I couldn't walk out and get a job doing something.[1]

Because failure can hurt financially and emotionally, many people make it their primary goal to avoid it at any cost. Rather than tackle new customer problems or attempt anything novel, they execute tried and true business solutions. However, when executing on an innovative solution, you may uncover problems you hadn't considered yet. Many people will try to hide these problems, but the successful entrepreneur will diligently work their way to solutions. The path to a solution is not always clear, so many people refuse to commit themselves to timetables. They linger contemplating what to do next and avoid taking any risks. This moment of truth is what often separates the innovator from the dreamer. Entrepreneurs must make the tough calls to move projects forward.

Most people don't want to be identified with a company that fails. Our upbringing and education equate failure with being wrong. We soon learn that taking risks is not a good idea—better to act only when you're certain of being correct. Yet in a changing world, an entrepreneur can never be certain of being right. A failure to try is a failure to learn.

---

1. We don't convert ideas into simple, specific, realistic action plans.
2. We fear the unknown.
3. We fear our solution might fail.
4. We fear our solution isn't perfect.
5. We can't say no to other things.
6. Figuring we need a home run every time, we don't even go up to bat.
7. We avoid tasks we don't like.

FIGURE 6.1 Psychological Roadblocks that Impede Action

Fear of the Unknown

Implementing a new solution is like walking on unfamiliar ground. Without being able to read the terrain, it's impossible to predict where you'll end up, and the new solution will bring its own set of new problems or opportunities in the form of new fuzzy situations. Hence it's more comforting to stick with knockoffs of what's already on the market. Innovation, however, requires bold, competitive moves.

Fear of Imperfection

Too much of our education is based on choosing the right answers to questions. Under this system, a flawed or imperfect solution must be wrong. People prefer to wait until the perfect solution occurs, an unrealistic hope.

We Can't Say No to Other Things

For many people, it's easier to keep busy with routine, familiar tasks than to tackle anything new. This is particularly true of failure or imperfection that might harm esteem, career, or wallet. It's this thinking that leads many people to focus on the simplest items on their to-do lists in order to gain a quick sense of accomplishment. In fact, the to-do items that involve implementing new solutions and entering unknown territory are usually so time consuming and so risky that they're left undone. Complex problems require more work to solve, so entrepreneurs work on the easier issues at the expense of successfully mapping the big picture of what's required to get to market. The best entrepreneurs, however, tackle the thorniest business issues. Good problem definition and solution generation can increase confidence to mitigate this risk.

The Importance of Creating a Specific Action Plan

Procrastination needs no elaborate explanation. Suffice to say that most of us encounter it all too frequently. One reason that we put things off is that we fail to translate our ideas into simple, specific action plans. Without detailed action steps, an abstract idea for a solution remains just that. How often have you left a problem-solving meeting feeling unsure about what you were supposed to accomplish? What's missing is a clear plan showing exactly who was supposed to do what, when, where, and how. The more specific, clearly understood, easily visualized, and realistic yet challenging the plan, the more motivated and committed people are to accomplishing it.

This is the sixth step in the creative entrepreneurship process: planning action. In this step, the entrepreneur must provide motivation and commitment to act by developing a clear, creative implementation plan, a "road map to success." Entrepreneurs are facilitators of action inside a company. They set the direction of the company, marshal the resources and people needed to move in that direction, and

Problem statement: _____

Idea selected: _____

	What will be done	How will it be done	By whom	When	Where
1					
2					
3					
4					
5					
6					
7					
8					

FIGURE 6.2 Action Plan

identify the challenges their teams need to overcome. An action plan like the one in Figure 6.2 helps to build commitment to action through the closure principle. Once you've started something, you want to see it through to attain a sense of completion.

So How Do You Create This Action Plan?

As in all the previous steps in our process, you first suspend judgment and extend effort to create a list of difficulties that you might encounter in bringing your product or service to market. Use prompter questions like those in Figure 6.3 to help you uncover these difficulties.

1. What new problems might this idea create?

2. Where might there arise some difficulties?

3. Whom will this idea affect? Who will gain or benefit? Who might be concerned?

4. How should this idea be introduced?

5. When is the best time to introduce it?

FIGURE 6.3 Prompter Questions for Anticipating Difficulties in Implementing a Solution

Based on this list—still deferring judgment and extending effort—you must generate a list of answers to the following prompter question: "What specific steps might I take to get the ball rolling on this solution?" (Figure 6.4). Make your answers as simple, specific, and action-oriented as possible. Start each one with a verb. Avoid philosophizing.

As in all previous steps, your next task is to select the most important step to take. Write this step on Figure 6.2 under the heading "what will be done." Then write "how it will be done" in the next column. In the third column, "by whom," place your own name. In the next two columns, "when" and "where," put specific times and places where you will accomplish the "what" and "how."

Getting Unstuck

Sometimes the hardest thing about getting started on a project is knowing where to start. A clear starting point gets ideas in action. If you're having difficulty creating an action plan, David Allen[2] is a productivity expert who provides easy steps for managing and completing projects. In *Getting Things Done: The Art of Stress-Free Productivity,* Allen observes that most people struggle with achieving their goals because of cluttered minds. Most people have too much going on in their heads, and as a result, they are not able to put their attention on what needs to be

---

Idea selected: _____

_____

Diverge: What specific steps might we in this group take to get the ball rolling?

FIGURE 6.4 Action Plan Divergence

done. He likens the condition to a computer with multiple applications and windows open on the desktop. The more programs open on a computer, the slower the computer. Sometimes it even locks up. It happens to people too. Allen warns that any undone task that you wish were done is lying in the subconscious waiting to be addressed. As long as it remains undone, it operates like an open loop, which takes attention away from the task at hand. This lack of focus, in turn, leads to work taking longer to accomplish and with less effectiveness. The best work occurs when the mind is clear and focused on what it's doing. So how do we close those loops operating under the surface of our consciousness? Allen instructs a person to take a sheet of paper and set aside 15 minutes to write down everything they can think of that they would like to get done. It doesn't matter if it's a big life-changing goal or a tiny task. Write it down. Allen's point is that if something came to your mind over that 15-minute period, that means it was an open loop in your subconscious waiting to be closed. It's an item that you're concerned enough about that your brain doesn't want you to forget it. Therefore, your brain is not operating at its full capacity because it's spending some of its bandwidth keeping track of all these undone tasks and goals.

By writing down everything you can think of, the concerns are now captured on paper. That capture allows your brain to relax a bit because it now knows that the items won't be forgotten or lost. Attention can be placed more fully on the task at hand. It's likely that the first time you do this exercise, you'll have a very long list. It might even require more than one sheet of paper. It will probably include a range of items from "ask my business mentor to see my pitch" to "find and remodel a retail space." The point is if you think it's something you'd like done, you write it down on the list.

Now that you have a list of everything on your mind, what do you do with it? You next must determine what tasks to complete first. Allen instructs us to examine our list and mark all the activities that could be completed in two minutes or less. He then tells us to get busy completing those tasks. These are tasks that can be easily crossed off our list, and by doing so, we delete items from our minds to be concerned with. Additionally, by removing small tasks, it allows us to concentrate better on bigger and more pressing goals. However, grander goals can often take a long time to cross off a list, so we often procrastinate on addressing them. For example, "ask my business mentor to see my pitch" only takes a quick phone call to complete, but "find and remodel a retail space" might take a year to do. The retail space can seem overwhelming when compared to the phone call. Allen recognizes this mental trap and encourages us to add another step in achieving progress toward its completion. By asking ourselves "What's the one thing I could do now to get this project going?" we are able to find an action that will get the ball rolling. Once started, the closure principle clicks in again, and we look for the next little step to get us closer to our goal. Therefore, the big project becomes a series of small, doable tasks. Once started, it's amazing how many big tasks move from wish-list status to being nearly finished.

People often find Allen's system liberating. Doing the list exercise once per week can greatly organize an entrepreneur's work schedule. Improved execution is a sign of professionalism to stakeholders and a stress reliever for the entrepreneur. The best entrepreneurs have relentless focus on what the company needs to achieve. Reducing the clutter of undone task assignments and making movement on critical jobs is implementation at its best. A company will run even better when the entire management team utilizes the practices from this chapter.

Company Action Planning

In the previous section, we examined how an individual can plan to accomplish their tasks and goals. Different people on the management team will have different obligations. Individual accomplishment, however, is not sufficient to create a successful company. Startup operations require a coherent plan for getting to market. In other words, the action plan for a company is its startup strategy. In this section, we provide a method that utilizes tools and skills from earlier steps in our process to create a strategic plan for the company. A full-fledged business plan is useful to a management team but will be allayed to a later time in the startup process. At this point in the process, the entrepreneurs must first determine what the overall strategy of the company is before it solidifies its operational design.

Strategy Guidelines

In our work as teachers and consultants, we view strategy development and implementation as a process. It begins with a preconsult, a meeting involving the management team to plan the strategy sessions. The primary intent is to get a solid understanding of the company's situation and objectives. The next step is determining who will be involved in the strategic-planning process. It is important that people who will be responsible for the implementation of the plan are in the group. Since this is a startup, the strategy group is typically composed of the entrepreneurs, key employees, and investors.

A session begins with an overall discussion of the company's background and issues, its industry, and market trends. This discussion provides the landscape the company is competing in. Next, it is important that the group test the relevance of any existing vision or mission. For startups that may or not have a vision or mission, this also generally proves an appropriate time to create one or both. The group then performs a diverged SWOT analysis capturing many internal and external factors affecting the company. It is common to generate a list consisting of 100 to 200 strengths, weaknesses, opportunities, and threats. The group then pares the SWOT down to roughly 10 percent of the factors they project will most impact the future success of the company.

From the converged SWOT, a list of possible challenges to the company is developed. The converged facts from the SWOT are converted into "How might we" statements. This list is then converged down to key challenges facing the company. At this point, entrepreneurs begin to see new challenges emerging that they overlooked at the beginning of the analysis. The new perspective helps develop more innovative strategies for the company.

Entrepreneurs use the selected challenges to serve as a springboard for building a strategy map using the "why-what's stopping" analysis that was detailed earlier in this book. Once the map is complete, the group now discusses and labels each Post-it note on the map to determine whether it addresses the company's vision, goals, strategies, or tactics. The team now has a more coherent idea of where the company will go in the future. This strategy helps coordinate future activity and ensures resources are directed toward achieving a common company vision (Figure 6.5).

Two typical areas of concern for entrepreneurs are how to translate the high level direction embedded in the vision and mission into goals and strategic challenges and how to get alignment in their company between what they are doing

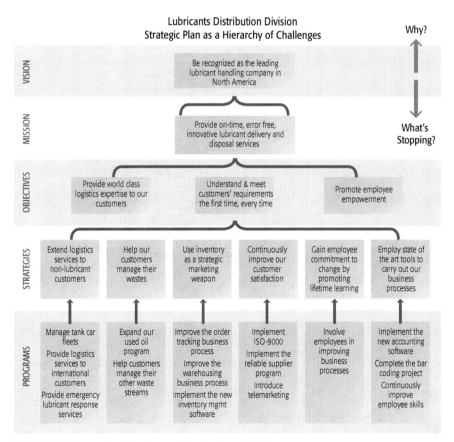

FIGURE 6.5 Example: Lubricants Distribution Division

tactically (marketing, operations, and finances) and their strategic direction. Lack of alignment can lead to the wasteful use of limited resources rather than a series of coordinated, deliberate challenges as part of a strategic effort. However, alignment occurs by utilizing the "why-what's stopping" analysis, covered in Chapter 3. This tool enables the group to build a logical strategic map that shows the interrelationships of the various challenges, from the tactical to the strategic.

At the very top of the strategic challenge map is the organization's vision. Immediately below is the organization's mission. Below the mission are goals (objectives). The group continues to build down, identifying strategic challenges supporting each of the goals, and then identifying possible initiatives (programs) to address the strategies. These are at the tactical level. The group may opt to prioritize the various initiatives and then collaborate to identify who is responsible for each initiative. Typically, this involves assignment of resources, reconciliation with budgets and timelines, and reporting and monitoring protocols. After the team has developed a converged strategy map, additional action planning is covered. The team discusses what initiatives, programs, and solutions can be developed for tactical support of meeting the chosen strategies.

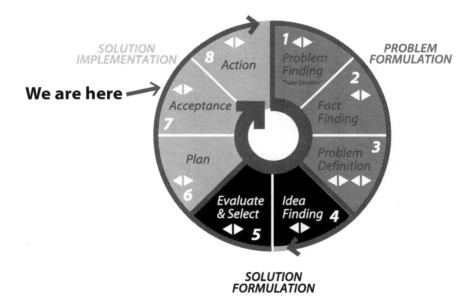

Step 7: Gaining Acceptance

During your action planning, you probably identified people whose support you'll need in order to successfully bring your product or service to market. In fact, you might have listed as one or more of your action steps the need to gain acceptance from one of these people. Why? There are a number of reasons.

When you ask someone to take a personal risk by participating or supporting your solution, you are asking them to venture into the unknown. You must figure out how to reduce their attendant discomfort, or you will not get their approval or the participation you need. Since entrepreneurial ventures are shrouded in uncertainty, anything that can demonstrate indicators of potential success should be sought. Steps 1 (problem finding), 2 (fact finding), 3 (problem definition), and 4 (idea finding) helped develop business concepts that address a significant customer problem. Step 5 (evaluation and selection) identified the strongest opportunity by evaluating ideas with subject matter experts and potential customers. Through this vetting process, the top idea garnered proof that the concept has good potential for success in the target market. Step 6 (gaining acceptance) evidences the needed proof for acquiring the resources and support required to bring a new product or service to market. When an entrepreneur can show proof of concept, they increase their legitimacy among their stakeholders. This proof of concept helps to alleviate stakeholder fears associated with the liabilities of newness[3,4] and small-ness[5,6] (see Figure 6.6). Alleviating (or at the very least mitigating) these worries leads to increased stakeholder confidence in the endeavor.

Proof of concept is a legitimacy-enhancing, value-adding part of an entrepreneurial narrative.[7] As Figure 6.7 shows, an increase in legitimacy corresponds with a decrease in risk, thereby making it easier to gain other resources critical for new venture growth.[8] And, as a reduction in risk of failure occurs, the chance of success rises, which naturally leads to a more positive valuation of a company. That is, as risk goes down, the certainty that the business will be successful goes up, and, as figure 6.8 shows, as certainty goes up, the valuation of a company increases.

However, while you may believe you've gathered enough proof of concept to get to market, you'll likely need to convince others of your decision. Seeking approval or agreement on anything involves "selling" people. You may be uncomfortable having to sell others on the merits of a seemingly valuable solution. You

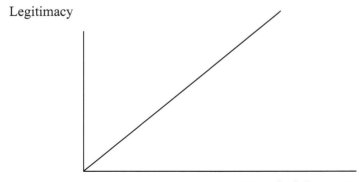

FIGURE 6.6 Proof of Concept and Legitimacy

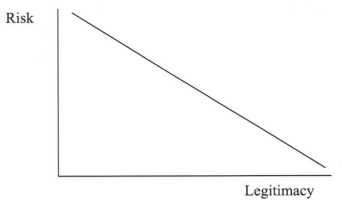

FIGURE 6.7 Legitimacy and Risk

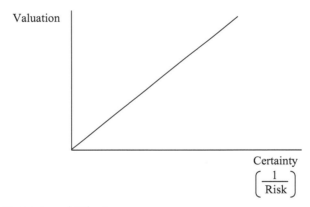

FIGURE 6.8 Certainty and Valuation

might believe the product or service is so good that it should sell itself, but this is rarely the case. In fact, innovative products and services are often harder to sell because they usually mean greater change in the market. This change will require the approval of many stakeholders who will determine if the product or service becomes a reality. Therefore, entrepreneurs seem to always be selling. For example, one gap in the supply chain may prevent the product from being sold. Thus, you have to become an effective salesperson with not only the customer, but also investors, suppliers, distributors, and employees.

How to Sell Ideas

Here are some ideas on how to build your skills in this step of the creative entrepreneurship process (Figure 6.9). One of the major skills is reducing the discomfort that new ideas bring. This is a very important consideration in entrepreneurship because a lot is at stake for everyone involved with the enterprise. The entre-

- Give others some control, be sensitive to the people aspects of your change.
- Spread ownership of your ideas.
- Give others credit at every opportunity.
- Show others that they have already used the concept.
- Leave something for the listener to change or improve.
- Involve others in fleshing out the implementation details.
- Don't make it easy for others to say no.
- Present your idea at a good time.
- Let your enthusiasm be contagious.
- Acknowledge your own misgivings.
- Ask your listeners to 'do' not just 'listen'.
- Use attractive visual aids.
- Appeal to all five of your listeners' senses.

FIGURE 6.9 Reducing Others' Discomfort with New Ideas

preneur is trying to gain support to acquire resources to make their vision a reality, investors are looking to avoid making bad bets, and customers are wary to spend money on a potentially disappointing product. As Stevenson and Jarillo state, "Entrepreneurship is the process by which individuals pursue opportunities without regard to resources they currently control."[9]

Within this perspective, the key tasks of an entrepreneur are to create a compelling vision of future opportunities and to facilitate the acquirement of resources needed to make it a reality. However, without having a reliable brand and track record, the entrepreneur faces challenges in gaining the support they need. As a result, a common mistake among entrepreneurs is that they try to impress their stakeholders with long, technical explanations of their product and business. This tactic often backfires, as the listener gets lost in the details and can't understand the big picture. Instead, a more effective approach is to present ideas in simple and concise terms. If an investor or customer has difficulty grasping an idea, they'll become defensive and shut down. The more the entrepreneur talks, the more they come across as unconfident of their idea, or worse, as a con artist. The less someone understands what the product or business is going to do, the more they will fear being involved with it. If you make the idea you're trying to sell simple, the listener will trust you more, knowing that you have done your homework and are comfortable with the idea yourself. Clear and concise answers that address the exact questions you are being asked show deep understanding and careful consideration of what your product or company is actually trying to accomplish. Unclear and rambling answers demonstrate an under developed concept.

One way to prepare concise and clear answers is to anticipate the listener's possible objections and prepare your responses to them. Here the entrepreneur actually becomes coach and teacher. Anticipating objections increases the investor's or customer's confidence in your ability to successfully deliver a solution you have promised. This confidence, in turn, opens the listener up to hear more about your product or company, which helps them to better understand the idea itself.

When an entrepreneur is selling their idea, the most effective way to win support is to ensure that the listener understands how the idea will benefit him or her.

If I am a rational decision-maker, and if the entrepreneur's proposal benefits me or my organization, then I would be illogical or foolish to oppose it. On the other hand, if the entrepreneur's proposal benefits only them, then it is difficult for me to see why I should go to some trouble and risk supporting it.

Even better, clearly explain how your idea helps solve an important customer problem. The customer will obviously appreciate that, and an aggressive investor is always looking for the next big breakthrough. The planning instrument in Figure 6.10 can be helpful in preparing your pitch. It can also provide you a way to be flexible in a conversation with a customer or investor. Your knowledge and

1 Selected idea: _____

_____

2 The listener is: _____

3 What problem of the listener will this idea help solve? _____

_____

4 What specifically do I want the listener to do?

I want the listener to: _____

_____

_____ on/by _____

5 Why should it be done? (list benefits)	Evidence? (How might each benefit be understood?)
A.	
B.	
C.	
D.	

6 What are the listener's possible concerns?	How might these concerns be overcome?
A.	
B.	
C.	
D.	

FIGURE 6.10 Selling Your Idea

application of the first five steps of creative problem solving can change the nature of a meeting from a sales call to a solution session. You can provide an overview of how you reached your solution by explaining the opportunity you recognized, the specific customer you are addressing in that opportunity, and the business solution that alleviates the problem. As the dialogue takes place, be open to suggestions that the customer or investor provides for making the solution better. However, by preparing ahead for the meeting with the instrument in Figure 6.10, you might have prepared answers that alleviate specific concerns that arise. Those objections to the product or service that are not addressed might be worthwhile considerations for going back to an earlier step in the process and improving the business deliverable. By using this planning instrument over and over again, you can improve your skills in gaining acceptance for your new ideas. Practice your use of the instrument by role playing. Ask a colleague to serve as a guinea pig and give you advice on improving your presentation.

More Ways to Sell Ideas

Here are some points to consider when you're creating and pitching your idea. Find a way to involve the listener and others affected by supporting your idea. This gives them some control over what happens. Remember that an idea that seems obvious to you might appear risky or complicated to others. For example, asking a hospital client to buy a new surgical instrument might dredge up memories of past grievances training doctors and nurses on new handling procedures. To them, your idea is an inconvenience if they've used another instrument for a long time. You'll need to show them that you're sensitive to their time constraints. Demonstrate how the instrument can be easily used and attain better surgical results. Better yet, if you've included surgeons and nurses in earlier steps of this process, explain how the instrument was designed with the input of others like themselves. If someone else contributed to elements of the design, even ever so slightly, make sure that you acknowledge that input. It will add credibility to your design. You'll show more proof of concept because it's clear you did your homework on the customers' needs. Or have the surgeons and doctors that you consulted with in the solution contact the potential customers about the product. Chances are they will since they will want to see the product make it to market. Again, be open to any input for improving the product from the potential customer. Rather than ask for a yes or no answer on the product (which means running the risk of their saying no), give the listener the choice of two yeses: "Would you like to buy the product as is, or do we need to make some modifications to meet your needs?" Involve them in developing further details of how the change should be incorporated into the product or service, and then bring the modified product back for a potential sale. This approach shows you care about making the customer happy with your product. You can use the same approach with potential investors by asking, "Can we close this deal today, or are there business issues we need to address to make you more comfortable being one of our partners?"

One way to lighten uncomfortable situations like a sales call or an investment pitch is to make the idea as attractive as possible. These meetings are as much about performance as they are about information. The listener is sizing you up as much as the idea. Therefore, it is imperative to make your sales presentation or business pitch fun and engaging. Let your enthusiasm for your idea be contagious. Acknowledge any misgivings they may have about treading into the unknown with you, and then explain how you firmly believe in your concept by emphasizing how you plan to address those concerns. All businesses have risks, but the successful entrepreneur is able to explain how they will address contingencies to mitigate those risks. Involve your listeners in doing something as you present your concept rather than allow them to just sit back and listen. Encouraging them to "do" rather than "listen" will help them better understand the concept. Use visual aids that are as attractive as possible or that require their assistance, or that involve listeners' senses besides the obvious one of sight. Let them touch, smell, or taste a prototype. Let them hear what your product sounds like or what others have said about it. Ask for their opinions. Remember Zig Ziglar's adage: "Don't sell the steak, sell the sizzle." Couple the business opportunity with demonstrations of the product or service. Make the sales call or investment meeting interactive in order to build familiarity with your customer and ease their reservations with you and your idea. Another factor that can affect the nature of the meeting is when you meet. Avoid proposing your new idea when people are not in the right frame of mind to accept it—late Friday afternoon, first thing Monday morning, 10 minutes before lunch. Take great effort to deliver on the factors you can control in the presentation.

Business Models

Once a proof of concept has been established, entrepreneurs will focus on how to get to market. Entering the market may require acquiring capital from investors to garner the resources needed to deliver the product or service and create a fully functioning organization to support the activity. In other words, the entrepreneur will need to sell their business concept to investors for securing an investment to support startup activities. One instrument that has gained popularity in the entrepreneurial community for meeting this aim is the business model.

Through the problem-finding and problem-solving stages, the entrepreneur collects, analyses, and reflects upon gathered information and feedback in order to develop a concept of what a nascent venture might be. Using what he or she has learned, a business model can be proposed. This model can then be iteratively improved, just as the product or service idea was (and will continue to be), resulting in a proof of concept for the business model. The important criterion for meeting proof of concept status in this stage is that the product or service is feasible from an economic standpoint. Because the business model helps to explain how a venture is expected to create a profit,[10, 11, 12] it can be both a barometer of the business's viability and a second, concomitant place to employ the problem-solving skills utilized throughout the entrepreneurship process. Specifically, a value proposition encompassing what the entrepreneur is offering the customer via a problem solution provides a general idea as to the eventual profitability of the enterprise, and the value proposition can be iteratively modified, in conjunction with the product or service being designed, in order to maximize overall value.

A narrow viewpoint of the business model would conclude that the business model is simply the value proposition, but a more thorough review of the literature finds that the term 'business model' can refer to a range of ideas from "how a company does business"[13] to an emphasis on an inclusive model.[14] A popular framework for business models, and one especially good for a design-centered approach, is provided by Osterwalder and Pigneur.[15] It presents a company's business model as typically addressing nine components: key activities, key partners, key resources, cost structure, customer relationships, customer segments, value propositions, channels, and revenue streams. Developing a business model using these building blocks as guidelines results in a thorough business model, which can be iteratively designed by modifying individual components as needed in order to "fit" the model to both the market and the product. A business model is an excellent instrument the entrepreneur can utilize for pitching (selling) the company to investors.

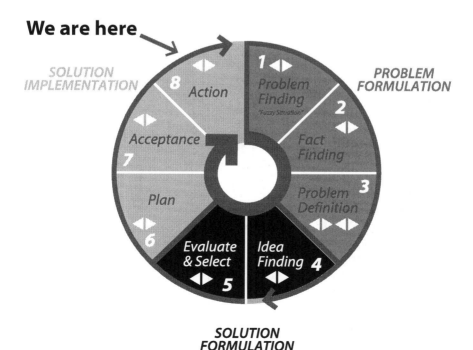

Step 8: Taking Action

Taking action is a specific eighth step in the creative entrepreneurial process. By now, you've discovered a great customer problem; uncovered intriguing facts about the market, industry, and product; created an outstanding business solution; made a foolproof action plan; and gained support for bringing the concept to market. But unless you take the plunge, all your work until now will have been wasted. Creativity is as important here as anywhere else around the wheel.

If you find it hard to take action, you're hardly alone. Most of us have trouble encouraging others to take necessary action, even when we know exactly what to do. Yet, that is what the best entrepreneurs do every day. They mobilize people to perform needed duties and gain consent where needed to make a product or service a future reality in the marketplace. After all, employees, customers, investors, suppliers, and distributors usually have many options as to what they will support in a free market system. You should always be trying to show why they should be on board with your company. If entrepreneurs cannot incur action from themselves and others, an idea will wither away into oblivion.

Further hindrance to action occurs when we are somewhat fuzzy about the necessary action. Having won acceptance and approval for the overall business idea, you still have to go from putting the idea down on paper to putting it into play. This becomes a test of confidence and overcoming negative thoughts like "How do I overcome my own fear of the unknown? How do I overcome my fear of failure? How do I overcome my fear of the imperfect? How do I overcome my own procrastination?" and "How do I become not just an 'action thinker' but an 'action taker'?"

If you learn to use the process covered in this book, you'll find ways to solve these particular problems, just as you solve any other kind of problem. Successful entrepreneurship is ultimately a practice in ongoing problem solving. Overcoming obstacles and sticking points determine who actually wins in the market and who fails due to not overcoming challenges. A startup is an exercise in solving problems that arise as you actualize your business concept. In essence, once the customer problem is identified and solved, getting to market requires relentless operational and marketing problem solving. Begin by determining your company's major roadblocks to getting to market. Come up with ten or fifteen specific ways to overcome each. For any particular solution you are trying to implement, think of ideas to help you propel yourself and others into action. Figure 6.11 provides a list of specific techniques that might prompt you into action.

How to Prompt Yourself to Act

The first three techniques address three common fears that prevent action: fear of the unknown, fear of failure, and fear of an imperfect solution. One technique

1   Write down the worst thing that can happen.
2   Share your plan with others.
3   Develop a strategy to minimize your discomfort and a way to turn failure to your advantage.
4   Ask yourself: 'If I wait, how much better will a later solution be?'
5   Use the closure principle.
6   Break big tasks down into smaller pieces.
7   Learn to 'reverse-prioritize' (learn to say no.)
8   Set deadlines for yourself (in writing if possible).
9   Share your deadline commitments with others.
10 Promise yourself significant rewards on meeting deadlines.
11 Use the 'broccoli first' principle—do the part you hate the most first to get it out of the way.

FIGURE 6.11 Ways to Spur Yourself to Action

for conquering fear of the unknown is called "writing down the worst that can happen." The worst outcome is seldom so daunting when you see it on paper instead of simply rolling it over and over in your mind. Developing a strategy to cope with the worst-case scenario can help reduce this fear. If the worst outcome is a cost you can afford to endure in the process of reaching a higher goal, then you'll more likely rationalize taking action. Some entrepreneurship scholars call this principle "affordable loss."

In order to overcome the fear of failure, why not share your intentions with other entrepreneurs? By doing so, you might obtain ideas to improve your company's chance of success. This helps you realize that your situation is hardly unique; other companies have faced setbacks and survived. This technique helps you develop a strategy to minimize problems associated with potential failure. You might even turn a short-term failure into a new opportunity as you adapt to what you learn by bringing the product to market. It helps you realize that fear of failure is the price of taking a risk on the way to success.

Think of Babe Ruth, considered by many as the greatest player in baseball history. Other batters with two strikes against them might have shortened up on the bat in order to reduce the risk of striking out, but Ruth swung just as hard as ever. As a result, he struck out more often than any other player, but he also hit far more home runs per at bat (1 every 11) than anyone else. Asked what he thought about when he struck out, he said, "I think of home runs." He saw more failures as the necessary price to pay for a bigger goal—more home runs. Failing on small goals is a way to achieve success with bigger goals. A failed sales pitch might uncover what a customer doesn't like about your product. It becomes an information session for modifying your business. A rejection from a group of investors may provide feedback for modifying your business model. Production setbacks may help you locate the type of employees you need to hire for the company. These are all proverbial swings at the ball from a business sense, and without stepping into the batter's box, you'd never get these valuable insights.

If you've been deliberate and adaptive throughout this process, what you'll probably find is that your business solution will be neither a complete success nor a complete failure, but something in between. Consider it as a first pass on which you can build toward real market success. You will likely need to adapt your product and business approach more than once, as your actions involve people, things, and events in unpredictable ways. We will speak in more depth on this layer of complexity later in this chapter, as the people factors oftentimes present more problems than the technical or financial issues will.

The third fear is that your product or service might be less than perfect, and haven't we all been taught that if a solution is imperfect, it must somehow be wrong? Think of school exams of the true-false, multiple-choice variety with either right or wrong answers. Carrying this mindset over to our company, we often look for the flaw in a solution rather than looking at the solution as a whole. In order to overcome this fear, simply ask yourself, "If I wait, will a better solution present itself?" You will probably realize that no amount of time will bring you the perfect solution. In fact, if you wait much longer, your opportunity for establishing yourself in the market may be lost. Think about it: If only perfect products survived on the market, there would be no need for new customer solutions. Customers would already have what they need, but we know this isn't the case because there are always unaddressed problems waiting for solutions.

The fourth technique uses the psychological phenomenon called closure. We have a natural desire for closure, for hearing the second shoe drop, for completing what we've begun. For example, you invoke the closure principle when you write your daily to-do list. If by the end of the day you have not checked off several items as complete, you will lack a sense of accomplishment or closure. This knowledge propels you into action. Many writers use the principle in order to "break the ice" of a blank screen on their word processor. They get themselves started by simply typing in nonsense. Having begun to fill the screen, they feel compelled to continue writing until something valuable begins to emerge. Similarly, you can employ closure in starting your business by setting up sales calls, no matter how much of a long shot the customer may be. More comfort demonstrating your product will occur as you modify your pitch to potential customers. In fact, it's likely you'll be told no several times before you make a sale. But each no is an opportunity to hone your pitch.

The fifth technique works on the same principle. People often struggle starting a business because they view the exercise as a single, large task that is too big to handle. Consider the act of writing a business plan for potential investors. It is an overwhelming document to write for many new entrepreneurs. The "pepperoni principle" can help with tasks like this. Visualize the giant task as a lot of smaller pieces to be bitten off a slice at a time. In trying to get your mind around larger tasks, make closure work for you. Deliberately set aside a large enough block of time to start and complete the task without interruption. So if you're writing a business plan, don't think about the entire document, but instead focus on each segment one piece at a time. Treat the industry section as if it was the only thing you had to write at that moment. Then move onto each additional section with the same attitude. Once a few sections are written, momentum will build and the business plan will eventually be written. If you're facing roadblocks to getting to market, delegate a few smaller tasks to other members on your team to build momentum, and put deadlines on the tasks to ensure the desired results are achieved on time.

The sixth technique is called "reverse prioritizing." Think of this technique as starting at the bottom of your priority list. Decide what items are relatively unimportant and refuse to do them. Instead, get started on the action steps that will lead to really getting the company up and going. This single skill will take you further toward making your product or service a reality than almost any other skill that we've discussed in this book. People often avoid committing themselves to act on important matters by purposely tying themselves up in more trivial activities. In the class business book *Up the Organization*, Robert Townsend, former highly successful president of Avis, kept the following question posted on the wall before his desk: "Is what I'm doing or about to do getting me closer to our objectives?" This reminder continuously saved him countless worthless trips, meetings, and lunches. It helped him to reverse prioritize, triggering him to act only on important matters. For the busy entrepreneur who faces an ambiguous and uncertain future, we could reframe Townsend's question to "Is what I'm doing or about to do going to get me closer to making my business a reality?" This mindset will create great focus and help the entrepreneur make better decisions regarding their time, money, and other resources.

Two other techniques—setting deadlines for yourself in writing and sharing your deadline commitments with others—combine the principles of closure, goal setting goal, and visualization. The latter principle is described by Maxwell Maltz[16]: when we clearly visualize success in accomplishing a specific task, we automatically trigger a mechanism hidden within our ourselves that moves us toward that success. Spelling out your deadlines makes them more clear, turns them into tangible, visible goals, and starts closure working. Telling others about your deadline further builds closure, as you have committed not only to yourself but to others. Entrepreneurs often make commitments to others by establishing milestones. Milestones are targets the company expects to reach in moving the business from concept to reality. The public accountability that comes with establishing milestones lights an emotional fire under the entrepreneur to deliver on their business promises.

Another technique, promising yourself rewards on meeting deadlines, employs motivational and behavior modification theory. The idea here is that rewarding a particular behavior is a way to stimulate its occurrence. For example, promising to treat your management team to lunch at a nice restaurant when the company makes its first sale will trigger the action.

You have probably known the last technique, "broccoli first," since childhood. It is one that your mother might have used to encourage you to eat everything set before you. Once you got through the broccoli, everything else tasted better. Similarly, accomplishing the most unpleasant task first may make the others seem easier. In starting a business, early action steps are often such unpleasant tasks. Addressing legal and governmental issues, for example, are not as fun as designing a corporate logo or testing a new version of a product. This is to be expected, but after you get through these steps, you begin to see your business having more legitimacy. The excitement you experience of owning an official business makes the early discomfort worthwhile.

Having come up with ways to trigger you into moving from thinking about action to taking action, you now must take steps to achieve completion. You must diligently involve yourself in bird-dogging (ensuring that others are getting their action steps done), clearing roadblocks, and adapting your plan as the startup process rolls along. Always remember that no one wants your business to succeed as much as you do. Others can easily be drawn away by competing opportunities. Persistence is important here. Recall Thomas Edison's quote: "Genius is 1 percent inspiration, 99 percent perspiration." As the final step in the process of creative entrepreneurship, this is the one that most requires your hands-on attention in order to avoid dropping the ball. Accomplishing this eighth step is like playing a football game with only seconds left on the clock and the goal line only a yard away. While everyone on the field knows the play, it's still up to one ball carrier to make it happen. The entrepreneur depends on many people to make their business a reality, but any follow through by anyone else will be dependent on the discipline and work ethic displayed by the founders.

Perpetual Motion around the Wheel

In the preceding chapters, we discussed a circular creative process designed to mainstream entrepreneurship and help you dramatically overcome the odds faced with creating a breakthrough product or service. These previous steps focused on addressing problems from a customer standpoint. However, once you're to the point of getting the product to market, problem solving doesn't stop. In fact, problem solving is a way of life for successful entrepreneurs. Adapting to changing market conditions, technical innovations, operational challenges, financial concerns, and people issues, among others, requires a nimbleness of mind and execution. Good problem-solving skills differentiate the persistent entrepreneur from the also-rans in the marketplace. Better yet, a good creative problem-solving process helps the entrepreneur systematically and deliberately overcome the roadblocks—also known as "sticking points"—to building a thriving business.

When faced with any complex problem where a simple solution isn't handily available, the entrepreneur can utilize the eight steps to whatever issue is faced. Let's revisit the process so that we can see how an entrepreneur might address a common startup problem.

Consider this story: A new sports nutrition company discovered that the local health food store that initially expressed interest in its healthy cookie had changed its mind. Dan, the entrepreneur who founded the company, was a personal trainer and nutritionist. He had made all the initial contacts with the market himself and was depending on the health food store order to leverage production of the cookie. He was low on funds and needed to make a sale soon to build momentum for his company. So Dan's problem was making his first sale. Many entrepreneurs would go into survival mode and hustle endlessly until the first sale was made. However, Dan also ran a busy personal training business that took up a lot of his time. He believed he had a good product but he needed to find that first customer who would validate his concept on the market. Dan came to us for assistance on his problem. After asking him fact-finding questions about the problem, we were able to apply the "why–what's stopping" analysis to help Dan reframe it. The real problem wasn't "How might Dan find more time to make his first sale?" The real problem was "How might Dan build a free sales team to sell his cookie?" This was an interesting challenge because Dan had limited funds, but he really believed in his product. Who could he find that would want to help him get his product on the market without being paid? Who was as interested as he was in having the product on shelves and would help make that possible? After diverging on possible solutions to this challenge statement, we decided to see if any students in our classes would like to help Dan out. So we pitched the product to a class of entrepreneurship students and asked if anyone would like to explore potential markets for Dan. Two athletes in the class expressed interest. Alex was on the university's baseball team, and Hunter was a competitive bodybuilder. Both said they would love to see a product like Dan's for sale because they didn't like traditional energy bars. Working with Dan, they targeted different possible markets that might contain highly interested customers. The partnership paid off, as they were able to convince the baseball team to include the nutritional cookie as part of their training meals. Local gyms soon followed in carrying the product, and as of this writing, Alex and Hunter are in the finals of a business pitch competition to secure more financial support for Dan from angel investors.

The sales challenge is just one problem that Dan has had to solve, and there will be many others along the way to his company's sustainability. But the process covered in this book helped him get through a major challenge he was facing. Once you see problems as new opportunities for further improvement and innovation inside the company, you'll know to launch yourself on your next cycle around the wheel.

Bottlenecks and "Battlenecks"

Entrepreneurs face many sticking points, but one of the biggest roadblocks to overcome in any organization is bottlenecks. Bottlenecks are points or activities that create inefficiencies in the overall system or process flow. There might be a manufacturing or other operational issue that is slowing the product's delivery to market. Creative problem solving can help uncover the underlying issues causing the bottleneck, just as we saw in the example of Dan. However, one type of bottleneck can be particularly debilitating to entrepreneurial success. We call these bottlenecks "battlenecks" because they incur extra emotional costs on the entrepreneur. Battlenecks are people-centered interference or obstructions blocking new ideas. Investors, suppliers, and distributors often dig in their heels to protect the status quo. Since your business idea must go through them in order to be implemented, their voices can sway or otherwise influence decisions regarding your company's future. Overcoming battlenecks requires time and energy planning and marshaling forces to defeat resistance efforts.

Bringing innovative products and services to market is very different from selling solutions that address routine customer needs. Why do so many new ideas fail? It has to do with people. We often don't consider the full impact their involvement with us will have on them. We think others will like our product or service as much as we do, but this isn't always the case. We have to deliver clear and concise messages that explain why customers will love this product and why it will bring good returns on any investment. If this isn't done, human nature will limit the receptiveness of the audience. People naturally look for flaws in new ideas. Therefore, it is incumbent on an entrepreneur to take steps to reduce others' uncertainty with a new idea. However, if stakeholders were involved in the earlier steps of our process, familiarity with our company and solution will help overcome this natural roadblock.

Let's look at more ways we can reduce discomfort with new ideas:

1. Try giving others some control; be sensitive to the "people" aspects of your pitch. When pitching your idea to a customer, supplier, distributor, or investor, paint a picture of how your business will make their lives better. What is pertinent to a customer may not be so for a supplier, and vice versa. Be sensitive to who you are talking to.

2. Spread ownership of your idea far and wide. When you are pitching an idea, include the names of others who provided valuable feedback in shaping the product, service, or business. Demonstrate that the business is built on input from other experts and professionals. This recognition of others will build your credibility as a good future partner.

3. Give credit to others whenever possible. If the person or group you're pitching to provided particular help on shaping your business concept, point it

out when appropriate in your presentation. One, they'll appreciate that you listened and applied their advice. And two, they may have forgotten what was said in past conversation, and giving credit serves as justification for why you took particular steps in building your business.

4. Note where the product or service has already been used, even if a unit hasn't even been sold yet. When a product or service is new, it is important for the entrepreneur to demonstrate any proof that the concept has a bright future. Beta tests, demonstrations, and free promotions are valid proofs of concept if you have early user feedback that can support your claims. If the product is already on the market, even on a small scale, make the case why its success can be scaled to new users and places.

5. Be open to changing the product or service based on input from the audience you're pitching to. Show that you're open to making changes and improvements to the product or service. This display of openness will evidence your intent of putting the best product or service on the market you can.

6. Ask for advice on fleshing out implementation details. If a stakeholder gives you advice on how to make your product better or your business more successful, don't fake understanding if you're unclear about how to implement it. Ask follow-up questions to clarify their advice, and request that they give you contacts and sources that can help you address any shortcomings you have on the topic. Most investors will appreciate your willingness to learn and improve as an entrepreneur.

7. Make it easy for others to say yes to your idea. If a potential customer or an investor is wary of your company, ask them what they're chiefly concerned with. After they provide their answers, ask them if they would be interested in considering your product or company further if those issues were addressed. If they respond yes, get to work improving your concept, and schedule the next pitch to show the better version.

8. Pitch your ideas at a time and place that is good for them. Be understanding of your audience. The setting where a pitch is made will have a great impact on how receptive they are to your idea. For example, some customers may appreciate you coming to their house to pitch your product because they can see it while staying with their children. Others may find a pitch in their home obnoxious. When in doubt, ask them where and when a good time to pitch is.

9. Let your enthusiasm be contagious. The biggest fan of the product or service should be you. Customers and investors want to know that you fully believe in your product or service, and they also want to know that your company is comprised of true believers too. After all, a business is a reflection of the people in it.

10. Acknowledge your own misgivings. If you have had struggles in building the business, noting how you overcame challenges can demonstrate your

persistence and grit. Investors know that entrepreneurs will be faced with both professional and personal hurdles as the company grows. Providing examples of how you overcame sticking points to starting the business will demonstrate you have the right stuff to be a successful entrepreneur.

11. Ask your listeners to "do," not just "listen." If you have a product, put it in their hands. If you have a service, have them tell you about the last time they faced the customer problem you're addressing. Bring your audience into the presentation. Do your best to help them get a good picture of what you are selling.

12. Appeal to as many of your listeners' five senses as you can. You can give them an even better picture of your product and company by thinking about how to help them experience what you are selling. Touch, sight, sound, smell, and taste are powerful avenues for sending signals about what your product or service actually is. Give them information in stimulating ways.

13. Use attractive visual aids. If you're not capable of creating your own professional slides or videos, hire an expert to do so. Sloppy depictions of your idea will downgrade the audience's perceptions of what you are trying to sell them. Remember everything you say, do, and show is a direct inference to what you will do in the future.

14. Ask for others' opinions and show that you truly value them. Confidence is an important entrepreneurial trait, but arrogance is not. The entrepreneur needs to demonstrate that they are open to others' opinions for making the business better. The biggest flaw in decision making is not being aware of our own biases. Listening to others demonstrates that you're an entrepreneur who will make informed decisions.

If the above suggestions are followed, you will get strong support from the stakeholders you need to make your business successful. Demonstrating respect for others' views builds ownership and commitment among the audience that will help in implementing the company's strategy. An entrepreneur who demonstrates humble inquiry and a good work ethic has a better chance of overcoming the battlenecks found around any innovative product being brought to market.

Summary

The previous chapters focused on the design component (problem definition and solution generation) of our creative entrepreneurial process. This chapter explained how to get a solution to market. Implementing an idea in an entrepreneurial context requires action planning (Step 6), gaining acceptance for the solution (Step 7), and taking action (Step 8). These steps help an entrepreneur demonstrate proof of concept of their idea to others. After all, startups must overcome the liabilities of newness and smallness. As proof of concept increases, a startup gains legitimacy, reduces its perceived risk, and drives up its valuation. Good selling skills help the entrepreneur further proof of concept and attain acceptance from important stakeholders, such as customers, investors, suppliers, and distributors. Business models are another tool that helps entrepreneurs tell this story. If the entrepreneurs are successful in Steps 6, 7, and 8, they are well on their way to finding their place in the market. However, they are still in the early stages of their entrepreneurial journey. Action will reveal new problems that need to be addressed, so entrepreneurs revert back to Step 1 solving the next round of challenges that face them. Therefore, the best entrepreneurs are first and foremost masterful problem solvers. Solving a customer problem leads to an abundance of other challenges to overcome in marketing, operations, and venture financing, among others. The next chapter concludes the book with an overview of the eight steps and tips for better collaborating with others to find these solutions.

Notes

1 Barrier, J. M. (2007). *The Animated Man: A Life of Walt Disney*. Berkeley, CA: University of California Press, p. 39.
2 Allen, D. (2015). *Getting Things Done: The Art of Stress-Free Productivity*. New York, NY: Penguin Books.
3 Singh, J. V., Tucker, D. J., and House, R. J. (1986). "Organization Legitimacy and the Liability of Newness." *Administrative Science Quarterly*, 31(2): 171–93.
4 Bruderl, J., and Schussler, R. (1990). "Organizational Mortality: The Liabilities of Newness and Adolescence." *Administrative Science Quarterly*, 35(3): 530–47.
5 Freeman, E., Carroll, A., and Hannan, M. T. (1983). "The Liability of Newness: Age Dependence in Organizational Death Rates." *American Sociological Review*, 48(5): 692–710.
6 Aldrich, H. E., and Auster, E. (1986). "Even Dwarfs Started Small: Liabilities of Age and Size and Their Strategic Implications." *Research in Organizational Behavior*, 8: 165–98.
7 Martens, M. L., Jennings, J. E., and Jennings, P. D. (2007). "Do the Stories They Tell Get Them the Money They Need? The Role of Entrepreneurial Narratives in Resource Acquisition." *Academy of Management Journal*, 50(5): 1107–32.
8 Zimmerman, M. A., and Zeitz, G. J. (2002). "Beyond Survival: Achieving New Venture Growth by Building Legitimacy." *Academy of Management Review*, 27(3): 414–31.
9 Stevenson, H. H., and Jarillo, J. C. (1990). "A Paradigm of Entrepreneurship: Entrepreneurial Management." *Strategic Management Journal*, 11: 17–27.
10 Afuah, A., and Tucci, C. L. (2000). *Internet Business Models and Strategies: Text and Cases*. New York, NY: McGraw-Hill Higher Education.
11 Chesbrough, H. W. (2003). "A Better Way to Innovate." *Harvard Business Review*, 81(7): 12–13.
12 Hedman, J., and Kalling, T. (2003). "The Business Model Concept: Theoretical Underpinnings and Empirical Illustrations." *European Journal of Information Systems*, 12(1): 49–59.
13 Gebauer, J., and Ginsburg, M. (2003). "The US Wine Industry and the Internet: An Analysis of Success Factors for Online Business Models." *Electronic Markets*, 13(1): 59–66.

14 Osterwalder, A. (2004). "The Business Model Ontology: A Proposition in a Design Science Approach." Doctoral thesis. Lausanne, Switzerland: The University of Lausanne.
15 Osterwalder, A., Pigneur, Y., and Tucci, C. L. (2005). "Clarifying Business Models: Origins, Present, and Future of the Concept." *Communications of the Association for Information Systems,* 16(1): 1.
16 Maltz, M. (2002). *The New Psycho-Cybernetics*, 1st edition. Upper Saddle River, NJ: Prentice Hall.

7
CONCLUSION

We've now covered the eight steps of the Simplexity creative problem-solving process and demonstrated how to adapt it to entrepreneurial ventures. Let's now review the previous six chapters of this book. We discussed earlier how important it is to separate content from process. Customers and subject matter experts can provide us great insight into what we can work with in shaping new ideas, but it's up to us to facilitate this knowledge into feasible and viable products and services. We also outlined the circular process of creative problem solving that you can use to design an innovative business concept for a startup. Many entrepreneurs do not have a deliberate approach to developing ideas, and as a result, they struggle in crafting a unique identity in the marketplace. In this chapter, we will conclude with some final thoughts on how to hone your ability to design winning products and services and get to market. Here we'll outline further skills you need in order to use the creative problem-solving process to full advantage. If half the battle is in understanding the difference between managing process and managing content, then the other half is developing these necessary process skills.

Remember our equation that summarizes these distinctions. Quality Results = Content + Process + Process Skills. Few entrepreneurs truly understand this equation. Concerned only with content and unaware of the power of both process and process skills, they end up with inferior products and services. Opportunity recognition should be seen as a starting point to designing a deliverable, not as an end in itself. The best ideas are shaped by extensive fact finding and problem definition. Now that you've gotten this far in the book, we believe you're much less likely to make this mistake.

Three process skills required to implement our creative process are deferral of judgment, active divergence, and active convergence. These three skills help to make each of the eight steps in this book work. But even these process skills aren't enough. In order to separate the eight steps of the wheel from each other, you must develop and use a fourth process skill: *vertical* deferral of judgment. We next discuss this important skill in more depth so that you can more effectively apply the contents of this book.

Vertical Deferral of Judgment

Imagine jumping, for example, directly to Step 4 from Step 1. You recognize a customer problem, skip learning more about the problem, and go right to building a solution without considering whether there is a better challenge to address. No matter how well you execute either Step 1 or Step 4, you're likely to design an inferior product or service. Recall our hot wax example from an earlier chapter. After the team had found a good problem (Step 1), it had immediately jumped to searching for possible solutions (Step 4) to an assumed problem definition of "How might we create a carnauba wax formula outside the competitor's patent?" The team skipped Steps 2 and 3, fact finding and problem definition. Recall also the green-striped bar example in which the team failed to do Steps 1, 2, and 3. The team members didn't actively search out and find the problem themselves but were forced into it; they didn't fact find or define the problem. Instead they began their process in Step 4, divergently searching for possible solutions to the assumed problem definition of "How might we create a green-striped bar that people will like better than Irish Spring?"

In both cases, the teams were able to use the two-step ideation-evaluation process *within* one step of the process, but because they lacked skill in vertical deferral of judgment, they leapt prematurely to a later step of the process. Had they been able to defer judgment, they would have moved from Step 1 into Step 2, fact finding, and then Step 3, problem definition, ultimately discovering a much better challenge before entering Step 4. If you picture the three process skills of deferral of judgment, active divergence, and active convergence *within* any step as *horizontal* skills, then the fourth process skill, *vertical* deferral of judgment, becomes the skill that allows you to *move stepwise* through Simplexity.

Here are skills that will help you practice the process of deferral of judgment:

- Know the difference between a fuzzy situation and a well-defined problem. Too many entrepreneurs recognize a possible opportunity but miss out on bigger prospects by not exploring the problem space more. Fact finding and problem definition help an entrepreneur find less obvious problems that competitors may have overlooked. Solving more important problems for customers can be the edge an entrepreneur needs for overcoming the liabilities of newness and smallness.
- Know the difference between defining and solving problems. Vertical deferral of judgment is a deliberate way to help the entrepreneur recognize the biases of themselves and others. Taking the time to fact find and facilitate clarification of what those facts mean with others helps the entrepreneur get a better

picture of the reality of their market and industry. While there will always be some degree of interpretation and judgment, recognizing the need to better understand a problem space and thoughtfully choosing which challenge to leverage become crucial steps to designing better solutions.

- Dig out pertinent facts before trying to define a problem. We believe you can never go wrong with taking time to do good fact finding. You have to be open to what a stream of facts can uncover. Therefore, patience is a prerequisite for getting a good understanding of a problem space. A good facilitator has to be comfortable with tempering a group's drive to get to a solution. However, we have often found in problem-solving sessions that taking a little extra time to let participants pull out a few more facts before moving into problem definition can change an entire session. A hundred facts might set the stage to trigger an unexpected insight that sends the team onto a new set of problems to address. Remember, the original problem you begin with is only a starting point for finding your customers' real problem.

- Turn premature critical evaluations into "How might we?" challenges. We have emphasized the importance of withholding judgment throughout our process. Still, it's human nature for people to be critical of new ideas. "Killer" phrases like "that's impossible" and "that will never work" are automatic responses common in the business world. That doesn't have to end conversation in your company if you're prepared to deal with it. In fact, those comments can help you uncover new opportunities for better innovation execution. The responsibility rests on the entrepreneur to manage the negative tendencies of others by turning their critiques into challenges that can be addressed. For example, if you have an idea for a more flexible rock-climbing shoe, someone might fire back that the materials used in those products tend to be rigid for durability. You can acknowledge that thought by reframing it as "How might we find a flexible fabric that is also tough?" This challenge statement might lead you to think about garments besides shoes that have these desired properties. You can then turn the critique back to the group and ask them to explore other clothing products that are flexible but tough. Maybe the first responder market has pants and jackets for SWAT teams and forest-fire fighters that are light but durable. Or what about special combat units that have to be prepared to go to battle in a wide range of climate conditions? Approaching all critiques in this fashion turns your company culture into one that is proactive rather than reactive. You evidence a solution orientation, and as you apply this approach, you model the creative problem-solving skills you want others in your company to have as well.

- Understand that new solutions that don't work perfectly are not mistakes, but learnings and new facts that you can use as the basis for your next trip around the wheel. As Walt Disney once said, "The way to get started is to quit talking and begin doing."[1] A business idea can seem so perfect when it exists in the mind, but reality hits when it goes to market. However, when you're testing an idea with your market, you're a step ahead of those afraid to take the plunge. Using the creative solving process you've learned in this book, you now have a system for taking those setbacks and turning them into opportunities to refine your business. For example, let's say that you create a consulting workshop to help freelance musicians better manage the business side of their profession. After you hold your first workshop, you may discover that they're bored when you cover contracts, but they ask a lot of questions when you address expense deductions and tax filing. You made some mistakes in what you thought musicians might appreciate in your workshop. That's okay. The next time you run the session you might tailor the workshop to cover financial strategies that generate more musician wealth.

- When a customer asks for help on a new problem with the product or service, avoid immediately giving advice. Instead, stay in fact finding so that the customer can help you think your way through the problem. You want to be sure that you're addressing the real problem, and the only way to be sure you're doing that is by asking questions about it. If you provide an answer that doesn't address the root problem, the customer will be frustrated with your solution. Take the time to use this customer interaction as a fact-finding opportunity to improve the product or service in the future. You also demonstrate your sincere interest in ensuring your customers are happy with your company and its performance.

- Recognize that team members are likely in different steps of the entrepreneurial process. Some people in your company may be thinking about what segment of the customer base to address while others are busy drawing up new products that could be sold on the market. That's a mistake. It's your responsibility as an entrepreneur to move your team through the process in sync. Always remember that a business concept comprises a solution to a big problem that a specific customer has. If any aspect of this formulation differs between team members, confusion will exist inside your company. A creative problem-solving process assists entrepreneurial pursuits by coordinating the creation of new products and services. Facilitating groups of subject matter experts, potential customers, investors, and cofounders ensures that ideas are moving along with clarity and agreement.

- Avoid leaping to action immediately upon discovering a customer problem. Instead follow Step 1 *through* Step 8 through the Simplexity process rather than jumping from Step 1 *to* Step 8. Jumping from Step 1 *to* Step 8 is like "ready, fire, aim"; proceeding from Step 1 *through* Step 8 is like "ready, aim, fire." In the former, you'll find yourself running back and forth and getting nowhere; in the latter, you'll find yourself creating on-target, workable solutions to well-defined problems. The entrepreneur is limited to the resources he or she has access to, so it is prudent to create products or services that have been vetted through the entire creative problem-solving process on the market. A little time and thought is a price well worth paying for cash-strapped entrepreneurs.

Realize that problem solving does not always yield immediate results. An entrepreneur has to be very patient when launching innovative products and services into the marketplace. New ideas often require customers to process and understand what you're selling. Let's look deeper at the way new ideas are processed.

Learning and Inventing: Two Parts of a Continuous Process

The distinction between the *availability* and the *use* of knowledge is a crucial one for an entrepreneur. In William J. J. Gordon's conception[2] of learning and inventing, learning (gaining knowledge or understanding) and inventing (using knowledge or understanding) are regarded as two parts of one continuous process. Learning and inventing may be regarded as opposite forces which feed each other in turn. Inventing is characterized as a process of breaking old connections. Learning is characterized as a process of making new connections. When we invent, we "make the familiar strange" (by breaking old connections that compromise current understanding). This permits us to view old phenomena in new ways, although this can be uncomfortable at first. In contrast, when we learn, we "make the strange familiar" (by making new connections between new—and thus strange—phenomena and our current understanding). This permits us to view new phenomena more comfortably. Thus, the processes of inventing and learning follow one another in a continuous cycle (see Figure 7.1).

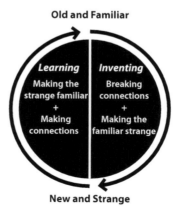

FIGURE 7.1 Two Parts of a Continuous Process

A continuous process of inventing and learning

On the left-hand side of Figure 7.1, new paradigms (ways of thinking and doing) become established. New processes are learned and become well-known and comfortable habits. On the right-hand side, old, established paradigms are broken. New processes that produce better quality or new goods or services are invented to replace previous ones. When an old *familiar* paradigm such as a well-established buying routine is broken, the new one replacing it feels very *strange* and uncomfortable to everyone affected. They are experiencing a process of *un*learning, *breaking* connections with past understanding and letting go of old habits and beliefs. As time goes on, the new product or service becomes less strange and more familiar. This is a learning process—making new connections and adopting new habits and beliefs.

Unlearning

A well-known example of unlearning—that is, the breaking of old patterns and the adoption of new beliefs—is the demise of the phlogiston theory, first propounded in the seventeenth century by scientists such as Johann Becher (1625–1682), Georg Stahl (1660–1734) and later by Joseph Priestley (1733–1804). Phlogiston theory, which lasted for about 100 years, maintained that the reason some things burned and others did not was that some materials, like wood, contained lots of phlogiston and others, like metal, did not. Although phlogiston theory made sense and fitted many of the known facts, quantitative experiments gradually convinced chemists that it was incorrect.

According to phlogiston theory, when magnesium is burned, the residue (magnesium oxide or calx) should weigh less than the original magnesium because phlogiston is lost. In fact, the residue actually weighs more than the original magnesium, implying the unlikely possibility that phlogiston has negative weight. Antoine Lavoisier (1743–1794), however, showed that the increase in weight of the residue was exactly equal to the weight of air used up, thus removing the need to invoke phlogiston at all. The phlogiston theory officially died on September 5, 1775, the day Lavoisier presented his paper "Memoir on Combustion in General" to the French Academy of Science:

> The existence ... of phlogiston in metals, sulfur, etc., is then actually nothing but a hypothesis, a supposition which, once admitted, explains, it is true, some of the phenomena of calcination and combustion; but if I am able to show that these phenomena may be explained in just as natural a manner ... without supposing that ... phlogiston exists in combustible materials, the system ... will be found to be shaken to its foundations.[3]

The birth of modern chemistry can be said to have begun with the breaking of the familiar phlogiston paradigm and the adoption of the strange new oxidation paradigm of Lavoisier. Should a better explanation for combustion ever be discovered in the future, scientists will have to break the old familiar paradigm of oxidation and begin making a new, strange paradigm more familiar by making new connections once again.

Thinking Organizations

We can define a thinking organization as one that (a) recognizes the value of breaking old and outdated paradigms and replacing them with new and better ones and (b) knows how to do so. A thinking organization can both unlearn and invent. It is proficient in efficiency thinking (perfecting current routines), adaptability thinking (breaking old routines and creating brand new ones), and flexibility thinking (operating effectively when there are no routines to follow in ambiguous, unexpected circumstances). Thinking organizations engage the innovative abilities and creative aptitudes of all of their employees.

Few organizations, however, have the skills or expertise to do this, and in particular, they lack a framework for sustained and disciplined creative thinking. In this book, we described a structured innovation process that allows entrepreneurs to think creatively in a collective, synchronized way, not only to improve routine work (efficiency) but also for the non-routine work of adaptability. This process, Simplexity, combines the apprehension of knowledge (understanding) with the creative utilization of such knowledge into a single framework. The process consists of four stages (Figure 7.2). Stage 1 is the proactive acquisition and generation of new information and possibilities, the sensing of trends, opportunities and problems. Stage 2 is the conceptualization of new challenges and ideas, Stage 3 is the development and optimization of new solutions, and Stage 4 is the implementation of the new solutions.

Recall that we all have our own personal unique blend of these stages, our creative problem-solving profile or style. Each of us prefers different steps and stages in this process. Maybe you prefer the first two steps, problem finding and fact finding. You might really enjoy interacting with the customer and studying the competitive landscape of your industry. You are more likely to be a generator and prefer to use the three horizontal process skills within these two steps than within the other six. Someone else might be inclined toward being a conceptualizer, optimizer, or implementer. They prefer to use the three horizontal process skills within the latter six steps. It's these individual preferences that make the process skill of vertical deferral of judgment such a vital one. This is the process skill that prevents you from leapfrogging prematurely to your preferred stage; it ensures that you move systematically from stage to stage.

If you want to design and implement a creative business concept, you must learn to use the Simplexity process with others to mainstream innovation, and you must develop all four process skills (active divergence, active convergence, deferral of judgment, vertical deferral of judgment) to make the process work, both within and among its steps. Let's practice putting together the process skills and the process. We'll start by selecting a fuzzy situation (the content) that matters to the customer and then walk

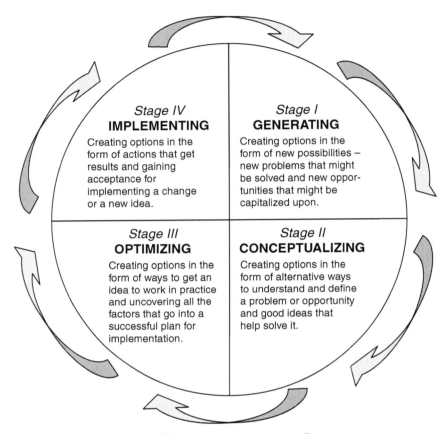

FIGURE 7.2 The Four Stages of the Simplexity Innovation Process

through all eight steps of Simplexity. In other words, let's practice putting together the entire equation from earlier chapters: Quality Results = Content + Process + Process Skills. If you need help working your way through this exercise, refer to the example later in the chapter called "I want to offer a better travel experience for tourists."

Simplexity from Start to Finish

Step 1: Problem Finding

Remember that you start this step by sensing and anticipating customer problems. Call these problems "fuzzy situations" to emphasize that you shouldn't prematurely assume anything about them. Keep in mind that the real customer you're solving a problem for may not be the end user of your product or service. So as you answer these questions, think about which customer you're actually serving with your business. You will need to design a product or service that is pleasing to the end user, but it must also address the problems of the real customer as well.

A. Diverge

Let's start by setting aside judgment. Use the prompter questions below to list fuzzy situations you might like to address. Practice your process skill of active divergence to come up with more than ten fuzzy situations.

Problem Classification 1a (B2C)

Questions to uncover the *present problems* the customer may have if they are a *consumer*

- What are the customers' major gripes and difficulties?
- What opportunities are the customers missing in their lives?
- What small problems do your customers have that could grow into big ones?
- What barriers impede your customers from being more successful?
- How could you improve the quality of the products or services they currently buy?
- What are their most difficult people problems?
- What goals do they fail to attain year after year?
- What crises do these customers often face in their lives?
- What issues are these customers often afraid or embarrassed to bring up?
- What areas of their life are hard to plan for?
- What problems do people like themselves have that they'd like to avoid?
- What solutions could you modify that are currently serving the customers?

Problem Classification 1b (B2B)

Questions to uncover the *present problems* the customer may have if they are a *business*

- What are the organization's major gripes and difficulties?
- What opportunities is the organization missing for better performance?
- What small problems does the organization have that could grow into big ones?
- What barriers are impeding the organization from growing?
- How could you improve the quality of the products or services they currently sell?
- What are the organization's most difficult people problems?
- What goals does the organization fail to attain year after year?
- What is likely to be the next crisis in the organization's industry?
- What issues is this organization likely to ignore or bury?
- What makes planning difficult for this organization?
- What problems experienced by other organizations would they like to avoid?
- What competitors' ideas could the organization adapt?

1._____

2._____

3._____

4._____

5._____

6._____

7._____

8._____

9._____

10._____

B. Converge

Now practice your process skill of active convergence. Select one problem that truly concerns the customer and that you'd like to create a business around. Since you're trying to develop your skill, make sure the problem you select is neither the most difficult to solve nor the most trivial. Describe the problem in writing in fifteen words or fewer. Don't include a lot of detail, and don't try to solve it right away—remember that your fuzzy situation is merely a starting point. Your brief description completes the first step of the Simplexity process.

Step 2: Fact Finding

A. Diverge

Now diverge again. List as many simple, specific, clear answers as you can to each of the following six fact finding questions. Defer judgment: don't analyze your answers as you go, no matter how trivial or irrelevant they may appear. Try to capture complete thoughts in sentences.

1. What do you know, or think you know, about this fuzzy situation?

1._____

2._____

3._____

4._____

2. **What do you not know about this fuzzy situation, but that you'd like to find out?**

1._____

2._____

3._____

4._____

3. **Why is this a problem, especially for the customer?**

1._____

2._____

3._____

4._____

4. **What solutions have you or others already thought of or tried?**

1._____

2._____

3._____

4._____

5. **If this problem were resolved, what would the customer have that they don't have now?**

1._____

2._____

3._____

4._____

6. **What might you be assuming that might or might not be true?**

1._____

2._____

3._____

4._____

B. Converge

Now converge again. Circle a few of the most intriguing facts on the above list. Look for things that stand out as particularly meaningful or important, and that perhaps surprise you. There's no special number to select, perhaps three or four.

1. _____

2. _____

3. _____

4. _____

Step 3: Problem Definition

A. Divergence

Defining the customer problem is so important you actually diverge and converge twice in this step. Keep your eye on your key facts, set aside your judgment, and list several optional problem definitions.

Phrase each problem definition as a challenge beginning with "How might the customer …?" (Let's say you're starting a travel company. Challenges might be "How might the customer get a better travel experience? How might the customer have a more entertaining guide on the trip? How might the traveler bring their children on the adventure? How might the traveler learn the history of the region on the trip? How might the traveler not get bored as they move from one location to another?") Write down at least seven such challenges.

1. How might the customer … _____

2. How might the customer … _____

3. How might the customer … _____

4. How might the customer … _____

5. How might the customer … _____

6. How might the customer … _____

7. How might the customer … _____

B. Initial Convergence

Now converge again. From your seven statements, select the one that you feel best represents your best opportunity at this point. Get ready to diverge a second time.

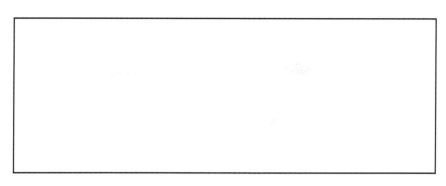

C. Final Divergence

This time you'll diverge using the "why-what's stopping" analysis. To begin, write down your selected "How might the customer?" challenge statement. Then ask yourself the question "Why?" That is, "Why would the customer want this challenge met by you?" For example, if your stated challenge is "How might the customer have a more entertaining guide on the trip?" then your why question might be "Why would the customer want a more entertaining guide on the trip?" Next, answer your question in a simple, concise, but complete sentence. In our example, perhaps an answer is "the customer would have a more memorable experience they won't forget." Write down your particular answer above your original challenge statement. (Keep in mind that these particular answers are only examples of countless other suitable possibilities.)

Now transform your answer into a new challenge. For example, the second statement above might be rewritten as "How might the customer have a more memorable experience they won't forget?" Write down this new challenge statement above the former one. (Again, this particular challenge is only one example of numerous possibilities.)

Now let's go the other way. Return to your original "How might the customer?" That is, "What's stopping the customer from having this challenge met?" In our example, the "What's stopping?" question might be "What's stopping the customer from having a more entertaining guide on the trip?" Perhaps the answer is "travel guides are often just locals who know the area but don't know how to perform." Write down your particular answer below your original challenge statement.

Now, using your imagination, transform this answer into a new challenge, again beginning with the phrase "How might the customer?" In our example, a new challenge might be "How might the customer travel with guides who turn the tour into a performance?" Write down this new challenge statement below the former one.

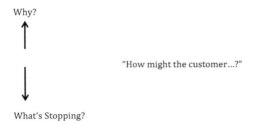

Why?

"How might the customer...?"

What's Stopping?

You could do a much more thorough analysis by asking, "Why else would the customer want ...?" or "What else is stopping the customer from ...?" several more times in both directions. For each of the resultant challenges, you could repeat the "why-what's stopping" questioning to create even more challenges. The more time you spend on this analysis, or the more frequently you repeat these powerful questions, the better you'll understand the customer problem space.

D. Final Convergence

Now it's time to make your final convergence in this step. From all of the challenge statements in your "why-what's stopping" map, select the one that you feel best describes the customer's *real* problem. (Incidentally, there's nothing stopping you from selecting more than one challenge—except perhaps lack of time.) With your problem definition in hand, you're ready to move from the problem-*finding* stage of the Simplexity process to the problem-*solving* stage.

Step 4: Idea Finding

A. Diverge

The previous step of discovering important customer problems addresses the "What's needed?" question from the market perspective. Now we turn to the "What's possible?" side of the business concept by converting the customer challenges into company challenges. We achieve this transformation by changing the "How might the *customer*?" challenge statements into "How might *we*?" challenge statements. We have identified what we need to address for our customers, and now it's our job to find ideas to solve these problems. For example, if your converged customer challenge from the previous step is "How might the customer travel with guides who turn the tour into a performance?" then your company's challenge statement might be "How might we prepare our guides to turn tours into performances?"

Now it's time to diverge again. This time, you're searching for answers rather than for questions. Convert your selected customer challenge statement into your company's challenge statement. Write down your "How might we?" challenge statement.

> "How might we . . .

Lay aside your judgment. Brainstorm at least 10 potential solutions to meet this challenge.

1._____

2._____

3._____

4._____

5._____

6._____

7._____

8._____

9._____

10._____

Keep your ideas simple and concise. Begin each statement with a verb to emphasize action. Deliberately create radical ideas you can build upon. Think of ideas that would probably bankrupt your company, land you in jail, or put you on the front page of the *Wall Street Journal*. Prompt further ideas by asking yourself questions like "What new ideas might colleagues at other companies offer? What ideas might a competitor offer? What ideas might one of my business heroes suggest? What would your worst enemy suggest (then reverse it)? What if you were flying a mile high on the back of a large bird and could see yourself below? What solutions might you see from that vantage point that aren't obvious to you at ground level? What other points of view might you take to generate even more ideas, like from your suppliers, distributors, or investors?" Perhaps you could double your list to 20.

1._____

2._____

3._____

4._____

5._____

6._____

7._____

8._____

9._____

10._____

11._____

12._____

13._____

14._____

15._____

16._____

17._____

18._____

19._____

20._____

B. Converge

Now let's converge on your ideas. Circle the four best bets. (There's nothing magical about the number four, of course, but you should attempt to whittle down your list to a manageable number for further evaluation.) Remember to choose ideas that are concrete, that are easy to understand, that point the way to an easy next step, and above all, that aim directly toward solving your chosen challenge.

1._____

2._____

3._____

4._____

Step 5: Evaluate and Select

A. Diverge

Now it's time to evaluate your list of potential solutions. Ideally, you want to select one good candidate or a combination of several. You might even end up with a modified version of one of your original ideas.

To get started, set aside your judgment again. List at least fifteen potential criteria that you might use in measuring the worth of these selected solution ideas. Remember that useful criteria must be specific, clear, and simple. Think about considerations your company will need to meet to be successful in implementing a business solution. Extend your effort to think of a wide range of criteria; don't be too quick to hone in. When you think you've finished, try to add five more potential criteria to your list.

1._____

2._____

3._____

4._____

5._____

6._____

7._____

8._____

9._____

10._____

11._____

12._____

13._____

14._____

15._____

16._____

17._____

18._____

19._____

20._____

B. Converge

Now it's time to converge. From your criteria list, circle four that you feel are most important for your company to be successful in providing the solution. To refresh your memory about developing valuable criteria, refer back to the guidelines for effective evaluation in Chapter 5. Make sure you know exactly what your selected criteria mean.

On the grid below, list your selected solution ideas vertically on the left, then list your selected criteria across the top. Using a simple numerical rating scale with 0 for poor, 1 for fair, 2 for good, and 3 for excellent, judge each solution in turn against the first criterion. Remember not to rank the solutions. Instead, rate each one individually. You may find all of your ideas are excellent or all are poor, or any conceivable combination. Then move on to your second criterion and repeat your evaluation procedure and so on for the remaining criteria.

If you believe that some criteria are more important than others, you can weight them accordingly to reflect their differing effects. Suppose that you believe that the criterion of materials cost is three times as important as another criterion, say, manufacturing time. Simply multiple each of the materials costs ratings by three. (You might not have to weight the criteria at all. Even if you do, remember that this is not intended to be a rigorous method. Its main intent is to help you carefully think through each of your ideas.)

If you wish, add up the ratings horizontally for each solution idea. These totals are useful guides to your final selection, but you're not committed to any particular idea at this point. One of your lower scoring solutions may be the right one if you

	Selected Criteria				Totals
Selected Ideas					

FIGURE 7.3 Selected Criteria

believe in it strongly enough to do what it takes to overcome the hurdles suggested by its low rating. For example, suppose a very good idea rated very low for material costs and very low for ease of finding committed suppliers because of its extreme novelty but was a super idea on all other counts. You might pick it, realizing that it will take a lot creativity, persistence, and hard work on your part to overcome these barriers. On the other hand, you might find that none of your selections is good enough. If so, return to the beginning of Step 4 to generate new solution ideas. You might even bring in a new group of subject matter experts and colleagues to see what solutions they might suggest. Or you can backtrack even further. Perhaps you need a more imaginative problem definition. Perhaps you missed important facts. On the other hand, you might like two solution ideas equally: perhaps there's a way to combine them into a single solution, or you could prototype the best ideas and see which ones receive the most interest from customers and investors.

Now write down your final selection below at the beginning of Step 6 as your solution to take to market. Remember that you must know exactly what you mean by your solution. This may require refining a business model or iterating a prototype numerous times before you commit to creating a company around it. If there is any ambiguity in the business concept, take the time to clarify it. You may need to include the coaching and involvement of others to help you do this.

If we want to further ensure we're confident with bringing the product or service to market, we can consider whether it meets IDEO's criteria for good proof of concept:

1.   Will the solution be truly *desirable* to this customer?
2.   Is it *technically feasible* for us to produce and deliver the solution?
3.   Is it *economically viable* for us to produce and deliver the solution?

The Jackson and Messick methodology can also be used to confirm the innovativeness of our solution:

1.   Unusualness. Is the product or service surprising?
2.   Appropriateness. Does the product or service make sense?

3. Transformation. Does the product or service make me look at the world in a new way?

4. Appreciation. Do I savor the experience every time I use this product or service? Do I still find something new about it? Do I deepen my enjoyment of it with use?

If a concept passes this thorough assessment, it's time to prepare it for market. So, having designed a solution, you're ready to move into the next phase of the Simplexity process, solution implementation.

Selected solution:

Step 6: Planning Action

Now let's continue our diverging-converging process into the implementation phase. Remember that your ultimate goal is to take action, creating a valuable solution for your customer and a good business opportunity for you and your investors. You need to exercise just as much creativity in these last three steps as in the first five.

A. Diverge

Begin diverging again. Keeping an eye on your chosen solution, write down at least one answer to each of the following six questions:

1. What new problems might this idea create for others and myself?

1._____

2._____

3._____

4._____

2. Where might you encounter difficulties implementing this idea?

1._____

2._____

3. _____

4. _____

3. Who might be negatively affected by this idea? (Whose life might become more difficult if I attempt to bring this idea to market?)

    1. _____

    2. _____

    3. _____

    4. _____

4. Who would benefit from this idea? (Whose life would get better if I successfully bring this idea to market?)

    1. _____

    2. _____

    3. _____

    4. _____

5. How might I introduce this idea to my different stakeholders (customers, investors, suppliers, distributors, employees, etc.)?

    1. _____

    2. _____

    3. _____

    4. _____

6. When might be the best time to introduce this idea to market?

    1. _____

    2. _____

    3. _____

    4. _____

Now continue diverging. Imagine yourself alone in a movie theater, watching yourself on the screen as you successfully implement your business idea, creating a valuable company. A great director has made a movie about your rise to entre-preneurial success. What are you saying, hearing, and doing? Who else is in the movie? What are they doing and saying? Where is the movie taking place? When? How do you feel as you watch? It's important to visualize yourself taking specific actions with specific results. Write down your answers to these questions.

1._____

2._____

3._____

4._____

Let's diverge further. Putting aside your judgment, quickly list at least ten simple steps that you might take toward putting yourself into this movie scene. Don't worry about getting the steps in any "correct" order. Include even unusual steps. Write down each thought as it occurs to you. Prompt yourself with questions like "Whom could I call? What could I buy? Where could I go? What would I need?"

1._____

2._____

3._____

4._____

5._____

6._____

7._____

8._____

9._____

10._____

B. Converge

Now it's time to converge. From this list of possible actions, circle the one you believe you should do first. Make sure it starts with an action word and is simple, clear, and specific. On the action plan below, write this action under the heading "What will be done." However, make sure you don't write it as number one or two. Write it as perhaps the third or fourth step so that you leave space both above and below it on the action plan: you may discover earlier necessary actions as you build your action plan.

Now write your own name under the heading "By Whom" for this first step. Then fill in the blank under the heading "How will it be done." This makes your action step more specific. For example, if your action step were to make a sales call, you would specify how you make that sales call: by phone, by checking a list of prospects from a mailing list, by delegating the task to another member on your team. Under the heading "By When," write down a specific date and time for taking this action. Then under the heading "Where," write down the specific place in which you plan to take the action.

You'll likely think of further action steps that should be carried out either just before or just after your first step. In either case, repeat the procedure above. Perhaps you can nail down only a few action steps right now—subsequent actions might depend on how your first steps turn out. Leave room for exercising creativity as your action plan unfolds. Recall the famous adage: Plan your work and work your plan.

What will be done	How will it be done	By Whom	By When	Where

You now have a simple plan for implementing your chosen solution. You can also work on your company strategy during this step, as outlined in Chapter 6. Once you have a plan of attack for your company, you're ready to gain further acceptance of your concept from others.

Step 7: Gaining Acceptance

It's quite likely that your action plan included getting support or approval from at least one other person or company. Whose approval might you need? Whose support might you need? Write one of the important names below.

Continue diverging. Might your idea solve any of this person's problems or help them reach an important goal? Pick one of the most important problems or goals and write it down here.

Diverge again. Write down three benefits this person would derive if your idea made it to market. Now converge. For each of the three benefits, write down at least one way in which you might illustrate or prove the benefit or in which you might clarify the benefit for the key person or company.

	Benefits	*Clarify the Benefits*
1.		
2.		
3.		

Now list at least three objections that you anticipate this key individual or company might raise to your solution. Remember that new ideas cause discomfort for all of us. Converge again. For each objection, write down at least one way in which you might show the person or company how it can be overcome or minimized.

	Objections	*Overcoming the Objections*
1.		
2.		
3.		

You can tailor similar plans for each individual you will have to sell. With each decision-maker, begin by establishing their particular problem or goal that you will help to solve. Frame your presentation to reinforce the idea that you plan to help them solve an important problem. Make sure you have enough time to explain the solution's benefits and to overcome objections. Also, as covered in Chapter 6, this step is also a good time to refine a business model that can be shown to investors.

Step 8: Taking Action

A. Diverge

Now apply the two-step diverging/converging thinking process one more time. Write down whatever you think might prevent you from taking the first step in your action plan. Circle the most important impediment, then list at least three ideas for overcoming it.

	Impediments	Ideas for Overcoming the Impediments
1.		
2.		
3.		

B. Converge

If you're actually working on your business right now, set this book aside, and go and carry out one of these ideas for overcoming this impediment. Having removed it, now carry out the action step. Repeat this for each action step.

For more complex problems that you may come across in getting your product or service to market, follow the eight steps of the process to find solutions to overcome any sticking points holding back your business.

"I Want to Offer a Better Travel Experience for Tourists"

If you haven't already taken a look at the following example, here's a sample of how the Simplexity process works in practice. We call this example "I want to offer a better travel experience for tourists." George had decided he wanted to become an entrepreneur. He thought about some of the aggravations he'd had lately in his life, so he applied the process to creatively solve a customer problem. George had repeatedly become frustrated with taking forgettable trips to what should have been interesting locations. Here's how he created a business idea by walking his way through Simplexity from start to finish.

Step 1: Problem Finding

A. Diverge

1. More reliable dry cleaning in the area that didn't damage shirts

   _____

2. Children scoring low on math tests

   _____

3. Frustrations finding baby sitters who show up on time

   _____

4. Taking forgettable trips because the travel companies lack imagination

   _____

5. Yard service does poor job trimming trees

   _____

B. Converge

> "I want to offer a better travel experience for tourists."

Step 2: Fact Finding

A. Diverge

1. What do you know or think you know about this fuzzy situation?
   1. Travel guides often don't seem to know much about the area.

      _____

   2. Travel guides act more like guardians than teachers.

      _____

   3. Travel guides are too boring.

      _____

4. The trips would hold no interest for our children.

___

5. It seems like we don't learn anything we couldn't find out in a book.

___

6. We move too quickly through areas without really enjoying them.

___

7. We miss out on opportunities to interact with the locals.

___

2. What do you not know about this fuzzy situation (but you'd like to know)?
    1. Do all travel companies operate like this?

___

    2. Is it just me? Are other travelers satisfied with their tours?

___

    3. Do some places have better experiences than others?

___

    4. If so, what makes an experience better?

___

    5. Would it cost too much to make a trip truly interesting?

___

3. Why is this a problem for the customer?
    1. Customers spend a lot of money on these trips and they only take one per year.

___

    2. Customers feel deflated when they spend so much time and money on a forgettable trip.

___

4. What solutions have you or other companies already thought of or tried?
   1. My college alumni group organizes tours to foreign countries, but they *lack a personal touch.*

   _____

   2. Disney offers "Adventures by Disney," but it's really expensive.

   _____

   3. My church organizes mission trips overseas, but there's little time for exploring when you're there.

   _____

5. If this problem were resolved, what would the customer have that they don't have now?
   1. The customer would have better memories to share with others.

   _____

   2. The customer would know more about the place they visited.

   _____

   3. The customer would feel they got their money's worth on the trip.

   _____

6. What might you be assuming that may or not be true?

   1. I'm assuming other travelers are as frustrated as I am.

   _____

   2. I'm assuming that more information could be provided by guides.

   _____

   3. I'm assuming I could find or train better travel guides.

   _____

B. Convergence

1. Travel guides are too boring.

_____

2.   We miss out on opportunities to interact with the locals.

3.   I'm assuming I could find or train better travel guides.

Step 3: Problem Definition

A. Initial Divergence

1.   How might the customer tour with more entertaining travel guides?

2.   How might the customer be more engaged with locals on the tours?

3.   How might the customer do more interesting activities on the tours?

4.   How might the customer learn more about the history of the places?

5.   How might the customer have a guide who shows more enthusiasm?

6.   How might the customer have a more memorable trip?

B. Initial Convergence

"How might the customer tour with more entertaining travel guides?"

C. Final Divergence

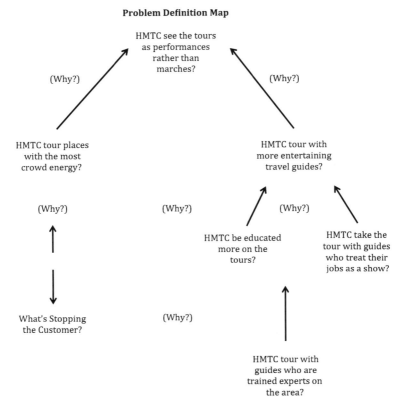

Problem Definition Map

FIGURE 7.4 Problem Definition Map

D. Final Convergence

"How might the customer tour with more entertaining travel guides?"

Step 4: Idea Finding

A. Convert Customer Challenge Statement into Company Challenge Statement

One possible formulation is:

> "How might we prepare our guides to turn tours into performances?"

B. Diverge

Selected problem definition:

> "How might we prepare our guides to turn tours into performances?"

- Hire Broadway performers who want to travel
- Hire theater students to be tour guides
- Send tour guides to local colleges for history classes
- Prepare scripted tours for the guides to learn
- Get employees at the sites to take part in the show
- Have guests take part in the show
- Give the guides acting classes
- Hire history students to be guides
- Hire retired teachers
- Set up shows at sites
- Hire local actors
- Perfect the stories told

C. Converge

Hire theater students to be tour guides
Perfect the stories told
Hire local actors
Prepare scripted tours for the guides to learn
Give the guides acting classes

Step 5: Evaluate and Select

A. Diverge

Possible criteria:

Talent availability	Amount of involvement on my part
Trainable	Potential enjoyment by guests
Time to develop	Probability of attainment
Repeatability	Potential to scale
Cost to develop	Quality control
Cost to train	Crowd disruptions

	Talent availability	Trainable	Crowd disruptions	Totals
Selected Ideas				
Hire theater students to be tour guides	1	2	2	5
Perfect the stories told	2	3	3	8
Hire local actors	1	2	1	4
Prepare scripted tours for the guides to learn	1	1	2	4
Give the guides acting classes	1	1	2	4

B. Converge

Criteria grid:

Step 6: Planning Action

Selected solution:

Perfect the stories told

A. Diverge

1. What new problems might this idea create for others and myself?
    I will have to have the stories written.

---

2. Where might you encounter difficulties implementing this idea?
    I will have to research the area more and make sure the stories are accurate.

3. Who might be negatively affected by this idea? (Whose life might become more difficult if I attempt to bring this idea to market?)
    If I use my current guides, they may not want to take the time to learn the stories.

4. Who would benefit from this idea? (Whose life would get better if I successfully bring this idea to market?)
    The customers would have a much better tour experience.

5. How might I introduce this idea to my different stakeholders (customers, investors, suppliers, distributors, employees, etc.?)
    I could post a video of a guide telling a story on our company website.

6. When might be the best time to introduce this idea to market?
    I could gradually have the guides work a story or two into their tours.

The "movie theatre scene"

> The tour guide has the travel group looking around spellbound by all the events that took place in that spot.

What specific steps might I take to get the ball rolling?

Buy books on the area's history

Attend a writing class

Hire a local writer to draft some stories

Offer internships to local students to write stories

Find a local historian to visit the sites with so that I can have stories to tell

Have a theatre expert advise me on how to tell the stories

B. Converge

Idea selected:

Perfect the stories told

What will be done	How will it be done	By whom	By when	Where
Buy history books	Shop online	Me	Tonight after work	Amazon
Read history books	Dive into books	Me	Start Saturday for 2 weeks	Home office
Draft outlines of stories	Pen and paper	Me	Two weeks from today	Home office
Contact local writer	Call university for contacts	Me	Three weeks from today	Home
Hire writer	Interview and select	Me	One month from today	Coffee shop
Perfect the stories told	Read and approve stories	Me & writer	4 months from today	Writer's office and my home office

Step 7: Gaining Acceptance

Whom do I need to convince?
No one but myself.

Step 8: Taking action

Potential impediments that might prevent you from taking the first step?
None

Follow the Process in Teams

In the previous example, we provided an entrepreneur who chose to build his company alone. However, many entrepreneurs will choose to be a part of a founding team comprising people with varying subject matter expertise, connections, resources, and cognitive styles (generators, conceptualizers, optimizers, and implementers). Teams offer many advantages over starting a company alone.

However, teams can be more challenging when team members have different visions, opinions, and thinking styles. Fortunately, committed use of a reliable process not only leads to better solutions, it leads to better teamwork.

This book has focused on using a research-supported and practice-tested process to design new products and services that a successful business can be created around. We recognize that most entrepreneurs will facilitate this process with others, such as co-founders, potential investors, target customers, and subject matter experts. Therefore, we conclude this book with guidance on using the process with others in achieving a mutual company vision. By using the Simplexity process and process skills to conduct meetings, you can help your startup team work much more effectively. Concept development, strategic decisions, resource acquisition, and market entry, among many other things, are complicated problems all entrepreneurs face. If your team hopes to fully understand these problems and come up with timely, quality solutions that keep the company moving forward, then it has to draw on wider knowledge from a broad range of people—especially since the team must deal directly with the company's customers, investors, suppliers, and distributors. How the team works together in the early days of the company will shape what the organizational culture becomes. A company built on respectful and productive working relationships is more likely to have an environment that attracts and keeps talent as the company grows. The founding team sets the initial conditions that shape what the company can become. Team members using a common process to creatively work through problems can reduce many of the tensions found in startups. Let's look at how you can build better teams in a startup.

Toward More Productive Teams

A lot of big decisions take place in a startup, and each one holds dire consequences that established companies have the luxury of absorbing. Startups with limited funds don't bounce back from bad strategic decisions like corporations with more cash on hand. A Fortune 500 CEO can quickly be replaced with a leader with a business pedigree by a board of directors, but a startup company is often not given the same chance of redemption. As we learned during the financial crisis of 2008, society holds that some corporations are "too big to fail." More people are concerned with the billion-dollar corporation's survival because of the rippling effect of destruction that takes place if it goes out of existence. Startups don't get that benefit of a doubt from the market. Entrepreneurs must rely more on themselves to survive. As we've emphasized throughout this book, the best way to weather these challenges and create effective solutions is to turn the entrepreneurial process into a team sport. Many legendary companies were built not by a lone entrepreneur but instead by effective partnerships and teams. Consider Steve Jobs and Steve Wozniak (Apple), Bill Gates and Paul Allen (Microsoft), Walt and Roy Disney (The Walt Disney Company), Sergey Brin and Larry Page (Google), and Steve Jobs, Ed Catmull, and John Lasseter (Pixar). The common lesson is that entrepreneurs hoping to make their teams more productive must meet several critical challenges, as follows:

- How might each member make a valuable contribution?
- How might each member support team decisions?
- How might members commit to implementing the team's own recommendations?
- How might the team focus on clearly defined challenges?
- How might the team develop and consider many alternative solutions?
- How might the team define how and when to implement its solutions?
- How might the team members listen to, share, and accept each other's ideas?
- How might the team members identify and resolve conflicting priorities and interests?
- How might team members agree on what's important?
- How might the team members assign themselves clear action steps?
- How might the team work well together?

Interpersonal Skills for Better Teamwork

If team members hope to meet these challenges, they need to learn a few skills besides the Simplexity process skills. Earlier in this chapter, you practiced your own skills in applying the entire Simplexity process to your own customer problem. When your company is founded by a team, you have to use the same skills, but you need to employ another set of interpersonal skills at the same time. These skills include active listening to others, supporting team members to help them say what they're thinking, and speaking clearly and simply to help others understand your thoughts.

Active listening means deliberately paying attention to what others are saying. The point is not to agree or disagree with their comment, but to try to completely understand what they're saying. Don't interrupt except to encourage clarification. Ask open-ended questions that permit speakers to enrich their thoughts. Value whatever is said, and avoid judging by your words or actions. Summarize their comments out loud to make sure you've understood.

Supporting others means automatically accepting that they're saying what they really think. Whether you agree isn't important. What's important is that you hear everyone's point of view. Don't debate or try to persuade team members to alter their comments to suit your thoughts. Otherwise, you will never enrich your own thinking or the thinking of the team. Effective problem solving comes from expressing differences of opinion or fact, not from suppressing them. Assume that others have useful information and ideas but that they might not want to express them, perhaps because they lack self-esteem or they assume that everybody already knows their ideas. Speaking in friendly, warm terms encourages others to share their thoughts and feelings. They will contribute more readily to the team if they believe you will build on their ideas and respond openly and spontaneously to their thoughts. When you do offer your own thoughts, make sure others realize you are trying to enrich the pot, not deliberately challenging them. One of the most effective ways to do this is by explicitly recognizing another person while you're adding your own contribution by stating something like "I'd like to build on what Fred said" or "yes, it's what Fred said, *and.* ..." This collegial approach builds a more creative atmosphere inside a startup where people feel more secure to offer their input. And as we've seen throughout this book, the more facts we uncover through collaborative dialogue, the better the process works. Collaboration leads to better solutions, which is a major outcome of our entrepreneurial process.

Speaking clearly and simply means several things. Express your thoughts in complete, simple sentences rather than single words or phrases. Avoid jargon that comes naturally to you but that may be foreign to others on your team. Only use terminology that is familiar to them as well. If they realize that you're trying to help them understand, they will appreciate your efforts and listen more readily. An effective leader is conscious of not only what they want to say but also how they say it. Avoid ambiguous terms that might be easily misinterpreted, and stay away from flowery language that intimidates others. For example, rather than saying, "We need to leverage our value proposition to expand our market reach in new geographic targets in the second year," say something like "we should plan to open a new store in our neighboring town next year" or "we need to find another nearby town with 1,000 potential customers to open a second store by next year." In this case, don't assume your teammates know what your definition of a value proposition is. For different people, the phrase "value proposition" might mean the product or service you're selling, the benefits your company provides the customer, the rationale for your company's existence, or any combination. If a technical term is used, be sure and clarify what it means for your company.

As an example, in one consulting session, we heard the phrase "leveraging the value proposition" spoken by the CEO. When we asked the team if they knew what the value proposition was, everyone nodded their head. We then asked each person to write on a slip of paper what the company's value proposition was. When we requested each person to reveal what they thought it was, each had a different answer, so we spent another ten minutes helping the team craft the value proposition together. They concluded that their value proposition was "to sell reliable data-gathering instruments for research scientists around the world." We requested that the team use that phrase, "reliable data gathering," rather than "value proposition" throughout the rest of the session. The team agreed and was pleased when the session enabled them to create a clear and concise strategy for entering a new sales region of Canada.

The best communicators take a disciplined and empathetic approach to considering what the listener will appreciate hearing. They don't ramble endlessly with technical jargon and steam-of-conscious "out-loud" thinking. They consider what is pertinent to the conversation and have the discipline to keep extraneous matters to themselves. This professional and considerate approach to conversation engages their listeners instead of wearing them out. Although clear and simple speech looks easy on the surface, it's actually one of the most challenging skills an entrepreneur must develop.

Team Skills for Better Teamwork

These interpersonal skills help team members to use their process skills in the group. They encourage the team members to defer judgment, actively diverge, and actively converge when they're working together. But just as the members must learn these interpersonal skills, so the entire team must learn an additional set of team skills: achieving consensus, providing feedback, and building cohesiveness.

Achieving consensus is the best way (but not necessarily the shortest way) for team members to converge together. Consensus doesn't mean the team unanimously agrees on one of several options. It means putting together the team's best thinking to make a choice that every member will support—even if it wasn't the member's own first choice. Neither does consensus mean taking a simple vote or living by "majority rules." While this approach saves time, it deters carefully thinking things through. Just because the majority was thinking the same way about a situation, it doesn't mean that any of them thought it through carefully or that they had all the important information. (How many voters carefully analyze all of the options or issues before casting their vote in a federal election?) When the team takes the time to hear and adapt everyone's best thinking, it is more likely to make the best choice or even create a new one. When new information is provided by a minority, for example, it can spark fresh thinking by an open-minded majority.

Here are four guidelines for reaching consensus:

- View differences of opinion as a help, not a hindrance. Don't argue for your choice just because it's yours. While keeping an open mind, focus on making a good decision, not on trying to prove your point. Deferring judgment on differences of opinion while the team converges helps members listen to one another and assemble their different viewpoints into the most creative end result instead of simply pinpointing whose idea won or lost. The final decision belongs not to one person but to the team as a whole.
- Offer your best thoughts, no matter how different or unusual they seem.
- If others have different viewpoints, don't change your mind just to avoid disagreement. Find out why the disagreement exists, then support the decision

that best accounts for everybody's viewpoint. If you think a teammate is making inappropriate assumptions, find a neutral way to voice your questions or doubts. You can turn differences in viewpoints into a positive thing: "It's really interesting to me that you and I see the same alternative so differently. Tell me more about how you see it. I'll bet I missed something that could really add to my understanding." The other person might respond positively and want to know more about your viewpoint in turn.

- Avoid deciding from among options without holding a healthy discussion. Trade information to ensure that everyone is using the same criteria to judge options. If people view options in different ways, you have to discover why the difference exists. Usually it's because people think different criteria are more or less important or because they lack the same level of understanding of the options. You won't get at these differences by simply flipping a coin or holding a vote without discussion.

It's especially difficult to build consensus in startup teams comprising experienced business people and senior scientists. Many team members with these backgrounds have gotten where they are in their careers through hard work and competition with others. They have learned to point out the flaws in others' choices as a way of showing their superiority. If a team member is jockeying to grab the top reins rather than working toward true consensus and the best result, they may be following their own hidden agenda. The problem gets worse if the CEO, fearing being labeled a tyrant, hesitates to drive the group toward consensus. Empowering individuals is one thing; abdicating authority is another. If the CEO doesn't play a full role in building consensus, team members may simply jockey for political position instead of putting their hearts into teamwork.

Another important skill is *providing feedback* to other team members and to the team itself. Just as ground control keeps a rocket on its correct launch path by making adjustments based on electronic feedback from the vehicle, so a creative team keeps its performance on track by providing continual feedback on its use of the creative process skills. However, since most teams focus strictly on content rather than process, most team members lack skill in giving each other helpful process feedback. They may even shy away from providing feedback. Why?

How to Improve Feedback

Many of us are used to getting only negative feedback (in school, at home, on the job), given only in a judgmental manner. Many performance appraisal systems, for example, work only by evaluating your past performance—especially by pinpointing your failures—rather than looking at ways to improve your future behavior. We then react defensively to feedback and find it difficult to subject others to the same negative experience. Few of us understand that the purpose of feedback is not to judge but to help us improve. Positive feedback is equally important: it's just as helpful to learn what you are doing well as to hear what you could improve.

Here are seven more principles for improving your skills in giving useful process feedback.

* Most important, your feedback must be based on trust and intended to help someone else. If your feedback is merely self-serving, keep it to yourself. As others learn that your feedback is intended to help them improve their performance, they'll trust you more, and they'll be more likely to risk changing how they work. Not only does feedback based on trust directly improve results, but it further builds trust among teammates. It's a self-fulfilling process. Research shows that trust is an important factor in building high-caliber teams. In these teams, people actually ask for feedback instead of shying away from it. Imagine a startup company composed of teammates willing to provide and receive feedback as a way of doing business. Milestones will be reached much faster when the team works together to make important decisions.
* Feedback is most effective when it's requested. When you ask someone else for their feedback, you make it easier for them to respond truthfully, for better or worse. They are also more likely to follow your lead and solicit feedback for themselves. A company culture focused on shared learning instead of power plays builds better team camaraderie. Lessons learned can be incorporated more quickly into developing a positive company culture and smoothly running systems.
* Feedback should be descriptive, not evaluative. Describe someone's behavior in a factual way, not in a way that evaluates them. It's much more useful to say, "When Tom began discussing the financial repercussions of missing the scheduled product launch, you appeared to lose interest, and Tom seemed upset about it," rather than to say, "You don't listen well. You won't last in this company." The latter attacks their self-esteem and puts them on the defensive.
* Not only was the former approach more likely to motivate the listener to improve, but it was also much more specific. When feedback is specific and includes examples, the recipient is more likely to know exactly what to do. If you are the recipient, check the feedback for clarity. It's better to take the time to pinpoint exactly what was meant than to alter your behavior based on misunderstood information. The more specific the feedback, the clearer it is. If the listener is still misunderstanding your message, consider using a metaphor or story to help them comprehend your intent. Then ask them to explain how the metaphor or story relates to the current situation.
* Time your feedback so that the person is most likely to act on it. Feedback usually works best shortly after a particular incident occurs. If you wait too long, the individual may be unable to clearly connect your comments with their behavior. However, this isn't *always* the case. It might be more useful to

wait until the person appears especially receptive to feedback or even asks for it. If they appear to be in a defensive mood, you might wait for a better time. Effective teams often provide a regular time for debriefing, which allows people to prepare themselves to give and receive feedback. For example, if cofounders are pitching their business plan to a group of investors, scheduling a debrief to occur immediately after the pitch might be an ideal time to discuss how to tweak the presentation for next time. If the pitch was successful, a debrief is still useful for considering how to improve the relationship with the investors in the future. After an investment, the team will need to learn how to improve its relationship with the investors over time. Entrepreneurs who are open to feedback and hold regular debriefing sessions to reflect on mistakes and successes will quickly build a high-performing company. A startup comprising mature professionals who are able to adapt as needed can reach milestones much faster than a band of rebels fighting among themselves. Teams that cannot demonstrate this type of leadership are often forced to hire more experienced managers who can move a company toward its stated vision.

- Offer feedback in a manner that relaxes both parties. Remember that feedback is intended to help someone learn and change behavior. Recall that learning is much more effective when the learner is relaxed. Some people might use humor to create a relaxed mood. Others pay attention to their tone of voice, keeping it soft, friendly, and measured. Pick relaxing or neutral surroundings. Instead of calling someone into your office, you might meet for lunch or coffee. Steve Jobs often took long walks with people when he was trying to think his way through a tough business decision.

It's one thing to know these principles of giving useful feedback. It's another to gain the skills you need to apply them. Not only must you apply the skills yourself, but you must lead others in doing so, either in teams or individually. If you model good feedback behavior, others will follow your lead.

To help you model this behavior with a group, use the following debriefing questions: "What are we saying or doing that is helping our process? What are we saying or doing that is hindering our process?" Another way you could ask these questions after a particular situation, such as a sales call, investor pitch, or product test, is "What went well during this event? What didn't go so well, or what could have gone better?" Or, if you're holding a strategy meeting to assess the progress of the company, you could ask, "What is our company doing well? What isn't going so well for our company, or what can we do better?" Encourage the team to consider these questions not just after meetings but during any type of company activity. Reminding the team members to defer their judgment and actively diverge, ask them to come up with as many answers to the two questions as they can. Then encourage them to discuss and clarify what they feel are the more relevant points. Doing this helps the team improve its process skills. A third useful question is—if we're discussing how we're working together as a team in forming our company—"What are we learning about our process and process skills?" If we just finished a sales call, investor pitch, product test, or other event, "What did we learn from doing this that we didn't know before?" If we're assessing our company's progress, "What have we learned recently about our market and company that we didn't know before?"

If you're giving feedback to one individual, you can modify these questions: "Here is what you say and do that I really like in your interactions with others (list as many positive behaviors as you can)." "Here are some things you might try to do differently to improve your interactions with others (list a few of the most important opportunities for improving behavior)." Even better, ask the individual to tell you first what they feel they are doing well and how they feel they might improve. In other words, ask them to pose these two questions themselves. Then add your own thoughts to reinforce theirs and to contribute anything they might have missed. When they're invited to participate like this, people are more likely to act on your feedback. This method can be used in conversations with any stakeholder who is committed to the success of the company. Positive relationships built through good communication with cofounders, investors, employees, suppliers, distributors, and any other group in the organization's ecosystem will support the future growth of the company.

A third important team skill is to develop high team cohesiveness. Team members should feel strong bonds to others members and to the team itself. Team cohesiveness is necessary for good problem solving and creativity. Cohesive teams share their members' diverse experience more completely and support differing viewpoints and risky, novel ideas. This helps to avoid group think, which encourages members to follow the crowd into inadequate solutions instead of offering possibly controversial viewpoints. This false harmony is often a sign of a team lacking cohesiveness. However, the best founding teams recognize that everyone has biases and prejudices that might distort the reality of what the company is facing. Teams made up of members who respectfully challenge and question each other's positions make more informed and creative decisions on the path to market credibility.

When used correctly, the process skills of deferral of judgment, active divergence, and active convergence increase team cohesiveness, and just as heightened trust and better teamwork feed on one another, so greater cohesiveness improves the team's use of these skills. As team members learn the benefits of moving in sync between diverging and converging, they practice these skills even more. It becomes a way of doing business. Quality results come not from the work of any one individual but from the efforts of the entire team, and no one cares or wants to know who should get credit for any particular idea. The process of achieving quality results becomes as exhilarating as the results themselves. As many serial entrepreneurs attest, the journey can be as rewarding as the destination for those lucky enough to have had an exciting and successful startup experience. It's why they often turn the reins of a company over to professional managers and look for their next opportunity for starting a new business. Successful startups can provide as much emotional satisfaction as they do financial reward. Entrepreneurship, like sports, the military, and music, is an experience where being part of a cohesive team creates shared meaning and purpose in the members' lives. When members rely on each other for survival, cohesiveness keeps the team moving forward.

One way to develop this oneness is to provide feedback to the team as a whole instead of to individual members. If an individual behaves poorly, the entire team automatically behaves poorly. When good ideas surface or when good process skills are used, the leader must commend the entire team, not just the individual who came up with the idea or displayed good process skills. When a team meets to solve a problem caused by someone's mistake, the discussion focuses on the mistake made by the team, not the individual. When the team presents its results to investors or the press, it does so as a unit.

It's Up to You

In this chapter, we reviewed the eight-step entrepreneurial process that you can use to creatively design a new product or service and bring it to market. Entrepreneurship is essentially a process of discovering and capitalizing on opportunities. Therefore, the first five steps of our process focus on design (finding a problem and creating a solution), and the last three steps focus on implementation within an entrepreneurial context. Creativity skills, tools, and processes were adapted to this endeavor. Since most successful companies are built by a group of entrepreneurs rather than a lone founder, team building and feedback skills were discussed to maximize the use of the process. As we discussed in the opening chapter, proficiency with an innovation process has never been more important. The pace of change continues to increase. Even as opportunities arise more often than ever, there seems to be less time to address them. However, a startup team that works together as a cohesive unit can more efficiently seize their opportunities and overcome obstacles on the way to market. Simply put, entrepreneurs who take the pains to master the innovation process become adaptable. They learn to embrace change and flex to constantly evolving situations. While larger companies strive to be efficient and flexible, a truly innovative startup can establish a foothold in the market with their adaptability. Thus, they pose a threat to the status quo and disrupt industries and, in the process, create new value for customers and investors.

There has never been more opportunity in the world. Become innovative. Build an effective team. Get to market. Grow a company. It's the right time to take the entrepreneurial journey. In this book, we've tried to provide the ticket you need for the trip—the Simplexity process and process skills. Now it's up to you to put it to good use. It's up to you to lead your team, enchant your customers, and delight your investors.

Notes

1 Disney, W. (2001). *The Quotable Walt Disney*. Glendale, CA: Disney Editions, p. 245.
2 Gordon, W. J. J. (1956). "Operational Approach to Creativity. *Harvard Business Review,* 9(1). Watertown, MA: Harvard Business Publishing.
3 Lavoisier, A. L. (1777). "Memoir on Combustion in General." *Mémoires de l'Académie Royale des Sciences 1777,* 592–600. In Leicester, H. M., and Klickstein, H. S. (1952). *A Source Book in Chemistry 1400–1900*. New York, NY: McGraw-Hill.

INDEX

abstract thinking 12
acceptance, gaining 7–8, 172–3, 224
action: psychological roadblocks to 165–7; taking 8, 180–8, 194, 215, 224
action plan 166–70
action planning 7, 164–72, 222–4; company 170–2; personal 164–70
active convergence 18–19, 191; evaluate and select 222; fact finding 202, 218–19; idea finding 207–8, 221; planning action 212–13, 224; problem definition 202, 204, 219–20; problem finding 200; taking action 215
active divergence 18–19, 191; evaluate and select 222; fact finding 201, 216–18; gaining acceptance 214; idea finding 204–6, 221; planning action 210–12, 222–3; problem definition 203, 219, 220; problem finding 199; taking action 215
active listening 226
adaptability 27
additive rapid prototyping 120
aesthetics 145
affordable loss 181
Alba, Joseph 147
Allen, David 168–9
Allen, Paul 225
Allen, Woody 71
Altair Product Design 125
Apple (company) 28, 30, 225
Apple I computer 124
Apple Lisa 74
Arthur, W. Brian 61
asking the Else? question 87–88, 90
Aspelund, Karl 117

assembly line 31–32, 37
assumptions: unconscious 54–55; unwarranted 62–63
atomic bomb 113

Bardel, William 115
Basadur Applied Creativity 4
Basadur creative problem-solving profile 10–11
Baskinger, Mark 115
battlenecks 186–8
Becher, Johann 196
Bell, Alexander Graham 30, 36
Berger, Arthur Asa 42
bias 54, 99; local search 57
Biondi, Angelo 94
Birdseye, Clarence 62–63
blitzing 107–8
blow molding 126
bottlenecks 186
brainstorming 107
breakthrough collaboration 87
Brin, Sergey 225
broccoli first technique 184
Brown, Sunni 115, 116
Brown, Tim 145
Burton, Robert 54
business concept 112–13
business models 178–9
business to business (B2B) problems 47–49, 199
business to consumer (B2C) problems 46, 47–49, 199
business viability 145
buying decision, influencing 33–35

Catmull, Ed 226
challenge mapping 89–91; customer
     99–103
challenges 170–1
challenge statements 79–80, 90, 203–4
Chouinard, Yvon 81
Christensen, C. 57
closure 182
Coast soap 85
Colgate 84
collaboration, breakthrough 87
collaborative problem solving 53–54
Collins, Jim 72
Collins, John 82
company action planning 170–2
competitors, worldwide 2
computer-aided drafting (CAD) 119, 121
computer-aided manufacturing (CAM) 121
computer numerically controlled (CNC)
     machines 120–1
conceptualization 8, 9, 12, 18
conceptual prototyping 114, 119–23
confirming the selection of idea 145–8
consensus 134–6; achieving 228–9
content separated from process 19–22
convergence see active convergence
converging by consensus skills 134–6
Coolidge, Calvin 113
Corning 36
creative destruction 164
creativity 2, 146
credibility 122
criteria for selecting idea 132–44, 208
criteria grid method 137–42, 209
curiosity and fact finding 72–73
curiosity conversations 72–73
customer: deep understanding of 36–38;
     discovering who is the real customer
     33–38; interacting with 40; personal life
     of 43–44; public life of 42–43; resolving
     their problem 62; what is problem for
     60–61
customer challenge mapping 99–103
customer feedback form for product/
     service concept 151–5
customer fieldnote form 40–41
customer problems 197; solving 3–8, 25
customer solutions 111–12

deadline commitments 183
decision-making 54
deep dive 38–42
deferral of judgment 18–19, 53, 106, 191

deliberately building radical ideas 108–10
desirability, human 145
Detroit Automobile Company 165
Disney, Roy 37–38, 225
Disney, Walt 32–33, 37–38, 75, 165, 193, 225
Disneyland 33
divergence see active divergence
dopamine 54
drawing, technical 116–17
drawing stage of a prototype 115–17

Eastman Kodak 36
Economic Rational Man 54
Edison, Thomas 30–31, 36, 75, 184
Edsel 75
effectuation 3
ego 58
Einstein, Albert 78
Eisenhower, Dwight D. 113
empathy 54
employee involvement 65
entrepreneurs 1
E.P.C.O.T., 33
ethnography 39
evaluate and select 7, 11, 132–61, 207–210,
     222; case study 136–7
experiencing 11, 71–72
Experimental Prototype Community of
     Tomorrow 33
expert feedback form for product/service
     concept 156–8
expressivity 122

fact finding 6–7, 51–75, 193–4, 200–2,
     216–19; case studies 67–71; and
     curiosity 72–73; by experiencing 71–72;
     follow-up 71–72; questions 58–64;
     seven strategies for 52–58; six fact
     finding questions 58–64
facts: converging on the most pertinent
     64–65; digging out the real 67–68;
     uncovering unknown 59–60
Fantasia 75
Fantasound 75
fear of an imperfect solution 182
fear of being wrong 67–68
fear of failure 165, 181
fear of imperfection 166
fear of the unknown 166, 181
feasibility, technical 145
feedback 145–6, 149, 229–33
feeling of knowing 54
flexibility 68–69

follow-up fact finding 71–72
forcing connections with ideas 108
Ford, Henry 31–32, 165
Ford Motor Company 31, 75
freewheeling ideas 107
functionality 122
fused deposition modeling (FDM) 120
fuzzy situation 5, 6, 25, 69, 192, 198–9;
   questions to clarify 58–63

Gable, Neal 32
gaining acceptance 7–8, 213–15, 224
Gates, Bill 225
G-code 120–1
generating ideas 9–11, 14, 18, 106–11
getting unstuck 168–70
Google 225
Gordon, William J. J. 195
Gorilla Glass 36
Grant, Adam 72
Grazer, Brian 72–73
Great Product, No Market mistake
   38–39
groupthink 136
guide on the side leader 16–17
Gyrus ENT 117

halo error 138
Hamilton, Laird 80
Hawkins, Jeff 119
Henry Ford Company 165
Herman, Tom 150
hitchhiking ideas 107
Honda 70
Honda Dream 71
Hoover Dam 113
Horowitz, Alexandra 99
human desirability 145
humble inquiry 72

idea finding 7, 105–30, 204–7, 221
ideas: deliberately building radical ones
   108–10; evaluating and selecting
   132–61; generation 8–9, 106–11;
   selling 174–8
ideation 11
IDEO 39–40, 117, 145
immersive problem-finding approach
   39–42
implementation 8, 9, 12–15, 18
information sharing 56
innovation 2, 3–8, 28; four quadrants
   of 8–9

innovation wheel 6–8
Innovator's Dilemma 57
interpersonal skills for teamwork 226–8
inventing and learning 195–6
iPhone 29, 36
Irish Spring soap 84–85
Ironman triathlon 82
Isaacson, Walter 29
iterations to idea 149–50

Jackson, P. W. 145–6, 209
Jobs, Steve 28–29, 36, 47, 74, 124, 150, 165,
   225, 226, 231
Johnson, Edward 36
Johnson & Johnson 69
journaling 40–41
judgment: deferral of 18–19, 53,
   106, 191; vertical deferral of 192–5;
   withholding 193

Kahneman, Daniel 54–55
Kawasaki, Guy 150
Kelleher, Herb 115
Kelley, Tom 39, 117
Kennedy, John F. 113
King, Rollin 115
knowledge, availability and use of 195
Koch, Charles 72
Koch Industries 72
Koppel, Ted 39

Laffley, A. G. 122
laminated object manufacturing (LOM) 120
Land, Edwin 29–30, 36, 75
Lasseter, John 226
Lavoisier, Antoine 196
leading 16–17
learning and inventing 195–6
legitimacy, increasing 173–4
Level 5 leadership 72
local search bias 57
look for the truth 58
Lynn, Gary S. 102

machine principles 124
Maltz, Maxwell 183
manufacturability 123
manufacturing processes 125–6
3M Corporation 28
Messick, S. 145–6, 209
Microsoft 225
milestones 183
Miller, Geoffrey 42

model building stage of prototyping 117–19
Model T 31
moving assembly line 31–32, 37
Mueller, Irina 148

negative attitude toward problems 25, 55–56
NeXT 165
Noller, Ruth 94
non-programmed problems 26–28

open mind 136–7
Oppenheimer, Robert 113
opportunity development 3
optimizing 8, 9, 12, 15–16, 18
Osterwalder, A. 179
outdoor sports and problem definition 80–82

Page, Larry 225
paired comparison analysis (PCA) 142–44
Palm Computing Company 102
PalmPilot 102, 119
Parnes, Sid 94
patent barriers 110–11
pepperoni principle 182–3
personal action planning 164–70
personal digital assistant 102
personal life of customer 43–44
phlogiston theory 196
phonograph 30, 36–37
picture collages 112
piggybacking ideas 107
Pigneur, Y. 179
Pixar 28, 226
planning action 166–70, 210–13, 222–4
Polaroid camera 29–30, 36
Polaroid company 75
Pooler, Jim 43
preconsult 170
preferences styles of problem solving 17–19
presentation prototyping 114, 125
Priestley, Joseph 196
problem defining 7, 192–5
problem definition 69, 78–104, 202–4, 219–20; case studies 84–87, 94–98; challenge statements 79–80; in outdoor sports 80–82
problem finding 6, 24–50, 198–200, 216; immersive approach 39–42
problem formulation 25–26
problems: avoiding negative attitude toward 25, 55–56; business to business

(B2B) 47–49, 199; business to consumer (B2C) 46, 47–49, 199; deep thinking about 98–100; programmed vs. non-programmed 26–28; uncovering 44–49; why is a problem for the customer 60–61
problem solving 3–8, 61–62, 184–5; collaborative 53–54; eight steps to 6–8; method of 10; preference styles of 17–19, 66–67; styles of 13
process leaders 16
process separated from content 19–22
process skills 8–9, 18–19, 63–64
procrastination 166
Procter & Gamble 59, 84, 122
programmed problems 26
project pillars 102
proof of concept 149–50, 173
prototyping 112–29; conceptual prototyping stage 119–23; considerations for 126–9; dimensions of 121–3; drawing stage 115–17; manufacturing processes 125–6; model building stage 117–19; presentation 125; rapid 119–21; stages of 114–26; working stage of 123–5
psychological roadblocks to action 165–7
public life of customer 42–43
pyramiding 73–74

question and asking the Else? question 87–88, 90

rapid prototyping 119–21
refined product/service concept form 157–62
Reilly, Richard R. 102
reverse prioritizing 183
rewards 183–4
Rhode, Mike 115, 116
risk of failure 173–4
Roam, Dan 115
rock climbing and problem solving 81
Rutan, Burt 113
Ruth, Babe 181

Sawyer, K. 147, 149
saying no to other things 166
say what you think 57
Scapa, James R. 125
Schein, Ed 72
Schoeniger, Gary 4
Schumpeter, Joseph 164

Scientific American 36, 37
scope, broadening 87–89
search divergently for possibly relevant
   facts 52–53
secrecy 56
selective laser sintering (SLS) 120
selling ideas 174–8
share information 56
shopping 42–44
Simplexity Creative Problem-Solving
   Process 4
Simplexity innovation process
   197–225
Simplexity process 65–66
sketch notes 116
Soarin' Over California ride 124
solid object printing (SOP) 120
solution formulation 105–30
solution implementation 163–89
solutions 111–12; that have been thought
   of or tried 61–62
Sorenson, Charles 37
speaking clearly and simply 227
Stahl, Georg 196
Startup.com (film) 150
stereolithography 120
storyboards 112
strategic plan 170–2
strategy guidelines 170–2
strengths, weaknesses, opportunities, and
   threats 170
subject matter experts 147
subtractive rapid prototyping 120–21
Sumner, Mark 124
Super Soaker 124
supporting others 226–7
surface prototype 114, 119
surfing and problem solving 80–81
Suzuki, Shunryu 55
SWOT analysis 170
systematic search 3

taking action 8, 180–8, 215, 224
Taulbert, Clifton L. 4
teams 224–9
technical drawing 116–17
technical feasibility 145
telephone 30, 36
telescoping method 45–46, 139–40
theme park 32–33, 37–38
thinking organization 197–8
tooling up 126
Toshiba Corporation 25
Townsend, Robert 183
trust, lack of 56
truth, looking for 58
Tuzman, Kaliel Isaza 150
Tylenol tragedy 68–69

unconscious assumptions 54–55
unlearning 196–7

valuation 174
value proposition 179
vertical deferral of judgment 192–5
viability, business 145
viewpoints, using several 53–54
von Hippel, Eric 73

Walt Disney Company 37, 225
WED Enterprises 38
Weeks, Wendell 36
Weisberg, Robert 147
what does one know about fuzzy situation
   58–59
what does one not know about fuzzy
   situation 59–60
"why-what's stopping" analysis 82–84, 88,
   90, 93–98, 203
working prototype 114, 123–5
worst-case scenario 181
Wozniak, Steve 124, 225
wrong, fear of being 67–68